Good Housekeeping

OCTOBER 1933
ONE SHILLING
NETT

WORLD HOUSEKEEPING *by* Comm. STEPHEN KING-HALL

Henry Handel Richardson – Vera Brittain – Lorna Reu
Winifred Holtby – Mrs. J.B.S. Haldane – J.W. Drawbell

Good Housekeeping

OCTOBER 1935 · ONE SHILLING NETT ·

Beginning R.C. Sherriff's *new novel*
· GREENGATES ·
REVIEW OF NEW WINTER FASHIONS

Good Housekeeping

SEPTEMBER. 1935 – ONE SHILLING

The Institute's Eleventh Birthday

Mary Roberts Rinehart · Naomi Mitchison
Noel Streatfeild · Countess of Oxford and Asquith
Christine Jope-Slade · Beverley Nichols

Good Housekeeping

SEPTEMBER 1936 – ONE SHILLING

INORDINATE (?) AFFECTION *by* Ethel Smyth
Richard Aldington · Countess of Oxford and Asquith
Anne Allardice · A.J. Cronin · Ursula Parrott

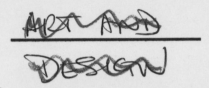

FOOD
Glorious
FOOD

FOOD *Glorious* **FOOD**

The Evening Meal

By Grace Noll Crowell

THE preparation of an evening meal
By any woman, anywhere, may be
A ceremony, beautiful to see,

Recalling clear, sweet evenings long ago
At Emmaus, or Bethany, when One
Beloved guest had come at set of sun.

And oh, that other quiet evening meal
Within an upper room—the grace He said
Above the scarlet wine, the broken bread!

An evening meal is such a gracious thing,
It matters not how plain may be the fare
So long as love and loyalty are there.

The supper hour—a magnet drawing home
The ones who have the need of food and rest!
All women know this hour of day is best.

Illustration by Alfred N. Simpkin

FOOD Glorious FOOD

Eating and Drinking with
GOOD HOUSEKEEPING 1922-1942

Compiled by
Brian Braithwaite
Noëlle Walsh

EBURY PRESS
LONDON

First published by Ebury Press
an imprint of the Random Century Group Ltd
Random Century House
20 Vauxhall Bridge Road
London SWIV 2SA

First impression 1990

British Library Cataloguing in Publication Data
Food glorious food: eating and drinking Good housekeeping 1922-1942
 I. Braithwaite, Brian   II. Walsh, Noëlle   III. Good housekeeping
 641.5

ISBN 0 85223 818 5

Printed and bound in Great Britain by
The Bath Press, Bath, Avon

CONTENTS

6 Foreword – Noëlle Walsh and Brian Braithwaite

9 The Business of Housekeeping – M and F Wooler

10 A Seasonable Luncheon – Florence B Jack MCA

12 Vegetable Dishes for Lent

15 For the Bachelor Woman: A Quickly Made Meal at the end of a Busy Day

16 Good Things from the Egg Basket – Florence B Jack MCA

19 About Grouse – Anticipating 'The 12th'

20 The Truth About Canned Foods – William G Savage BSc MD

25 To Please the Men

27 A Word in Praise of Mushrooms

29 The Humble Crumb Disguised

31 When the Cupboard is Bare

33 The Housekeeper's Dictionary of Facts

34 Cakes for Christmas – Florence B Jack MCA

36 The Adulteration of Food – Helena Normanton BA

38 Cookery As A Career for Women – Florence B Jack MCA

41 What should a Woman Eat? – Dr Cecil Webb-Johnson

45 Sweets for the Dance Supper

46 Serving Rice – E Edwards

48 Lenten Menus – Helen Clarke

53 The Housekeeper's Dictionary of Facts

56 Strawberries

61 Piquant salad dressings

64 Catering for a Dance

66 The Housekeeper's Dictionary of Facts

68 Selecting and Purchasing Beef – The Director of GHI

73 Cooling Drinks for The Party

79 The Housekeeper's Dictionary of Facts

82 Are You a Good Housekeeper? – Lady Violet Bonham Carter

85 Wayside Berries for Winter Preserves

86 A Christmas Dinner planned by the Chef of Good Housekeeping Restaurant

92 The Institute suggests uses for oatmeal and prepared oats

98 Marmalade Making

100 Quick Lunches for Spring-Cleaning Time

105 The Housekeeper's Dictionary of Facts

106 The Story of a Soup Plate – Marion St John Webb

111 Vegetables for the Gourmet

112 The Goode Housewyfe – Poems in the Elizabethan Manner by CWD

114 The Housekeeper's Dictionary of Facts

117 Home-made Liqueurs – Anne Benshaw

119 The Housekeeper's Dictionary of Facts

120 The First Meal of the Day – P L Garbutt

125 Some Cookery Books of Yesterday – Marion Ryan

127 The Weekend House Party

130 Meals for the Business Girl – Phyllis Peck

132 How Others Live

134 Favourite Foods of Famous Men – Florence White

138 Seven Christmas Puddings

140 Farewell to Pheasants – Michael Home

144 The Cooking of Game

148 The Fascination of Old English County Cookery – D D Cottington Taylor

152 The Pleasures of Picnics – Osbert Sitwell

155 The Housekeeper's Dictionary of Facts

156 What do you know about meat? – Rachel and Margaret Ryan

158 Coronation Catering – E J M Creswell

161 Selected Recipes for the Month

163 Do You Know…

165 Selected Recipes for the Month

166 Meals on a Tray – C F Palmer

170 Seasoning: A Subtle Art

175 Menu Making – Leonora Mary Ervine

177 Seasonable Salads – Olive Edwards

179 What Shall We Have for Supper? – N M Ramsay

180 Holiday Catering 1941 – E J M Creswell

183 How Do You Cook Fresh-Salted Cod?

184 Cottage Loaf – Marjorie Hessell Tiltman

188 Magpies Aren't Popular – Anne Blyth Munro

189 Food for the Picking

190 And Again – Potatoes – Christine Palmer

FOREWORD

ADVERTISING VIEWPOINT

Good Housekeeping has always been synonymous with food, and right from the first issue in 1922 food advertisers have been active and prolific in our pages.

I looked through hundreds of food advertisements to make the selection for this book and the final choice was a frustratingly difficult task, having to omit dozens which I would have loved to have included. Perhaps my favourite advertisement in the book is Cook's Farm Eggs on page 24. I love the skilful evocation of royalty with the appellation Queen Mother used in a completely non-royal sense, plus the little invitation for boys and girls in the top left hand corner to get a gift for mother.

As one progresses through the years there seems to have been a very positive need for hot drinks. Heavily advertised products were Ovaltine, Horlicks, Bengers, Bournvita, Beefex, Oxo, Bovril, Instant Postum, Allenbury's and Virol. And all our favourite breakfast cereals: Kelloggs, Post Toasties, Quaker Oats, Grape Nuts, All-Bran and Sunny Jim's Force.

I was also surprised at the cavalier indifference at the placing of advertisements in juxtaposition to one another. These days we are most sensitive about products which do not lie happily together: in pre-war days such delicacy was eschewed. I discovered baked beans next to toilet paper, Oxo adjacent to rat poison, mince pies alongside sanitary knickers, butter next to the Elsan and Golden Shred Ginger Marmalade sharing the page with Veet Underarm Hair Removing Cream!

It is interesting that Skippers (which every pre-war child will remember as a tea-time treat) were advertising in 1934 the rigorous inspection of The Man from Skippers, rather pre-dating The Man from Del Monte in these television days. I also liked the advertising for All-Bran which not only cured your constipation but offered the 'the sunny side of life — she's taken for her daughter's sister!'.

At the end of the 1920's refrigeration came into our lives and it is fascinating to read the measured arguments from Frigidaire, Kelvinator and Electrolux, as skilful as the hustling for the Parkinson New Suburbia gas cooker on page 96 with the advice to 'change your oven, not your butcher!'.

Many of the advertisers on these pages, right back to 1922, are still extant today. The selling methods may have changed but many of the products have not. Famous names are here, together with many which have been forgotten today, but I do admire the presentation, the artwork and the energy which food advertisers have always put into their selling.

I hope you will find their work as fascinating and enjoyable as I did in making the selection.

BRIAN BRAITHWAITE

Publishing Director

EDITORIAL VIEWPOINT

When Good Housekeeping first appeared in March 1922, food was the major preoccupation of housewives: pickling, curing, jam-making and preserving. Many were having to undertake culinary tasks for the first time since one of the effects of the First World War had been to deplete the number of women willing to enter domestic service, diverting them instead to industrial work. And those housewives who still managed to hold onto a cook were expected to keep up-to-date with new domestic equipment and keep to their housekeeping budget.

'Housekeeping is a business, and to attempt to run it on other than a business basis is simply courting disaster. A budget is essential…' so wrote the two principals of GH's school of home management in Clifton in the fourth issue. With a businesslike air, GH set out to inform the housewives of the twenties and thirties on everything from disguising the humble crumb to the truth about canned food. GH always had the last word on matters domestic, which was only to be expected from a magazine whose first test kitchen was sited at 1 Amen Corner! As proof of the seriousness of Good Housekeeping's determination to get things right, in 1924 the Good Housekeeping Institute was opened. There on the food side, a team of women worked primarily creating and testing recipes for inclusion in the magazine, but also offering their services as speakers and demonstrators at schools and women's institutes. Worried mothers of the-bride could even give their daughters as a wedding present a member of GH staff who would stay in their home and teach them the finer points of housekeeping.

Good Housekeeping also ran a restaurant in Oxford Street, a training school for home economists and, later on, a wartime meals centre where nutritious, well balanced meals could be purchased. The thirties also saw the publication of food leaflets and the beginning of GH's cook books.

Despite the distance in looking back more than 60 years, there are shocks of recognition at issues in the arena of food which were news then and are still potent today. 'The Truth About Canned Foods' (page 20) for instance, written in 1923, was 'inspired by the panic recently created in the public mind by certain tragic cases of food poisoning.' In the 'Adulteration of Food' (page 36), written in 1924, the author puts many of the country's food problems down to the same reason which is blamed today for the food scare problems of the recent years, inadequate laws: 'In 1875 we were the pioneers in passing the first Sale of Food & Drugs Act; nowadays other countries… have far surpassed us. The administration of our Acts is vested in local authorities with overlapping effects… whilst the Ministry of Health has inadequate power of supervision…' Plus ça change.

Perhaps the last word concerning food in this period should go to Florence B Jack MCA, director of the Good Housekeeping Cookery Department (page 38), 'The work of catering and cooking should not be depreciated, for it is even more necessary to mankind than the housing and clothing trades, and as a profession it should stand on an equal footing with medicine.' Hear, hear!

NOËLLE WALSH

Editor

Halcyon Days

Days with the Boys and Girls

Daddy pays his weekly visit to the village tuck-shop, to the unconcealed delight of the children . . . for it means the weekly tin of Mackintosh's Toffee-de-Luxe.

Sold loose by weight at 8d. per ¼-lb.; and in "Baby" Tins, 1/3 each; "Tall" Tins, 1/3 and 2/6 each; and in 4-lb. Family Tins. All the flavours are favourites with everyone, everywhere.

Egg and Cream-de-Luxe	Chocolate Toffee-de-Luxe
Cocoanut-de-Luxe	Almond Toffee-de-Luxe
Cafe-de-Luxe	Mint-de-Luxe
Plain Toffee-de-Luxe	De-Luxe Assortment

Mackintosh's Toffee-de-Luxe has the largest Sale in the World.

MACKINTOSH'S
Toffee-de-Luxe
The Quality Sweetmeat

THE BUSINESS OF HOUSEKEEPING

Making Budget

By M. and F. Wooler

Principals of the School of Home Management, Clifton

WERE it possible to ask a large number of women, each in turn, to say with absolute honesty whether the family income was being spent wisely and scientifically, the majority of the replies would be vaguely elusive, or indicative of a woeful ignorance of home finance.

Housekeeping is a business, and to attempt to run it on other than a business basis is simply courting disaster. A budget is essential, but beware of adopting an over-complicated s y s t e m. Thousands of housewives have, through this error, become so disheartened, or hopelessly mystified over elaborate book-keeping, that they have given up all idea of "keeping accounts," and have fallen back on a "rule of thumb" method that is never satisfactory.

The chief value of making a budget is that, having apportioned the family income under different headings it becomes a simple matter to adjust. We are all apt to be extravagant in certain branches of housekeeping and too economical in others. The budget, with its definite statements of expenditure, makes a common-sense proportioning of income possible.

It is obviously impossible to lay down hard-and-fast rules for the division of an income, as neighbourhood, social position, and the particular needs of each family must all be taken into consideration. Each housekeeper should make her own budget, and to help her in this we give a specimen Budget Sheet on this page. This the housekeeper may criticise, adding to this item and deducting from that, until from it she evolves the system that in her case is most practical.

The division of income given in the specimen Budget Sheet is not an imaginary arrangement. It has been carefully worked out in a family consisting of four adults—one of them the servant—

and has been proved, in this family, to be the best way of proportioning an income of £650 per annum.

Since meals are the most important

SPECIMEN BUDGET SHEET

For a family of four adults living in town.
Income £650 a year.

		Per annum £ s. d.
Shelter	Rent, Rates, Taxes, House and Personal Insurances, General Repairs	120 0 0
Food	13s. 6d. each per week	140 0 0
Heating and Lighting	Coal, Gas, and Electricity	33 8 0
Laundry	Everything but bed and table linen washed at home	31 4 0
Servant's Wages	Insurance included in Special House Policy	25 0 0
Dress	Clothes and personal expenses for three persons	140 0 0
Miscellaneous	Health, Entertaining, Charity, Library, Flowers, etc.	76 0 0
House Cleaning	Window and Chimney Cleaning, Cleaning Materials	32 8 0
Newspapers	1s. 6d. per week	3 18 0
Total		£601 18 0

item in housekeeping, we detail here a typical day's menu in this household of four adults, whose total weekly expenditure on food is £2 14s.

A Typical Week's Bills

	s.	d.
Butcher	14	1
Grocer	10	9
Dairy	8	11
Greengrocer	6	9
Flour and Bread	5	1
Fish	4	7
Poulterer	4	0
Weekly Total	£2 14	2

Menu

Breakfast: Porridge, sausages with fried potatoes, marmalade, bread and butter, watercress.

Luncheon: Kedgeree, beetroot salad, cheese biscuits.

Tea: Scones, brown bread and butter, spice cakes.

Dinner: Fishcakes, ragout of rabbit, baked potatoes, onions au gratin, apple pie, cheese, biscuits.

All cakes, biscuits, and scones are home - made. Dripping and margarine are used for cooking; butter for table use. First-quality imported meat used.

Having apportioned a sum to the various items of household expenditure, a system of book-keeping should then be started. This need not be an elaborate one; the simpler the better. Two cash-books with money columns and a cash-box will be required. One book will serve as Day Book, the other as Ledger. To keep the day-book all payments made should be entered on the right-hand page, or credit side, and all money received or drawn from the bank entered on the left-hand page, or debit side. This account should be balanced once a week or oftener by adding up both sides. If the credit side is less than the debit side, the money remaining in the cash-box should equalise it. This is called the Balance.

To start the Ledger the various entries in the cash-book will require to be sorted out and arranged under the different headings agreed on—such as Shelter, Food, Dress, etc.—and the amounts carefully noted in this second book. This need only be done once a month, or once a quarter. There will now be a clear statement as to how the money has been spent, and it will be seen at a glance whether or not the expenditure has been kept within the prescribed limits. A simple system of household book-keeping is the only sure means of regulating expenses.

FOOD
Glorious
FOOD

1922

Tried and Proven

This is the motto of the Department of Cookery. We offer these pages in all confidence, as they are developed by actual experiments and tests carried on in a fully equipped model kitchen. There need be no hesitation about using any of the recipes, success is assured if the directions are followed completely

The matter will be varied as much as possible in order to meet the requirements of every household, and an effort will be made to solve the difficulties of present-day catering. On all cookery problems we shall be pleased to give you the benefit of our experience and research. Inquiries are invited and should be accompanied by a stamped and addressed envelope. Address: "Good Housekeeping," 1 Amen Corner, London, E.C.4

A Seasonable Luncheon

Complete menu with directions for serving

THE service of luncheon takes several different forms. There is the simple meal, when the remains of the previous night's dinner are usually served, the early dinner, of two courses, of which children can partake, and the more formal luncheon of several courses. There are no hard-and-fast rules regarding the menu for the formal luncheon, and, provided suitable dishes are served, the arrangement may be left very much to individual taste.

Hors d'œuvre

These are not compulsory, but they are becoming more and more popular, and the menu that starts off bravely with some savoury morsel is bound to go off well through all its various stages. Hors d'œuvre, or appetisers, may be of many different things, and there are various ways of serving them. The following will offer a fair choice: olives, sardines, anchovies, pâté de foie gras, caviare, oysters, devilled or potted meat, smoked fish, sausage, pickles, small salads, and fruit in season. Small leftovers, too, may often be utilised for making many a tasty savoury. One of the daintiest ways of serving hors

These luncheon recipes are designed to serve four persons

d'œuvre is on a platter which contains divisions for several different varieties. This may be made of glass, silver, or china, and it adds a smart touch to the table, especially when filled with a spicy assortment in different colours. For the present season the following may be suggested: (1) Pickled beetroot, cut in very thin round slices and sprinkled with chopped green pickle. (2) Sliced hard-boiled egg, with salad dressing and parsley. (3) Celery stalks cut in inch lengths, filled with potted meat or cream cheese, and decorated with red pickle. (4) Smoked salmon, in very thin slices, or sardines. (5) Pickled red cabbage or chutney.

Hors d'œuvre of celery and cheese

Hors d'œuvre could also be arranged on little plates or saucers placed on a tray with a serviette on it, or if one kind only is being served, on any suitable dish.

Hot hors d'œuvre are occasionally served, but these are not so popular; they would be composed of such things as small patties, rissoles, croquettes, or savoury toasts. They should be served very hot on a pretty dish paper.

Spinach Soup

This is given here as an alternative to the hors d'œuvre, as many people prefer to commence a meal with something warm. Served in individual pots it will look attractive. *Ingredients:* 1 lb. spinach, 1½ pints light stock, 1 onion, 1 oz. butter, 1 teaspoonful cornflour, ½ pint milk, a pinch of nutmeg, pepper and salt.

Pick and wash the spinach and put it into a saucepan with the stock; onion chopped, and salt. Cook until tender and rub through a sieve. Then melt the butter in the saucepan, add the cornflour, and mix until smooth. Pour in the milk and stir until boiling. Add spinach purée, season to taste, and cook for a few minutes.

Spinach Soup served in individual pots looks attractive

Apricot Fool served in Custard Glasses

Croûtons of fried bread, or puffed rice crisped in the oven, may be served separately.

Fish Omelet

This is an excellent method of using a small amount of left-over fish of any kind. Take a teacupful of cooked fish and shred it finely, removing all skin and bone. Put the yolks of two or three eggs into a basin with pepper, salt, and one teaspoonful of chopped parsley. Work these together with a wooden spoon until pale and creamy, then add the fish. Beat up the whites of the eggs to a stiff froth and fold them lightly into the mixture. Melt a good tablespoonful of butter in an omelet pan, pour in the mixture, and stir until beginning to set. Cook until a rich brown on the under side, then fold over and turn on to a hot dish. Serve garnished with parsley and lemon, or with a border of buttered beetroot.

Buttered Beetroot

Cut some cooked beetroot into dice, sufficient to make one cupful. Melt a tablespoonful of butter or margarine in a saucepan, put in the prepared beetroot, and season with pepper and salt. Heat thoroughly and sprinkle with chopped parsley.

Fillets of Beef with Bananas

Cut four or five rounds fillets of beef, sauté them in butter for six minutes, or until sufficiently cooked, and season with pepper and salt. Place them on potato cakes (see below) of the same size, and on the top lay a small section of banana that has been sautéd in butter. Add two or three tablespoonfuls of water and one teaspoonful of meat extract to the pan in which the meat was cooked; stir until boiling, and pour round the dish. Garnish with finely-shred horse-radish.

Potato Cakes

To two cupfuls of cooked and sieved potato add a little melted butter, pepper, salt, and enough milk to moisten. Form into round, flat cakes, using a little flour; brush over with milk or egg and brown in the oven.

Salad

This may be composed of one or of several kinds of vegetables according to what is convenient. A nice green salad is generally to be preferred, and lettuce, endive, corn salad, and watercress should be obtainable. The green stuff should be carefully picked and broken or cut in pieces not too small, then thoroughly washed in several waters and shaken as dry as possible. A wet salad can never be a successful one. Arrange the vegetables neatly in a salad bowl or dish, and mix them lightly with any simple dressing. The following is easily made : Mix together one tablespoonful of wine vinegar with half a teaspoonful of salt and a pinch of pepper, and stir in gradually three tablespoonfuls of the best salad oil. A little made mustard and a pinch of sugar may be added if desired A few pieces of tomato or beetroot and

---

MENU

Hors d'œuvre

Spinach Soup

Fish Omelet

Buttered Beetroot

Fillets of Beef with Bananas

Salad

Apricot Fool

Cheese   Coffee

---

some slices of hard-boiled egg will give a touch of colour to the salad.

Apricot Fool

Rub some tinned apricot through a sieve, or press it through a potato ricer, using a small proportion of the syrup. To one cupful of the purée add one cupful of custard, sweeten to taste, and flavour with two or three drops essence of almonds. Keep in a cool place until wanted, then serve in custard glasses, with a little whipped and sweetened cream on the top. Garnish with a piece of apricot, or some crystallised fruit or flowers.

Fish Omelet garnished with Buttered Beetroot

The sweet served at a luncheon should always be very simple in character. A fruit compote, or the natural fruit in season, is usually considered sufficient ; or a savoury may replace the sweet, especially if an hors d'œuvre has not been served.

Cider Cup

This is a very refreshing drink and it is simple to make. Infuse a pint of good tea and strain it boiling hot over 2 oz. of loaf sugar. Allow this to stand until cold, then add the juice of two oranges, a few thin slices of lemon and a small glass of brandy. Just before serving mix with a large bottle of sparkling cider. Other fruits may be added if liked.

Coffee

A really good cup of coffee will make a fitting finish to the meal. The coffee ought to be well roasted and freshly ground, and one heaped teaspoonful allowed for each cup. The water must be freshly boiled, and it is also important to have the coffee-pot very clean. There are many kinds of cafetières, but the simple fire-proof china one with percolator makes as good coffee as any ; it requires no spirit lamp, and is easily cleaned. Heat the coffee-pot first with boiling water, then pour the water away and put in the required amount of coffee. Pour the boiling water gently and gradually over it, keeping the coffee-pot in a warm place, or standing in a deep tin with hot water, while the filtering process is going on. Coffee to be good must be very hot. It should be served black, but hot milk or cream may be served separately if desired.

Table Decoration

This need not be elaborate; a few flowers tastefully arranged are all that is required. Flowers, typical of the season, are the most pleasing in effect, and the early spring offers us a good variety. Growing bulbs, such as daffodils, tulips, and hyacinths set in unglazed pots, look very attractive; or a lovely picture can be made with a large bowl holding daffodils, narcissi, or pheasant's-eye, a r r a n g e d in holders to look as if they were growing. Crocuses, in colours ranging from white through the various shades of mauve to a dark purple, or the golden yellow variety, have a fresh, simple quality very charming on a luncheon table. The natural foliage should always be used if available, and the flowers should never be crowded.

Vegetable Dishes *For Lent*

All Recipes serve six unless otherwise stated

Scalloped Tomato Surprise is particularly novel

VEGETABLES can supply us with quite a number of delicious and savoury dishes, which will come in useful at any meal during the Lenten season. At this time of year when winter vegetables are on the wane, and the variety to be obtained is somewhat scanty, it is often found difficult to find a choice of dishes. Monotony in the vegetable service may, however, be avoided by trying various combinations. Two fresh vegetables may be used together, or a fresh vegetable with a tinned or a dried vegetable. Vegetables may also be combined with grated cheese or chopped nuts, and various seasonings used to give piquancy, such as lemon, herbs, and pickles. Tasty sauces may also be utilised in the manufacture of these dishes, and now that eggs are coming down in price they may be more freely used, and combined with cheese and some vegetable, they make quite a substantial dish, which might take the place of meat. It is wonderful what can be done with the old vegetables if one has a little ingenuity and a certain amount of pains is taken in their preparation. The following recipes are well worth trying, and they will no doubt suggest many other combinations.

Bean Casserole

Combine a pint of cooked haricot or butter beans with two carrots finely chopped and two onions thinly sliced. Heat with one pint of canned tomato for about ten minutes, and season with one and one-half teaspoonfuls of salt, one-eighth teaspoonful of pepper, and one tablespoonful of sugar. Lay in the bottom of a buttered casserole three or four hard-boiled eggs cut in slices, sprinkle them with salt and pepper, and pour over it the combined vegetables. Dot with butter, using two tablespoonfuls, cover, and cook in a brisk oven until the vegetables are tender.

Scalloped Onions and Peas

This is a delicious dish, in which one tinned and one fresh vegetable are used. Cook eight small onions or three large ones, quartered, in boiling salted water until tender. Drain, and place half of them in a buttered glass or other fire-proof dish, dot with one tablespoonful of butter, and sprinkle over them one-fourth cupful of coarse bread-crumbs which have been slightly browned in one tablespoonful of butter or margarine. Add an inch layer of tinned peas, about one and one-half cupfuls, which have been highly seasoned with one-half teaspoonful of salt, one tablespoonful of butter, and one-half teaspoonful of sugar. Then add another layer of the seasoned onions and cover all with three-quarters cupful of the coarse, dried bread-crumbs. Pour over all one cupful of milk or thin cream and brown in a hot oven. Tomato sauce may be used instead of the milk, and French beans instead of the peas.

OTHER LENTEN DISHES

In our next issue will be given some tasty and attractive ways of cooking and serving FISH.

Latticed Eggs make an attractive main dish for a family luncheon or supper

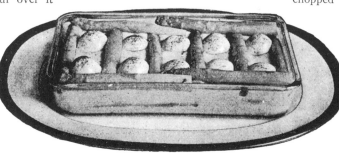

Celery with Cheese

This is another tasty bite. Measure one quart of celery cut into inch pieces and cook until tender in slightly salted, boiling water. Drain and place in a saucepan with one tablespoonful of butter, stirring for a minute or two. Then add one cupful of well-seasoned white sauce, two or three tablespoonfuls of grated cheese and one teaspoonful of lemon juice. Remove from the fire and serve on a hot dish, sprinkling one tablespoonful of cheese over the surface. Surround with a ring of chopped parsley, with here and there a bit of scarlet pimiento, and you will have a beautiful, as well as a tempting dish, for your pains.

Scalloped Tomato Surprise

Cook three large but delicate onions in salted water until soft but not broken. Lay them in the bottom of a buttered baking dish and with a sharp knife divide in quarters, not cutting entirely through the onions. Press the quarters slightly apart and between each two sections put one tablespoonful of the following mixture: equal quantities of grated cheese and fine bread-crumbs, mixed together, seasoned with pepper and salt, and slightly moistened with beaten egg. Carefully pour around three cupfuls of highly seasoned canned tomatoes to which has been added one-fourth cupful of bread-crumbs. Dot liberally with butter, sprinkle with fine crumbs, add more dots of butter, and bake in a hot oven one-half hour.

Eggs in Spinach Cases

This makes a very dainty dish. Line the bottom and sides of six small, buttered, fire-proof dishes with hot, very finely chopped and seasoned spinach, leaving a hollow in the centre of each. Break an egg into each dish, sprinkle with salt and pepper, and pour over a little melted butter. Set in a tin with hot water, and place in a moderate oven until the eggs are set. Pour a few drops of ketchup or sauce on the centre of each egg and serve at once.

Celery Custard

Combine one cupful of celery cut in ..ce with one onion finely chopped. ..ook both in one cupful of milk about ..ve minutes or until partially tender. ..dd salt and pepper and pour over two ..ggs beaten slightly. Bake in a buttered ..ish which has been placed in a pan of ..ater for about one hour, or until firm .. the touch. Sufficient for three or four.

Vegetable Croquettes

Very tasty croquettes can be made ..ith the remains of nicely cooked ..egetables, or a mixture of two or three ..inds together. Cut the vegetables into ..mall pieces, moisten them with some ..ood sauce, and season to taste. The ..ixture must be cold before it is used. ..oll out some scraps of pastry as thinly ..s possible, and cut out rounds three or ..our inches in diameter. Put some of ..e vegetable mixture in the centre of ..ch and wet round the edges. Double ..e pastry over and press the edges to-..ether. Brush over with beaten egg, ..prinkle with bread-crumbs, and fry in ..oiling fat or bake in the oven until ..ooked and nicely browned. These may ..e served with or without sauce as an ..ccompaniment.

Latticed Eggs

This is a combination of tinned as-paragus and eggs. Drain one quart of canned asparagus, being very careful not to break the stalks, and heat to the boil-ing-point. Prepare two cupfuls of medium thick white sauce well sea-soned; hard-cook six eggs. Halve the eggs crosswise, place a layer of sauce in the bottom of a shallow glass or fire-proof baking dish, then add a layer of asparagus, using one-half of the amount. Pour over this the remainder of the white sauce and on it place in regular lines the eggs cut in halves with the rounded sides up. Arrange the re-maining asparagus, cut in uniform lengths, in a lattice of squares around the eggs. Pour a little melted butter or margarine over all and set in a hot oven to heat through. Sprinkle with parsley or paprika pepper.

Turnips in Béchamel Sauce

This makes an excellent vegetable dish and will be found most delicate in flavour. Peel some white turnips and cut them in small dice. Cook three cupful of these in boiling water until tender; then drain and rinse with cold water to which a little vinegar or lemon-juice has been added. This will whiten and flavour the turnips. Fry a small onion chopped fine, one tiny carrot also chopped, in a tablespoonful of butter, till a pale golden tint, then stir in one and one-half tablespoonsful of flour and cook till the mixture bubbles. Now pour in half a pint of white stock or milk and stir till thick and creamy. Season with pepper, salt, and a few grains of cayenne, and pour over the turnips. Re-heat, and serve sprinkled with chopped parsley.

Tomato Toast with Cheese

3 Tomatoes	½ cup Milk
3 slices Bread	Seasoning
1 Egg	Cheese

Method.—Beat the egg until light, and add to it the milk, seasoned with salt and a little pepper. Cut the bread rather thick, halve the slices, and remove the crusts. Dip the pieces of bread into the egg-mix-ture, allowing them to absorb it. Then lift them carefully on to a greased tin, put a small piece of butter on the top of each, and brown lightly in the oven. Now lay two or three slices of tomato on the top of each slice of bread with more seasoning, and cover with thin slices of cheese. Bake in a hot oven, or under a broiler flame, until the tomato is tender and the cheese delicately browned.

DOWN ON THE FARM—
OR IN ANY HOME

Modernise your kitchen with a Valor-Perfection Oil Cooking Stove and forget your coal worries. Do away with all dust, dirt, and trouble. A woman's stove made as she would make it. Everything in sight and within easy reach. Easy to light. Clean and movable. No guess work—you know because you can see the progress of the cooking through the glass door of the oven. Don't cook in the dark—cook in the light and right way on a

VALOR-PERFECTION
Oil Cooking Stove

Made in Two, Three, and Four-burner Sizes
It saves Coal—Money—Time—Labour
Ask your Ironmonger to demonstrate
Send for free dainty Pamphlet
Please address your enquiry to the
ANGLO-AMERICAN OIL CO., LTD.
(108) Stove & Heater Dept.
**QUEEN ANNE'S GATE
LONDON, S.W.1**

USE
ROYAL
DAYLIGHT
OIL

AVAILABLE
EVERY-
WHERE

ANGLOCO

Successful home-making is not the monopoly of the married woman, as the delightful room above, belonging to two professional unmarried women, clearly shows

For the Bachelor Woman

A Quickly Made Meal at the End of a Busy Day

For the Bachelor Woman

THE woman who lives in rooms, or where it is difficult to get little tasty dishes prepared for her, will be glad to have the following suggestions. She is not often catered for in the ordinary cookery book, or it is only after wading through countless recipes that the few possible ones can be discovered. Dishes that require only a few minutes to cook and the simplest apparatus to prepare are the most welcome.

The following recipes could all be carried out on a gas ring or small oil stove, or even on a spirit lamp or chafing dish placed on a tray in front of the fire, and with the help of one or, at most, two saucepans.

With such a small outfit it is often possible to turn a cold and somewhat untempting repast into one that is not only tasty, but has some cheer and comfort as well.

Steamed Fish with Orange Sauce

White Fish.	1 gill Water
1 Orange	Seasoning
1 dessertspoonful Cornflour	A little Butter

Any kind of white fish may be selected, and it is preferable to have it filleted or cut in slices. Place the fish on a greased plate, season it with white pepper and salt, and cover with a lid or second plate. Then steam the fish over a saucepan of boiling water from 15 to 20 minutes. A few potatoes might quite well be cooked in the water underneath the fish if desired. To make the sauce, put the juice and grated rind of an orange into a small saucepan, and bring them to the boil. Mix the cornflour to a smooth paste with a little cold water, and add it to the other liquid. Stir constantly until it thickens, and cook 2 or 3 minutes. Add pepper and salt and a small piece of butter at the last. Pour the sauce over the fish, or serve it separately. This will be found excellent.

Cheese Dreams

Make some sandwiches with buttered bread and slices of cheese. The bread should be about one-fourth and the cheese one-eighth of an inch thick. Trim off the crusts and cut the sandwiches in convenient sized pieces. Then melt some butter in an omelet or frying-pan, put in the sandwiches and fry them until brown and crisp on both sides. Serve them very hot with a little highly seasoned sauce poured over each.

Creamed Shrimps

For Two Persons:

2 Eggs	1 teacupful White Sauce
1 teacupful prepared Shrimps	Seasoning
	Buttered Toast

Hard cook the eggs and cut them in thin slices. The shrimps can generally be bought ready boiled and shelled, or by the bottle or tin. Chop them rather coarsely. Heat the white sauce in a small saucepan, add a squeeze of lemon juice and other seasoning to taste. Then put in the eggs and shrimps, and let them heat gently. Serve on hot buttered toast.

Note.—The remains of a tin of lobster or salmon is also very good used up in this way.

Kidney Hot-Pot

For Two Persons:

4 Sheep's Kidneys	1 dessertspoonful Flour
1 Onion	1 gill Stock or Water
2 or 3 Potatoes	1 tablespoonful Fat
Seasoning	

The imported frozen kidneys may be used for this dish if they are allowed to thaw in warm water for some time before being used. Then dry them, split them, and remove the skin and white core. Put the flour on to a plate with some pepper and salt, slice the kidneys, and toss the pieces in it until they are well coated. Now melt the fat in a small saucepan, and cook the kidney in it until browned on all sides. Pour in the stock or water, and stir until boiling. Cut the onion in very thin and the potatoes in medium slices, and lay them on the top. Sprinkle with more pepper and salt, put the lid on the pan, and cook very slowly for half an hour. Shake the pan occasionally to prevent the contents sticking.

The addition of a few fresh mushrooms, peeled and cut in slices, would be an improvement to the hot-pot.

Mushrooms and Bacon

For One Person:

3 or 4 oz. Bacon	6 Mushrooms
Seasoning	

Wash and peel the mushrooms and cut them in thinnish slices. Remove the rind and rust from the bacon, and cut it in small thin pieces. Heat a frying-pan, put in the bacon and cook it for a minute or two. Then add the mushrooms, and cook both together for a few minutes longer. Add pepper and a pinch of nutmeg, and serve very hot.

DEPARTMENT *of* COOKERY

Conducted by Florence B. Jack, M.C.A.

First-Class Diploma, Edinburgh, Authoress of "Cookery for Every Household," "Invalid Cookery," etc

We Will Help You

to solve the problems which confront you in the preparation of those three meals each day. Whether it is a request for assistance in planning menus for special occasions, or merely a recipe which you desire, we will gladly give you the benefit of our research and experience. The Department of Cookery is constantly working for you in trying out new recipes and new methods in the Model Kitchen of "GOOD HOUSEKEEPING," 1 Amen Corner, London, E.C.4. Watch these pages for the results of this experimental work. Send a stamped addressed envelope with your inquiry

Good Things from the Egg Basket

THE egg lends itself so readily to different modes of treatment, and there are so many palatable and inexpensive ways of serving it, that it seems a pity there should be such a lack of variety in the way it appears on our tables. There is scarcely anything in the way of scraps that cannot be utilised in the making up of little egg dishes, the remains of fish, meat, game, poultry, vegetables, cheese, and even sauces can all help in making their preparation more tasty and appetising.

The purchase of a few dainty fireproof dishes, such as those illustrated on the opposite page, will give an air of refinement to egg dishes and enable them to be served up in an attractive manner. In many cases the eggs can be both cooked and served in the same dish.

To begin with the hard-boiled egg, let us see how the serving of this can be varied. An *Egg Fri-cassée* for one example is easy to prepare. Take the required number of hard-boiled eggs, shell them, and cut them in about eight equal-sized pieces; then for each four eggs prepare half a pint of good white sauce, and season it sufficiently with pepper, salt, a pinch of nutmeg, and some finely chopped parsley. Warm the eggs thoroughly in this sauce, being careful not to break the pieces, and serve garnished with croûtons of fried bread, or with small baked tomatoes or green peas.

Eggs and Cheese might be prepared

Sardine Eggs make a delicious cold savoury

in much the same way by adding grated cheese to the sauce instead of the parsley. The prepared eggs should be put into a fireproof dish and the hot sauce poured over them; then after a liberal sprinkling with more cheese, they should be browned in the oven or under the grill, and served in the same dish.

There are other sauces which could very readily be used for the reheating of hard-boiled eggs, such as brown sauce, tomato, curry, hollandaise, anchovy, shrimp sauce, etc., and the garnish too might be varied and one of the following used—mushrooms, rolls of bacon, boiled rice, fried onions, shrimps or prawns, according to individual taste and what happens to be available.

Another good way of serving any boiled eggs that happen to be left over is to make them into *Egg Croquettes.* Remove the shells from the eggs and chop them rather finely; then put them into a saucepan with an equal quantity of thick white sauce, and an equal quantity of white breadcrumbs. Season with pepper, salt, a pinch of nutmeg and a squeeze of lemon juice. Stir over the fire until all is thoroughly blended, and then spread the mixture on a plate and let it cool. When firm enough to handle, form into small cutlet shapes, using a little flour; egg and breadcrumb them, and fry in boiling fat until a golden brown. Drain on paper, and stick a small paper skewer or a piece of parsley stalk in the end of each. Serve up neatly, and garnish with parsley.

The croquettes may be made in any other shape preferred. A few chopped mushrooms or a little chopped ham or tongue added to the mixture will help to make it more tasty, and by dishing the croquettes on a border of spinach or mashed potatoes and pouring a good sauce round, quite a nice entrée can be served.

Egg Rissoles can be made by putting small portions of the same mixture inside rounds of very thin pastry before the egging, bread-crumbing, and frying.

Quite a variety of *Cold Savoury Dishes* can also be made from hard-boiled eggs. The eggs are cut in halves crosswise, the yolks removed, and a small piece cut off the ends of the white cases to enable them to stand. The yolks of the eggs are then blended with some butter and savoury ingredient, and the white cases refilled with this tasty mixture.

To make *Sardine Eggs*, for instance, pound sardines free from skin with the yolks of eggs and a little butter; then sieve the mixture, season to taste, and use it for filling the white cases. A pretty effect can be produced by putting the savoury paste into a forcing-bag with a star or rose pipe and forcing it out into the egg-cups. A little salad or aspic jelly may be used as a garnish.

This dish may be varied by using any kind of savoury paste, a purée of ham or game, cream cheese, or a curry mixture, etc., to mix with the yolks of eggs. Or a stoned olive may be stuffed with some of the savoury mixture and put in the centre of the egg case.

And now to turn to *Scrambled Eggs*. These too may be served in quite a number of different ways. One must first of all be able to produce the simple article, and to be a success this should be soft and creamy, resembling an omelet in texture. It requires some care to make scrambled eggs properly, and so often they are served tough and leathery, insufficiently seasoned, and sometimes floating in a sort of whey. The toast on which they are to be served should first be prepared, cut in

The serving of eggs is made more attractive by the use of fireproof dishes

convenient-sized pieces, and placed on a hot dish in readiness; then melt one or two ounces of butter in a saucepan, add half a teacupful of milk, or chicken broth is even better, and then three eggs slightly beaten. Season to taste, being careful to add enough salt. Now stir the mixture over a moderate heat until the eggs begin to set, then reduce the heat, and continue stirring until sufficiently thick. Pour the mixture at once over the prepared toast and serve immediately. Scrambled eggs should never stand, but be served up as quickly as an omelet.

Egg Cutlets

Now here are some suggestions for varying the simple scrambled egg. *First :* The toast itself may be made more tasty by spreading it with some savoury paste or potted meat. *Second :* Other ingredients may be added to the egg mixture, such as anchovy or shrimp sauce, chopped ham or tongue, a few green peas or asparagus points, smoked fish, a few shrimps or chopped prawns, or some chopped mushrooms. *Third :* A separate garnish may be added to the dish, such as rolls of bacon, anchovies, small baked tomatoes, grilled mushrooms, fried onions, etc. And *Fourth :* Scrambled eggs may be combined with

some other dish, as, for instance, stewed kidneys, chicken livers, stewed tomatoes, spinach, macaroni, risotto, and so on.

Or, here is rather a novel way of serving scrambled eggs cold; it is a little more elaborate, but will serve as a pretty luncheon or supper dish—*Scrambled Eggs in Tomatoes*. Choose even-sized tomatoes, cut them in halves, scoop out the insides very carefully, and turn them upside down to drain. Or, if the tomatoes are small, leave them whole, cutting only a small piece off the top to enable the inside to be removed.

Sieve the inside pulp from the tomatoes, and use it in preparing the scrambled egg. Fill up the tomatoes with nicely seasoned scrambled egg, and, when cold, coat over with mayonnaise sauce or any other good salad dressing. The addition of a little aspic would be an improvement. Garnish the tomatoes with thin pieces of green pickle and serve with salad.

One of the simplest ways of cooking eggs, and one which is much adopted by the French, is *Eggs sur le Plat*. To do this, melt a small quantity of butter in a fireproof dish, break the required number of eggs into it, season with pepper and salt, and put some small pieces of butter on the top; then bake the eggs in the oven, or cook them on the hot plate, until the white part is set, but not hard. Serve on the dish in which they are cooked. Small individual dishes are often used, and these are very fascinating—the eggs would then be called " *en Cocottes.*"

Eggs sur le Plat may be varied by sprinkling some savoury mixture over the dish before breaking in the eggs, such as chopped ham, tongue, mushrooms, herbs, parsley, shallot, grated cheese, etc., or by pouring over them when nearly cooked some good gravy, sauce, or cream.

Another way of varying *Eggs sur le Plat* is to pour a layer of sauce into the dish first, to break the eggs carefully into it, and then to cook them. A well-made bread sauce is very good used in this way, and with the addition of a little grated cheese a most savoury dish can be produced. A layer of tomato sauce, with eggs broken into it and a sprinkling of parsley over the top, is also good.

During the Lenten season, when egg dishes are apt to be very much to the fore, every housewife should put a little extra time and thought into the selection of such combinations as will lend substantial variety in the serving of this old-time friend. Try some of the suggestions given above; they will add zest to your springtime menu.

Another article on making eggs into omelets will appear shortly.

Scrambled Eggs in Tomatoes make an appetising luncheon dish

RASPBERRY CREAM CAKE.

Take a packet of Green's Raspberry Flavoured Sponge Mixture, and make up according to the directions given on back of the packet for Victoria Sandwich. When cold, spread one half of the sandwich with whipped cream, place the other half on top, and cover with thin water icing. Decorate with crystallised violets or glacé cherries as preferred. The cream should be whipped with just a teaspoonful of sugar.

Please retain this page or cut out the recipes for future reference.

GREEN'S SPONGE MIXTURE

This article is packed in eight flavours, viz.:— **Vanilla, Lemon, Madeira, Orange, Cocoanut, Almond, Chocolate, Raspberry,** also **Plain.**

Nothing else is required but two eggs with one packet to make a beautiful light Sandwich, Sponge Roll, or Cake. A child can use it. It is finished in a matter of about 15 minutes, cooking included. Delicious light Sponge Puddings may also be made from the Mixture, also Castle Puddings, Genoese, Madeira Cakes, &c. See Recipes on this page and in Recipe Booklet sent post free.

GREEN'S

The

Original

BRIGHTON

SPONGE
MIXTURE

Of Grocers and Stores Everywhere

To-day's Price

6½d.

Per Packet

Write for Recipe Booklet "G.H." giving additional recipes

H. J. GREEN & Co., Lᴰ·
BRIGHTON

GENOESE.

One packet Green's Sponge Mixture (preferably Madeira, Almond, or Lemon Flavour), 2 oz. butter, 2 eggs. **Method.**—Cream the butter, and add by degrees first a little of the Sponge Mixture, and then the eggs, which have previously been thoroughly whisked. Spread the batter over one of Green's Swiss Roll tins, and bake for 10 or 15 minutes. When cold, cut into fancy shapes and spread with water icing, coloured if liked. **Water Icing.**—Icing sugar and cold water mixed to the consistency of cream.

CASTLE PUDDINGS.

One packet of Green's Sponge Mixture (Lemon or Madeira Flavour), 3 oz. butter, 2 oz. flour, 2 eggs, a little milk.

Method.—Mix the Sponge Mixture and flour thoroughly. Cream the butter, add by degrees a little of the dry ingredients, then some of the egg (previously thoroughly whisked) until all is used up, taking a small quantity of milk to make all into a smooth batter. Grease about 1 doz. Castle pudding tins, put in batter, bake for 10 or 15 min. in a hot oven. Serve with Green's Custard, or as cakes for afternoon tea. These are delicious.

VALENCIA SPONGE.

One packet Green's Lemon, Almond, or Madeira Sponge Mixture, 2 eggs, a few almonds, a little sherry, 1 pint of Green's Custard. **Method.**—Beat the eggs thoroughly, add by degrees the Sponge Mixture. Put the batter into a well-greased mould, and bake in a moderate oven for 30 minutes. When cold, place the sponge in a glass dish and soak with sherry, blanch and cut up the almonds and decorate. Make a pint of Green's Custard and pour around the sponge.

SPONGE ROLL.

One packet of Green's Sponge Mixture and 2 eggs.

Method.—Break the eggs into a ba. in and whisk thoroughly with a good pinch of salt; add by degrees the Sponge Mixture, beating all to a smooth batter. Take a flat oblong tin, grease well with butter or lard and sprinkle with flour. Put the batter into the tin and spread evenly, place in a hot oven, and bake for about 10 minutes. Turn on to a sugared paper, spread with jam or marmalade, and roll quickly.

CHOCOLATE TRIFLE.

Make a sponge with Green's Sponge Mixture, and when cold, cut up. Take a packet of Green's Chocolate Blanc Mange or Green's Chocolate Mould, and make according to directions, using 1½ pints of Milk. When this thick "Chocolate Custard" has cooled a little, pour on to the sponge, sprinkle with desiccated cocoanut, and serve cold.

SPONGE SANDWICH.

One packet of Green's Sponge Mixture and 2 eggs.

Method.—Break the eggs into a basin and whisk thoroughly with a good pinch of salt; add by degrees the Sponge Mixture, beating all to a smooth batter. Take two round sandwich tins, well greased; sprinkle with flour and put half the mixture into each. Place in a hot oven and bake from 10 to 15 minutes. Turn on to a sugared board, spread with jam or marmalade, place together, and sprinkle with sifted sugar.

Photo: W. A. Rouch

The beautiful red grouse, which delights the hearts of both sportsmen and gourmets, is said to be peculiar to the British Isles

About Grouse—*Anticipating "the 12th"*

THE highly prized grouse will soon be in season. On the 12th of August grouse shooting commences, and from that date onwards the bird will be available for table use. Its flavour improves as the season advances, and it is not until September that the bird is at its best.

There are several different species of grouse, but it is the beautiful and delicious red grouse—or moor fowl—that is so much appreciated by gourmet and epicure. This bird is supposed to be peculiar to the British Isles. It is abundant on the moors of Scotland and in the north of England, and is also found on the heather hills of Wales and Ireland. France has also its *coq de bruyère*, which resembles our grouse very closely, but it lacks the special flavour which is peculiar to the British variety. The delicate flavour of the flesh is supposed to be due to the heather on which the bird feeds, or possibly to other plants or berries found in mountainous regions.

Grouse, like other kinds of game, requires to be kept a certain length of time before it develops its full flavour. The French describe this as the *fumet*; it is really a natural principle, which not only increases the savoury flavour of game, but softens the fibres, and acts as an aid to digestion as well. If game is cooked too soon it will be lacking in this peculiar flavour. It must not, however, be kept too long, or it will acquire a taint and become unwholesome. To keep a game larder requires some skill, and unfortunately it is impossible to draw up a table showing exactly how long the various game birds should hang before cooking. There are several different factors to be taken into account. For example, a bird that has been cleanly shot will keep better than one that has been torn and bruised, and one that has

fallen on dry ground will hang longer than one that lands in water. The length of time for hanging depends also on the age of the bird and the weather. An old bird will require to be kept a longer time than a young one, and a cold dry climate is much better for hanging purposes than a damp and muggy one. As a rule, grouse should hang at least forty-eight hours before it is cooked. The birds should remain unplucked and undrawn as long as possible. Hang them in a dry, cool place, and if possible where there is a current of air. If the birds happen to be wet they should be carefully wiped and then hung for a few hours in a warm kitchen, or in the sun, before being taken to the larder. When there has been injury to the skin the part should be liberally dusted with pepper to keep off flies. As soon as there is the least evidence of taint the birds should be plucked and drawn, and then cooked quickly once they have been prepared. If there is slight taint, this may generally be removed by soaking the plucked bird in milk, or by washing it in water with plenty of salt and a little vinegar. Dry thoroughly before cooking. If a plucked bird is not required for immediate use, it can be kept for a few hours longer if it is plunged into boiling water and allowed to remain for five minutes or so, then dried and dusted with pepper.

The most popular way to cook grouse is to roast it, unless the bird happens to be old, when some other method of cooking will have to be adopted. There are several recognised signs by which the age of a bird can be distinguished. In the young bird the breast is plump and firm, and the legs smooth and supple with a short, rounded spur, whereas in the old bird the legs are rough and scaly and the spur is much more fully developed. The plumage too of a young

bird is brighter and more glossy and the wing feathers are softer and not so firmly fixed.

To roast a grouse, first pluck and pick it carefully, squeeze out the inside, and then wipe it both inside and out with a damp cloth, but do not wash it. Work up a small piece of butter with pepper, salt, and a squeeze of lemon-juice, and put this inside the body with the liver. Truss like a fowl and tie a piece of fat bacon over the breast. Roast in front of the fire or in a good oven, basting frequently with butter or bacon fat. The basting is most important, as the flesh of grouse is inclined to be dry. From 20 to 25 minutes should be sufficient time for cooking. Grouse must not be overcooked or it will lose that juicy and delicate flavour for which it is so much appreciated. A few minutes before the bird is ready, remove the bacon fat from the breast, dredge it with flour, and return to the oven to brown. The method of serving and choice of accompaniments are matters of taste and of fashion. The toast underneath the bird, the fried bread-crumbs and bread sauce are no longer necessities. Something lighter, a garnish of watercress with one appropriate sauce and a few potato chips or straws, is more in favour. If a brown sauce is served, no strong spices must overpower the delicate flavour of the grouse. A fruit sauce, such as orange or lemon, has been fashionable of late, or some tart fruit jelly or fruit compote may be served.

Orange Sauce.—½ pt. light stock, ½ oz. butter, ½ oz. flour, grated rind of 1 and the juice of 2 oranges, 1 yolk of egg. Melt the butter in a saucepan. Mix in the flour, and pour on the stock. Stir until boiling. Add the orange rind and juice and simmer for ten minutes, stir in the yolk of egg, and strain before serving.

Capping the tins is an important process in canning, and in this illustration it is shown being done under thoroughly up-to-date, hygienic conditions

The Truth About Canned Foods

By WILLIAM G. SAVAGE, B.Sc., M.D. (London)

THERE exists a widespread prejudice against preserved foods generally, and against tinned or canned foods in particular, which is fanned by much ill-informed newspaper and other criticism, and which seems to acquire considerable justification from such deplorable tragedies as the catastrophe last August at Loch Maree. Undoubtedly public confidence is greatly shaken. The purport of this article is to set out the scientific facts of the case, so that the reader may be able to form a reliable opinion on the subject.

It is necessary to realise that we have to discriminate between dangers to health which are peculiar to this particular method of preserving food and dangers which are common to all foods, preserved or not preserved. This is a very important distinction. It is evident that disease germs may be conveyed into our bodies with any kind of food, either accidentally or from want of adequate care in seeing that the food is not contaminated. The scientist, in assessing the liability of food to convey disease, knows that the three factors which are of main importance are: is the food one which is eaten raw or cooked, is the food of such a nature that germs which have gained access can multiply in or on it,

THE panic recently created in the public mind by certain tragic cases of food-poisoning convinced us of the need for a definite statement of facts from an outstanding authority on the subject. Dr. W. G. Savage was the man chosen by the British Government to make full investigation of the canned food industries of England and America, and he has embodied the result of his investigation in a series of special Reports for the Canned Food Committee of the Food Investigation Board. This article, in which he gives a scientific, but lucid explanation of the actual causes of poisoning by food, will, we think, completely dispel the widespread doubt and distrust with which the whole subject is at present regarded.

and is it a food which is liable from its method of collection or preparation to bacterial contamination.

For example, milk is a great vehicle for the spread of disease, since not only is it liable to a good deal of bacterial contamination arising from want of care and cleanliness in collection, but also because bacteria find it a most suitable medium in which to grow and multiply (so that one or two harmful germs may become thousands before the milk is drunk) and, further, because it is largely consumed raw and without cooking. In

other words, milk has all the three dangerous qualities mentioned above, and this is why authorities are so insistent as to the need for its special care.

As another example, butcher's meat is much more liable than bread to convey disease, since the former may come from a diseased animal and bacteria will rapidly multiply in it, factors which do not operate with bread. Meat, however, is less liable to spread disease than milk, because the cooking it receives kills most bacteria and is a valuable safeguard.

These three factors must be kept in mind when studying the dangers of canned foods. Tinned foods, and most kinds preserved in glass, are foods which, after they are put in the tin or other receptacle, are subjected to heat, and this after the tin has been finally closed. The methods of preparing foods for canning are very varied, but in nearly all cases, in addition to this terminal heating after closure, the foods are heated at one or more stages in their preparation. It used to be supposed that the heating given them after the tins were closed sterilised the contents, and that was why they kept sound. Later studies have shown that this is not always true, and that some bacteria may survive. Fortunately, nearly all the harmful bacteria are of types which are killed at fairly low temperatures, and therefore in nearly all cases these, if present, would be killed by the heating given. The few exceptions will be discussed later on in this article. It can be very positively stated that these canned foods when sound always contain a very small proportion of the bacteria which the same food would contain if it was eaten unpreserved.

This side of the subject, therefore, can be summed up by stating that all foods may serve as a vehicle to convey disease germs, but that the canned foods are very much safer than the raw article as regards this danger because they are foods which are heated during or after preparation and so have this valuable added safeguard.

The other aspect of the problem is a consideration as to whether there are any special dangers peculiar to preserved foods. There are a number of possibilities all of which must be considered.

The commonest popular conception is that these foods may go bad in the tin and that persons eating them may become ill in consequence. Two special forms of food-poisoning will be discussed shortly, but apart from their occurrence there is no real danger from this source. It is undeniable that these foods may become decomposed within the tin, either because decomposing organisms have survived the heating given or because leaks developed and such organisms go in from outside. When this happens, however, the food becomes visibly unsound to eye and nose, and there is very little risk of anyone eating food in this condition.

Also the danger from this kind of decomposition is enormously exaggerated, since, in fact, such decomposition products are only very slightly poisonous. The old conception of ptomaine poisoning from decomposition changes is not true. There is no such thing as ptomaine poisoning, it is a " Mrs. Harris " of medicine, and the theory of it was founded upon faulty knowledge.

The intelligent reader may agree that obviously unsound tinned food will not be eaten, but yet have in his mind the possibility that there may exist a condition in which the obtrusive changes of decomposition may be only slight, so that the food might be eaten, and yet the changes be sufficiently advanced to make the food actively poisonous. Fortunately, as regards simple decomposition changes, there is no evidence at all that this occurs apart from the special food-poisoning cases now to be dealt with, which are not decomposition changes at all and are nothing to do with the food "going bad."

Two separate groups of bacteria may cause food-poisoning and constitute a real danger, but one which is not peculiar to canned or preserved foods. One group causes botulism, the other a variety of food-poisoning which is very much commoner.

Botulism is now a very rare disease, as will be realised when it is mentioned that only a few hundred cases have been recorded during the whole of the last twenty years. The outbreak at Loch Maree was of this character, but is the only outbreak which has been recorded in Great Britain. It is, on the other hand, an extremely fatal disease, and in that outbreak all the eight victims died. The germ which causes it (*Bacillus botulinus*) lives in soil and other places and very occasionally may get into canned foods, especially fruits and vegetables. It forms spores which are very resistant, so that the heating given the tins may not kill them, while the conditions in the tin rather favour their growth. Fortunately, if they grow they nearly always produce changes, such as a definite musty smell, which show that the contents are not good, while the tins themselves are unsound. With highly spiced foods such as some meat pastes these alterations in the food may be masked and overlooked, and this danger-sign be lost.

If infection with this organism was at all common it would make preserved foods very dangerous, but fortunately the liability of an outbreak of botulism from canned or other foods is a very remote one. The danger is reduced to very small limits in the first place by the rarity of this organism being present, by the fact that the heating given is a valuable safeguard, since probably only a few gaining access survive, and lastly by the fact already mentioned that if a tin is infected the tin and the contents nearly always become unsound and so are naturally rejected. A real but a very remote danger.

The other kind of food-poisoning is a good deal commoner, and the writer has records of over fifty such outbreaks. The food becomes infected with a special germ, allied to the organism which causes (Continued)

So scientific has food canning become that fully equipped laboratories, with trained chemists in charge, are a part of every big manufactory

The Truth About Canned Foods

typhoid fever, which has the very unusual peculiarity that the poisonous bodies which it produces withstand boiling. The heating given after the tin is closed should always, and usually does, kill the bacillus itself, but the poisonous bodies which it has already produced may be left undestroyed. Types of tinned foods which may become poisonous in this way are usually meat or salmon. The tin outside and the contents inside appear perfectly good, and no one by ordinary examination can detect that the food is poisonous. Persons eating such food are quickly attacked with illness (diarrhœa, vomiting, abdominal pain, and weakness) and may be severely ill for days, but fortunately the condition is rarely fatal.

It is, however, important to grasp the fact that while food-poisoning outbreaks due to the poison of this organism are not uncommon, they are not associated more with preserved foods than with fresh foods. Indeed, when they occur associated with fresh foods they are liable to be much more dangerous, and often cause death, owing to the fact that in such cases the living organism is often present as well as these heat-resisting poisons.

The public can adopt no precautions to protect themselves from poisonous canned foods of this type, and neither the vendor of the food nor the Local Authority officers who may have passed the tin as sound are to blame. The prevention of such outbreaks is a matter of proper supervision of the food at its source, and the prevention there of infection with this germ.

Progress lags because we do not know enough as to how the food becomes infected, and more research is required. Their occurrence is part of the general risk of infection from food which is not confined to, and is indeed less common in, canned as compared with fresh food. They should not occur, but as yet we do not know enough to always prevent them.

Another possible danger, and one peculiarly associated with tinned foods, is from tin poisoning. Undoubtedly some tin is dissolved and mixed in with the food, but the risk of any poisoning from this cause is a very small one, although it looms large in public estimation. The Great War was a gigantic experiment in canned food consumption, but the writer is unaware of a single case of tin poisoning resulting from the enormous quantities of tinned foods consumed.

Vitamins (those minute essentials to life) are damaged by cooking, and because canned foods are cooked foods such foods may contain little or no vitamin. This is not of much importance so long as these foods are only a portion of our diet. On the other hand a person who, for instance, lives on tinned sardines for breakfast, tinned beef with tinned fruit for dinner, finishes with tinned salmon for supper would run a serious risk of having insufficient vitamins in his daily food.

Summing up the subject, it may be said that canned foods, like any other food, may spread disease from being infected with harmful bacilli, but that from this point of view they are generally safer than raw foods, being cooked. They may be made very far from the places of consumption, so that their preparation demands careful supervision to see that sound and fresh food only is used, that they are handled properly, and properly treated.

Help Yourself.

When the bread is spread with Sailor Savouries, that's an invitation that any hostess is proud to give and any guest delighted to accept. They taste as good as they look. Sailor Savouries—remember—not just potted meat.

There is no purer product than Sailor Savouries, to which fact the makers testify by backing them with a £500 guarantee.

Whenever you want a change in the menu, or a meal quickly served, make use of Sailor Savouries.

Made in the following eight delicious varieties, all warranted true to description :—

Chicken & Ham. Bloater. Turkey & Tongue. Chicken, Ham & Tongue.
Ham & Tongue. Lobster. Salmon & Shrimp. Salmon & Anchovy.

If you cannot obtain Sailor Savouries, send 10½d., with your Grocer's name and address, and we will send you a full-sized jar, post free.

N.B.—Each jar is enclosed in a sun-proof carton which **protects it from light, heat, and dust.**

SAILOR SAVOURIES

*The name
" ANGUS WATSON "
on any ready-to-eat food
means the best of its kind.*

ANGUS WATSON & CO. LTD.,
17K, ELLISON BUILDINGS,
NEWCASTLE-UPON-TYNE.

8VR 3—34

Wives who are Queens—
of Home Happiness

There are thousands of homes where the wife reigns as Queen of Happiness over her family. Her affectionate rule starts the days with sunny smiles.

Father sets out to meet his daily responsibilities with a cheerful heart. The children leave for school radiant with the joy of living. A royal welcome awaits them on their return. With eager anticipation they take their places at the table, for well they know the good and satisfying fare that "Queen Mother" delights to provide for them.

Foremost in the kitchen of every Queen Mother, because of their importance in her loving preparation of good things to eat, are:—

Cook's Farm Eggs

What rich goodness Queen Mother puts into all her Made-with-eggs Puddings by using the money-saving Cook's Farm Eggs, now costing only 1/6d. a dozen large eggs.

Omelettes, Custards and Yorkshire Puddings

What delicious Omelettes they make, cheapest of all Egg Dishes and most easily and quickly prepared; what delightful baked and boiled Custards; what Yorkshire Puddings unrivalled in their appetising flavour and rich food value—and scores of other always-welcome Egg Dishes that every Queen Mother knows how to prepare.

Delicious Cakes

She uses Cook's Farm Eggs, too, in her rich Fruit Cakes, Madeira Cakes, Sponge Cakes, Queen Cakes, and many tea-time fancies loved by the children, including those jolly Birthday Cakes reserved for special occasions.

Cook's Beef Suet

Who doesn't love the steaming hot Savoury Puddings that Queen Mother makes with this splendid aid to good cooking?

What visions of delight are conjured up by the very names of these most popular, satisfying and economical of all puddings:—Golden Roll, Apple and Currant Roly-Poly, "Spotted Dick," Raisin, Currant and Jam Roll, Ginger and Lemon Roll, Marmalade Pudding, Toffee Pudding, and many others, including *that special one* for which Mother is herself famous.

With Cook's Shredded Beef Suet recently reduced in price by 3½d. per lb.—now costing only 6½d. for a full half-pound sealed carton—these nourishing, satisfying and delicious Puddings will be more plentiful and popular than ever.

Every Wife and Mother can reign Queen of Happiness over her family if she combines wise economy with good cooking by purchasing and using these two excellent aids—Cook's Farm Eggs and Cook's Shredded Beef Suet.

* * * *

Queen Mother's two Famous Aids to Good Cooking are sold by the best Grocers everywhere.

Cook's Farm Eggs
Cook's Beef Suet

Ask your Grocer To-day for these two Money-Saving Aids to Good Cooking.

Stuffed Cabbage is a delicious savoury dish that few men will fail to appreciate

When "Good Housekeeping" comes in at the door, monotony in diet flies out of the window

TO PLEASE THE MEN

All these recipes have been tested in the Model Kitchen

IF you want to know of something tasty, and something a little out of the common to please the men-folk, try the following recipes. None of them are difficult to prepare, they are all good, and ought to please the most fastidious.

Sole Matelote: In Normandy this is a favourite way of preparing the sole, or any other flat fish. It is very simple and very good.

Remove the dark skin from the fish, and trim off the head and fins. Grease a fireproof dish and place the fish on it with the skinned side downwards. Half cover the fish with cider and water mixed in equal quantities, sprinkle with salt and lay one or two sprigs of parsley at the sides. Cook in a moderate oven for 20 minutes, or rather less, according to the size of the fish. Remove the parsley, and thicken the liquid with a piece of butter the size of a small egg and a small spoonful of flour mixed smoothly together. Pour the sauce over the fish, and sprinkle very lightly with some fine browned breadcrumbs.

Scallops: These crustacea resemble the oyster in appearance, but are very much larger. They are delicate in flavour and make excellent eating. Care must be taken, however, to use them only when they are very fresh and in full season. The roe should then be a bright orange colour, and the flesh very white.

Remove the scallops from their shells and wash them very thoroughly until free from all grit. Then remove the beard and black part and let them drain on a cloth and cook as desired.

There are several ways of preparing scallops: *Fried Scallops:* Let them soak for ½ hour in a mixture of salad oil and lemon-juice seasoned with pepper and salt. Then drain, roll in flour, egg and breadcrumb, and fry in boiling fat to a golden brown. Or, they may be made into a *Fricassée:* Cut the scallops into three or four pieces, put them into a double cooker with a good white sauce to cover them, and let them stew about 30 minutes. Serve with dry toast. *Scallops au gratin* are also good; cook them in sauce as above, then turn them into a fireproof dish and sprinkle with grated cheese and breadcrumbs mixed. Lay a few small pieces of butter on the top and brown in a good oven.

Cannelon of Beef makes a very good meat dish and it is not difficult to prepare. You will require 1 lb. stewing steak, ¼ lb. fat bacon, 3 or 4 cooked potatoes, 1 dessertspoonful chutney or chopped pickles, seasoning, and 1 egg. Cut the meat and bacon in pieces and put them through the mincing machine. Chop the potatoes and add them to the mince, add seasonings, and bind together with the egg well beaten. Form into a roll, using a little flour, and place this on a baking-tin with some hot dripping. Bake in a good oven about 1 hour, basting frequently. Serve with brown or tomato sauce poured round. Garnish with a cooked vegetable, or a few rolls of bacon. This cannelon is also good cold served with salad.

Stuffed Cabbage: Choose a hard white cabbage of medium size. Remove the outside leaves, leaving a compact form, and trim away the hard part of the stalk. Then cut a round about 3 inches in diameter in the top of the cabbage and scoop out the centre, making a hole about the size of a tea-cup. Now wash the cabbage well and let it soak in cold water, whilst preparing the stuffing.

Take the remains of any cooked meat, including a little ham or bacon, and chop finely 1 cupful. Add 1 cupful breadcrumbs or cooked and sieved potato, season with pepper, salt, a little chopped parsley and onion, and a pinch of nutmeg. Moisten with a little milk or sauce. Mix well and fill up the cavity in the cabbage. Cover with a leaf, and tie the whole tightly in a piece of muslin. Plunge into a saucepan of boiling water and boil quickly for 1 hour or longer. Lift out, drain, and press out the water. Serve covered with a good white sauce.

If any stuffing is left over, it may be made up into small balls, browned in the oven with fat, and used as a garnish.

Ham Toast with Mushrooms makes a very tasty savoury. Chop finely 1 teacupful of cooked ham, using a fair proportion of fat. Put it into a saucepan with a piece of butter the size of a small egg and season with mustard and cayenne. Add 2 eggs, well beaten, and a little salt if necessary. Stir over the fire until thick. Serve on rounds of toast or fried bread and garnish with grilled or toasted mushrooms.

Cannelon of Beef garnished with crisp little rolls of bacon

Ham Toast with Mushrooms makes an excellent breakfast dish

Bring the sun of Spain to your Breakfast Table in the White Pot o' Dundee—

—There's no marmalade flavour like that of Seville's finest oranges preserved in the Keiller way.

This year's crop gives you Keiller's at its best, and the White Pot retains all the zestful flavour of the orange for you.

Try a pot of the new Keiller's Marmalade on your breakfast table to-morrow.

Up with the White Pots o' Bonnie Dundee!

KEILLER'S
DUNDEE WHITE POT
MARMALADE

EVERY GOOD GROCER SELLS IT

Kidneys and mushrooms combined, and tomatoes stuffed with mushroom, make appetising luncheon dishes.

A WORD IN PRAISE OF *MUSHROOMS*

Delicious recipes tested in our Model Kitchen

MUSHROOMS have been used as food from the earliest times, and for generations they have been cultivated in ever-increasing quantities. They are obtainable all the year round, but sometimes the price is so prohibitive that they become a delicious luxury, which the epicure alone is able to afford.

There are quite a number of edible varieties, but the common field mushroom (*Agaricus campestris*) is the one most generally eaten in this country. These should now be plentiful and to be had for the gathering by those living in the country, while town-dwellers should be able to buy them for a moderate sum. The housewife may well serve them occasionally to add variety to her daily meals—they are not particularly nourishing, but they are appetising and tasty.

When using mushrooms, care must always be taken to have them freshly picked; once they have become sodden and black they are no longer fit for food. The flesh should be white and brittle in texture, with a delicious odour. No powerful seasoning should be used in the cooking of mushrooms, their own delicious flavour must always predominate. Overcooking should also be avoided as it tends to harden them.

To prepare Mushrooms: Trim off the earthy end of the stalks, scrape the stems and peel the skin off the caps. If they are perfectly clean, do not wash them, as it is apt to spoil the flavour. The stems are often tough and require longer cooking than the caps, and on this account the peeled caps are often used in one dish, and the trimmings chopped fine and used for flavouring another dish. There are many uses to which mushrooms can be put—perhaps they are never so good as when cooked simply by themselves; but there are also many very good combinations, as the following recipes will show.

Mushrooms Suprème: 1 lb. mushrooms, 1 oz. butter, 1 tablespoonful chopped parsley, ½ gill hot water, celery salt, pepper, 2 or 3 hard-cooked eggs, ½ pt. white sauce, 6 rounds of toast.

Clean and prepare the mushrooms. Melt the butter in a deep saucepan, and add the parsley, water, and the stems of the mushrooms cut in small pieces. Cover and simmer for 5 minutes. Then add the caps of the mushrooms cut in halves or quarters, and season with celery salt and pepper. Re-cover and simmer about 10 minutes longer, or until the mushrooms are tender. Meanwhile prepare the white sauce and season it nicely. Slice the eggs and add them to the sauce. Pile the mushrooms on rounds of hot toast, pour the egg sauce over, and garnish with chopped parsley.

Lambs' Kidneys and Mushrooms: 1 lb. mushrooms, 6 kidneys, 2 oz. butter, 1 large onion, 1 tablespoonful chopped parsley, 1 tablespoonful flour, ½ pt. stock, seasoning, mashed potatoes.

Mince the onion finely, put it into a saucepan with half the butter and parsley, and cook until tender and golden-brown in colour. Add the flour and stir until blended, then pour in the stock and continue to stir until boiling. Wash the kidneys, cut them in halves lengthwise, and remove the skin and core. Then add them to the sauce, cover, and simmer gently until tender. Meanwhile clean and prepare the mushrooms and cut them in halves lengthwise. Put them into a separate saucepan with the remainder of the butter and a little water, and simmer until tender. Then combine with the kidneys and season with celery salt and pepper. Place a mound of well-seasoned mashed potatoes in the centre of a dish, sprinkle with parsley, and arrange round it the kidneys and mushrooms.

Mushrooms and Spaghetti: 1 lb. mushrooms, ¼ lb. spaghetti, 2 oz. butter, 1 onion, 2 tablespoonfuls minced red pepper, 1 tablespoonful chopped parsley, ¼ pt. stock, seasoning.

Cook the spaghetti in boiling salt and water until tender. Then drain, run some hot water over it and keep it warm. Meanwhile melt the butter in a saucepan, add the onion and red pepper both finely chopped, and cook for a minute or two. (Sweet red pepper can be bought in tins if the fresh is not available.) Then add the stock, the mushrooms prepared and cut in halves, and seasoning; cover, and simmer for 10 minutes, or until the mushrooms are tender. Put the spaghetti in a hot dish, sprinkle the parsley over, and pour the mushroom mixture on the top. Served with a green salad, this provides a luncheon dish well worth the making.

Tomatoes Stuffed with Mushrooms: 6 tomatoes, ½ lb. mushrooms, 1 oz. butter, 1 tablespoonful chopped onion, 1 tablespoonful flour, 1 gill milk, seasoning, 2 tablespoonfuls bread-crumbs, 6 rounds of toast, ½ pt. white sauce.

Select firm, fresh tomatoes of equal size. Wipe them and scoop out the centres. Season with pepper and salt, and turn them upside down to drain. Melt the butter in a saucepan, add the onion and the caps of the mushrooms skinned and cut in slices. Cover and cook slowly for 10 minutes. Meanwhile mix the flour with the milk, add them to the mushrooms, stir until thick, and season to taste. Fill the tomatoes with this mixture, sprinkle a few bread-crumbs on the top, and bake in a good oven about 10 minutes, or until the tomatoes are tender. Remove and serve on rounds of toast. A thin, well-seasoned white sauce may be poured over.

Mushrooms and Green Peas: 1 lb. mushrooms, 2 oz. butter, 2 cupfuls cooked green peas, 2 or 3 tomatoes, 1 onion, seasoning.

Prepare the mushrooms, separating the stems from the caps. Chop the stems and cut the caps in pieces. Divide the butter in three portions and put one of these into a saucepan with the water and mushroom stems. Cover and simmer until the stems are almost tender. Then add the caps and cook about 5 minutes longer. Melt another piece of butter in a separate saucepan, put in the onion finely chopped and cook it until tender and a golden brown. Add the peas and seasoning and make thoroughly hot. Serve on a hot dish and keep warm. Melt the remaining portion of butter in the same saucepan, put in the tomatoes, peeled and cut in pieces. Season and cook until tender. Pour the tomatoes on the top of the peas and arrange the mushrooms on the top. Finish with a sprinkle of paprika.

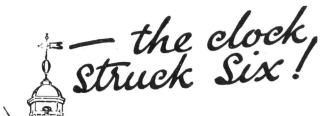

— the clock struck Six!

I had no idea it was so late! Nothing in for supper, either. I bought some Homepride Self-Raising Flour and made straight for home.

I started making the meat pasties directly I got in. I put the cold meat scraps through the mincing machine and added a little gravy and tomato sauce, seasoning with pepper and salt. Then I weighed out 1 lb. of Homepride, mixed in a pinch of salt and rubbed in $\frac{1}{2}$ lb. of lard to form a fairly stiff paste, using a little milk to moisten.

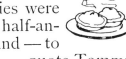

The pasties were ready in half-an-hour. And — to quote Tommy —"You could tell they were toppers by the smell of 'em!"

Homepride
SELF-RAISING
FLOUR

Our Daily Test Keeps It Best.

HOMEPRIDE MILLS
BIRKENHEAD, COVENTRY, CAMBRIDGE AND LONDON.

The best HOT POT *I ever made was prepared this way*

I REMOVED nearly all the fat from about two pounds of the best end of neck of mutton, and then cut it into chops. These I dipped in seasoned flour and laid in the bottom of a deep dish.

Finely sliced onions and potatoes, and some sliced beef kidney were then added—and then more chops, and so on until the dish was filled. Next I added half a pint of gravy, a tablespoonful of Lea & Perrins' Sauce, and pepper and salt.

The top I covered with raw potatoes, cut in halves, and then let the pot—covered, of course—cook gently for two hours in a steady oven.

Within the reach of everybody
9d., 1/2 and 2/- per bottle

Lea & Perrins'
THE ORIGINAL WORCESTERSHIRE
Sauce

28

Cut crusts of stale bread into small pieces and bake in a slow oven until a golden brown and crisp

The Humble Crumb *Disguised*

CRUMBS are one of the most useful and most adaptable commodities in the equipment of the modern housewife. To begin with, there is a well-founded sense of economy in the use of crumbs, for they are usually made from left-overs —scraps of bread, biscuits that have been broken, or cake no longer fresh enough for service at table.

If the left-overs are dry and crisp, they may be rolled or ground down in the mincing-machine, then sieved and stored in a jar for future use. The air should not be entirely excluded: the best plan is to cover the jar with muslin or cheese-cloth held in place with a rubber band. If the pieces are not dry, they should either be sieved and used at once or dried slowly in the oven and then ground down.

There are many different ways in which crumbs can be utilised. They will often extend a vegetable or a small amount of meat in such a way as to make it serve several persons. Bread-crumbs used with egg will form a coating on articles that are to be fried. Sprinkled over a *gratin* dish they add both to its flavour and to its appearance. They may also be used to thicken soups that are made with milk, besides doing good service in the many recipes which require crumbs of different kinds as the basis of the dish.

Crumb Omelet: Soak a teacupful of white bread-crumbs in a teacupful of milk for 15 minutes. Then add pepper, salt, and 3 well-beaten eggs. Melt 1 oz. butter in a frying-pan and grease the sides as well as the bottom. Pour in the egg mixture and cook slowly, shaking the pan and pricking the omelet frequently with a fork so that all is cooked. When brown underneath place in a moderate oven, 350° Fahr., to finish cooking the top. Fold over, turn out on a hot dish, and serve immediately, garnished with parsley. A little brown gravy or fried potatoes might be served separately.

Bread Rarebit: Soak 1 cupful white bread-crumbs in 1 cupful milk for 15 minutes. Melt 1 oz. butter in a double boiler, add the soaked crumbs, 1 slightly beaten egg, salt, and a little cayenne. Cook until the egg thickens, stirring constantly, and remove from the fire. Add ¾ cupful grated cheese and beat until the cheese melts. Pour on to hot toast or crisp biscuits and serve at once.

Girdle Cakes: Soak 1 cupful biscuit-crumbs in 2 cupfuls milk for fifteen minutes. Meanwhile mix and sieve 1 cupful flour, 2 teaspoonfuls baking powder, ½ teaspoonful salt, and 1 tablespoonful sugar. Add these to the soaked crumbs, along with one beaten egg and 1 tablespoonful melted fat. Stir well until smooth. Bake in spoonfuls on a hot greased girdle until brown on both sides.

Chocolate Cups: Dissolve 2 oz. chocolate in 2 cupfuls milk in the double boiler. When quite melted add a cupful of fine biscuit-crumbs, a good pinch of salt, and sugar to taste. Remove from the fire, add 1 beaten egg and ½ teaspoonful vanilla. Pour the mixture into greased cups, place them in a tin, pour in a little hot water, and bake in a moderate oven (350° Fahr.) until firm —about 45 minutes. Turn out and serve with milk, cream, or hard sauce. Serve either hot or cold.

Spice Pie: Add ½ cupful sweet biscuit crumbs to 1 cupful hot milk. Beat up 1 or 2 eggs and add them along with ¼ teaspoonful cinnamon, ¼ teaspoonful nutmeg, ½ teaspoonful ginger, a good pinch of salt, 2 tablespoonfuls treacle or syrup, and 2 tablespoonfuls brown sugar. Mix well together and pour into a pastry-lined tin or dish. Bake for ten minutes in a hot oven (450° Fahr.), then reduce the heat to 325° Fahr., and continue the baking until the mixture is firm and the pastry cooked—about half an hour. Sprinkle with sugar, cut in pieces, and serve hot or cold.

Holiday Pudding: Soak 1 cupful stale cake-crumbs in 2 cupfuls milk for ten minutes. Then add 1 beaten egg, a pinch of salt, the grated rind of ½ lemon, and sugar to taste. Mix well, pour into a greased pie-dish, and sprinkle the top lightly with ground cinnamon. Place in a tin with a little warm water and bake in a moderate oven about 1 hour.

Baked Apple Pudding: To 1½ lb. apples allow 6 oz. browned bread-crumbs, 2 oz. butter or margarine, 2 tablespoonfuls golden syrup, 1 gill water, and the grated rind of ½ lemon.

Peel, core, and slice the apples very thinly and put a layer of them into a greased pie-dish. Sprinkle some of the bread-crumbs over this, and lay on a few small pieces of butter. Repeat these alternate layers until all the apples and bread-crumbs are used up. The last layer should be crumbs. Mix the syrup, water, and lemon-rind together and pour them over the top. Sprinkle with sugar and lay on some more pieces of butter. Stand in a tin with a little water and bake in a moderate oven about 1 hour, or until the apples are cooked. A little cream or custard may be served separately.

Caramel Ginger Pudding: Soak 2 cupfuls of cake-crumbs in 1 cupful hot milk for 15 minutes. Put ½ cupful sugar into an iron or aluminium saucepan with enough water to moisten it and let this melt and become a golden brown colour. Pour immediately into one large or ½ dozen small moulds that have been well greased. Then add to the moistened crumbs ½ cupful flour, ½ cupful sugar, 1 teaspoonful ginger, ½ teaspoonful cinnamon, and a good pinch of salt. Mix thoroughly for a few minutes, add 1 or 2 beaten eggs and 2 tablespoonfuls treacle and beat again. Sprinkle over 1 teaspoonful baking powder, stir it in, and pour into the mould or moulds. Cover with greased paper and steam from ¾ to 1½ hours according to size. Stand a minute or two after removing from the saucepan, then turn out on a serving-dish and the caramel will run down as a sauce.

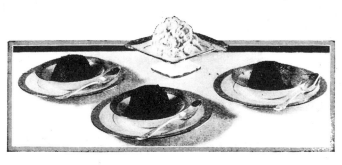

Using biscuit crumbs as the basis for Chocolate Cups results in a delicious dessert

Winter Chow-Chow is a pleasing addition to one's store of piquant sauces

When the Cupboard is Bare

THE best regulated household sometimes comes to grief as regards an adequate supply of home-made pickles, piquant sauces, jams, and jellies, and the early spring is apt to show a lack of these commodities. It may be that one has been unable during the preserving-season to prepare as much as was needed, or the size of one's family may have increased and the precious stores melted away.

The cupboard need not, however, go entirely bare, nor the family be wholly deprived of those little additions to the table which add so much to the attractiveness and enjoyment of what would otherwise be ordinary meals. Moreover, piquant sauces and tempting sweets stimulate the appetite and therefore aid digestion, and the meal so accompanied becomes more healthful and satisfactory, besides being vastly more enjoyed.

A plate of cold meat or plain hash is much more attractive if accompanied by a sauce that has some zest and tang. A plain pudding or a dish of rice becomes a real dessert if enriched by a little fine jelly or jam. Let us not allow our table to lack these appetising accessories at a time when summer fruits and vegetables have not yet come into season.

Winter Chow-Chow

Remove the outside leaves from a firm white cabbage, cut it in quarters and remove the hard stalk. Then shred the cabbage finely with a sharp knife, chop the shreds across, wash in several waters, and then drain well. Prepare also 2 cupfuls of chopped onion, and one red and one green pepper finely chopped. (The tinned variety may be used if the fresh is not available.) Mix these with the cabbage, sprinkle with 3 or 4 tablespoonfuls of coarse salt, stand at least four hours, then press out as much of the liquid as possible.

Put into a saucepan 1 quart of the best brown vinegar and add to it ½ lb. brown sugar, 1 teaspoonful celery seed, 2 tablespoonfuls each of black and white mustard seed, and 1 teaspoonful alum. Bring these slowly to the boil, pour over the cabbage mixture, and bottle in sterilised jars.

Emergency Chilli Sauce

Put into a saucepan 1 quart of tinned peeled tomatoes and add one onion and one green pepper, both finely chopped. Season with ½ teaspoonful celery seed or 2 sticks celery finely minced, 2 teaspoonfuls salt, ½ teaspoonful dry mustard, ¼ teaspoonful pepper, and a good dash of cayenne. Mix together and add 3 tablespoonfuls brown sugar and ½ teacupful of the best malt vinegar. Bring to the boil and simmer ¾ hour, stirring occasionally. Rub the sauce through a sieve, and if not of the right consistency, return to the saucepan and boil a little longer. Bottle and cork tightly.

Carrot Marmalade

Take some firm red carrots, wash and scrape them, removing all trace of black, but as little of the red part as possible. Cut them in pieces and cook in boiling water until tender, letting the water almost boil away. Then rub the carrots through a sieve and to each pint of purée allow 1 lb. preserving sugar and the grated rind and juice of 3 lemons. Put all together into a preserving-pan and boil, stirring frequently, about ¾ hour or until the mixture will jelly. A few blanched and shredded almonds may be put in at the last, and the addition of a little brandy will make the jam keep better. Pot and cover in the usual way.

This jam is excellent served as dessert with any plain pudding or with pastry.

Pineapple and Orange Marmalade

3 large oranges, 1 tin grated pineapple, 1½ pints water, and preserving sugar. Wash the oranges and soak them overnight in the above proportion of water. Next day boil them in the same water until quite tender, letting the water boil away. Then chop the oranges finely or put them through the mincing machine, carefully removing all the seeds. Measure the chopped orange and grated pineapple and to each pint allow 1 lb. preserving sugar. Put all together into a saucepan, bring slowly to boiling-point, and then boil until the marmalade will jelly. Pot and cover down in the usual way.

Note: Fresh pineapple may be used instead of tinned. Cut it in quarters and grate without peeling.

Dried Peach Chutney

1 lb. dried peaches, ½ lb. seeded raisins, 1 large onion, ½ pint brown vinegar, ½ lb. brown sugar, 1 tablespoonful salt, 1 tablespoonful mustard seed, 1 teaspoonful turmeric powder, 1 dessertspoonful ground ginger.

Wash the peaches and soak them overnight in cold water to cover. Next day cook them in the same water for ½ hour. Add the raisins and onion finely chopped and all the other ingredients. Then simmer slowly by the side of the fire for 2 hours or longer. Bottle and keep a week at least before using.

Grape Fruit and Banana Jam

1 grape fruit, 4 bananas, 1 pint water, 1 lb. sugar.

Wash the grape fruit and peel off the yellow rind as thinly as possible. Cut the fruit in half and, with a spoon, scoop out all the pulp from the inside, leaving nothing but the white skin. Remove the seeds from the pulp and put it into a preserving pan with the water and yellow rind. Boil these together for ½ hour, then strain and press out all the juice. Return the liquid to the saucepan with the sugar, and stir until the sugar is melted. Peel the bananas and cut them in slices with a silver knife. Add them to the syrup and cook altogether until the mixture will jelly. The banana slices should be kept as whole as possible.

Rhubarb and Orange Jam

1 lb. rhubarb, 3 large oranges, sugar. Wash the rhubarb and cut it in small pieces without peeling. Wash the oranges and grate off the rinds, taking the yellow part only. Then cut them in halves and scoop out the pulp. Put the seeds into a small basin and soak them in a little boiling water for ½ hour. Weigh together the orange pulp, rhubarb, and grated rind, and allow an equal weight of sugar. Boil the fruit first until reduced to ½ quantity, add the sugar and strained liquid from the seeds, and continue to boil until the jam will set.

The Housekeeper's Dictionary of Facts

Some Nuggets of Household Wisdom

When Carving Salmon

Silver or plated fish-servers should be used. Care must be taken to serve as little bone as possible, and not to break the flakes more than is necessary. The fish should be placed on the table with the thick part farthest from the carver, then cut across in fairly thick slices right through to the bone. When the top side is finished, the bone should be gently raised and the underside carved in the same way.

A Butter Economy

When cutting a large quantity of bread and butter or sandwiches, pour ½ pint of boiling milk over 1 lb. butter in a basin. Cool slightly and then work together with a wooden spoon until of a creamy consistency. This will spread easily on the bread and go farther than solid butter.

To Make Tea-cakes

Sieve ¾ lb. flour and 1 teaspoonful salt into a warm basin and make a well in the centre. In a small saucepan melt 2 oz. butter or margarine, add 1 teacupful of milk and make the mixture just lukewarm. Put ½ oz. yeast into a small basin with a teaspoonful of sugar and cream them together with a teaspoon, pour over them the warm milk and butter and strain all into the centre of the flour. Add also one egg well beaten and mix with the hand from the centre outwards, gathering in the flour by degrees. Beat the dough lightly for a few minutes, then cover the basin with a cloth and set it in a warm place, for from three-quarters to one hour, until the dough has risen to about double its original size. Turn out 'on a floured board and knead lightly until free from cracks. Form into three round cakes, place them on a greased and floured tin, and set them again to rise for about fifteen minutes. Bake in a good oven until brown and firm to

the touch. When nearly ready, brush them over with sugar and milk to give them a gloss. Split and butter the cakes and serve them hot.

To Pickle Beef

Put into a large clean saucepan 1½ lb. bay salt, ½ lb. brown sugar, 1 oz. salt-petre, and 1 gallon of water. Bring these to the boil, and boil from 15 to 20 minutes, skimming carefully. Then strain through muslin and use when cold. The beef used should be freshly killed. Choose a fleshy piece from the round or flank, about 5 or 6 lb., wipe it, and trim it carefully, removing the bone if possible. Rub it well with common salt and let it stand overnight. Next day rub off this salt, and put the meat into a large jar or basin. Cover it completely with the above pickling mixture and let it stand for 10 days.

Woollen Stockings or Socks

In spite of every care being taken, these have often a tendency to shrink when washed. A solution of the problem is to slip them on to wire hose-driers while still wet. These can be had in various sizes, they keep the hose in shape, and when dry they will be as comfortable to wear as when new.

Tussore Silk

This fabric should be ironed dry and on the wrong side—if ironed damp like other silk, it will feel hard and have a mottled appearance. If the colour becomes too light with washing, it may be restored by rinsing the silk in water coloured with a little clear tea, or in water in which a little hay has been boiled.

To Stiffen Chintz

Use size instead of starch, dissolving a small packet in ⅓ gallon of boiling water. When lukewarm, put in the chintz and let it soak one hour. Then

wring out, and hang up until dry enough to iron. Use a hot heavy iron and rub it with a little beeswax, as this will give a gloss to the chintz.

Things to Remember

(1) That lacquered brass must never be cleaned with polish, but simply rubbed with a leather or soft duster. When dirty, it may be washed with soap and water only, well dried, and polished with a little dry whitening.

(2) That the outside sills of windows should have the dust swept off them daily, and washed with some disinfectant when the rooms have their weekly cleaning. This will help to keep away flies and other insects.

(3) That a supply of candles should be kept in a tin box in the storeroom—if anything goes wrong with the lighting arrangements, the house need not then be plunged in darkness.

(4) That chimneys should be swept twice a year if a fireplace is much used, and a kitchen chimney at least three or four times a year. In addition to this, any soot that collects near the bottom of the chimney should be removed with a brush when the grate is cleaned.

(5) That cisterns should be properly cleaned by a plumber at regular intervals —and that they should always be kept covered.

Time-Saving Notions

Always remove the skin and bone from fish while it is still warm; they come away easily then.

If boiling water be poured over raisins that are to be stoned, the fruit will plump out and the stones may be quickly and easily removed.

When brown stock is needed for some dish and none is handy, dissolve a little meat extract in water and use this instead.

Potatoes mash smoothly and quickly if hot milk is used instead of cold.

FOOD
Glorious
FOOD

1923

The tea table on the 25th looks festive with Santa Claus presiding over "the cake."

Cakes for

Ꭹe Olde Ꭹule Time

Is the season for happiness and good will, and there is no better way of spreading cheer and fellowship than by providing perfectly planned meals. All the recipes and methods given here have been carefully tested, and we are always willing to help you with personal advice. Write, enclosing a stamped envelope for the reply, to the Cookery Department, GOOD HOUSEKEEPING, 1 Amen Corner, London, E.C.4

A S Christmas approaches, our minds turn instinctively to sweet things. Cakes, pies, puddings, and sweetmeats— all seem to fit in with the spirit of the season. A good supply of cakes is a real asset at this time of year, as they are always at hand for the frequent occasions when holiday hospitality can be shown by the serving of light and impromptu refreshments.

As all fruit cakes improve with keeping, the wise housewife will make them in good time and not wait until the rush of the holiday season is upon her. Recipes for Christmas cakes are legion, and almost every household has its own favoured one, passed down probably from one generation to another. For those who have not inherited such a recipe, or who would like to try something different, the following recipe will be found both good and reliable:

A Christmas Cake

½ lb. butter	½ lb. currants
½ lb. margarine	½ lb. sultanas
1 lb. castor sugar	¼ lb. orange and lemon peel
1 lb. flour	¼ lb. citron peel
6 eggs	¼ lb. sweet almonds
2 tablespoonfuls treacle	½ teaspoonful ground cinnamon
1 glass sherry or rum	namon
Grated rind of 1 lemon	½ nutmeg, grated

First prepare the cake-tin, choosing one 7 inches in diameter, or two of a smaller size. Grease it first with salad oil or unsalted butter, and then line it smoothly with two folds of thick white paper. The band of paper lining the sides should stand about 2 inches above the rim at the top.

Next, prepare the fruit. Wash and dry the currants, and roll them in a little flour. Pick the sultanas and rub them on the top of a sieve with a little

dry flour. Shred the peel finely, and blanch and shred the almonds. Mix the fruit together and leave it in readiness

Christmas Snowballs

in a basin. To mix the cake, put the butter and margarine (or all butter, if preferred,) into a large warm basin, sieve the sugar on the top, and beat them together with the hand or with a large wooden spoon until of a soft, creamy consistency. Sieve the flour and add it alternately with the eggs, treacle, and milk, beating the mixture well after each addition. When the mixture has been well beaten, add the spices, grated lemon-rind, and the prepared fruit last of all.

Turn into the prepared tin, and bake in a moderate oven (275° F.) about 3 hours. Test when ready by running a hot skewer or knitting-needle into the centre; it should come out dry. Leave the cake in the tin for a few minutes, then turn out and cool on a sieve

or wire stand. When quite cold, wrap in paper and keep in a tin box for a week at least before cutting.

Almond Paste and Icing

A Christmas cake is not complete without a layer of almond paste and a coating of white icing or frosting on the top: *To Make Almond Paste,* take ½ lb. ground almonds, ¼ lb. castor sugar, ¼ lb. icing sugar, 1 dessertspoonful lemon-juice, about 2 yolks of eggs, and 1 tablespoonful rum or other flavouring. Put the ground almonds into a basin, and sieve the two kinds of sugar on the top. Add the flavouring and enough yolk of egg to bind all together. Knead with the hand until smooth.

Put this on the top of the cake and smooth over with a wet palette knife. Or, if preferred, the cake may be split and half the almond paste put as a layer in the centre. The almond paste should be allowed to dry for a day or two before the white icing is put on.

White Icing: In the November issue directions were given for making Boiled Icing, but here is a recipe for Royal Icing, which is rather harder in character: To 1 lb. icing sugar add 1 dessertspoonful lemon-juice and from 2 to 3 whites of eggs. Sieve the sugar and put it into a basin with the lemon-juice. Add the white of egg by degrees, beating well with a clean wooden spoon. When the icing is of the right consistency, the spoon should stand vertically in it without falling. Spread this icing over the cake with a palette knife, coating first the top and then the sides, or the top only may be iced and the sides covered with a paper frill or ribbon. Leave the icing to dry before decorating the cake.

Christmas

By

The Director

FLORENCE B. JACK, M.C.A.

Whatever ingenuity you have, in the making of Christmas cakes you will find ample scope to exercise it

FOOD
Glorious
FOOD

1923

Decorating the Cake

The ornamentation of the Christmas cake provides ample scope for one's ingenuity. This may be simple or elaborate in character according to one's talent and the time at disposal, and a walk round the confectioners' shops will always furnish the novice with many new ideas.

If the cake has to be finished off quickly, preserved fruits, crystallised flowers, bonbons, or marzipan sweets will make a pretty and effective decoration. Small sprigs of artificial flowers, holly, or leaves, can also be utilised. When time permits, however, pretty designs in icing may be piped on the cake by means of a forcing-bag and tubes of different patterns, or "A Merry Christmas" or other suitable greeting may be written on, in a contrasting colour.

The Little House Cake

This suggests something of a novelty, which means very little more work than any other form of cake decoration. Make a round cake in the ordinary way, and when putting on the almond paste mould it into a point to form the roof, keeping back a small portion to make a chimney-pot. Then make the white icing, and colour a small amount of it brown with fine chocolate powder. Spread this on the roof and roughen it over with a fork. Next coat the sides of the cake with white icing and let this harden. With a little melted chocolate and small paint-brush cutline the bricks of the house and paint in the doors and windows. Colour any remaining icing with sufficient chocolate to make it stone-colour, and, by means of a forcing-bag and tubes, pipe round the edge of the roof with this to form eaves, put a narrow piping round the

door and windows, and indicate the door-handle. A small Father Christmas may be placed close to the chimney, and a few little dolls and animals will add life to the foreground.

Christmas Snowballs

These will delight the kiddies and the older folk too. Unlike the fruit cakes, they should be made fresh and not more than two or three days before they are

Tiny oranges and green leaves decorate this cake

required. Any white cake mixture will do, or you may use the following formula: 1 egg, its weight in butter, flour, and castor sugar, 1 tablespoonful of milk, flavouring to taste, and ½ teaspoonful of baking-powder. Put the butter into a warm basin, sieve the sugar on the top, and beat the two together with a wooden spoon until of a soft, creamy consistency. Add the egg and half the flour (sieved), beat well until thoroughly mixed. Then add the remainder of the flour and the milk, and beat again until the mixture is light and full of air-bubbles. Add vanilla or any other flavouring preferred, and just before using, stir in the baking-powder.

Have ready some small, round-bottomed cake-tins, greased, and dusted

out with a mixture of flour and sugar. Half fill them with the mixture, and bake in a good oven (375° F.) about 15 minutes, or until lightly browned and firm to the touch. Turn out of the tins to cool. If necessary, cut a slice off the top of the cakes to make them level, and put two together with some tart jelly between, thus forming a ball.

Or, the little cakes may be slightly hollowed out, and the cavity filled with some rich custard or thick cream before putting them together.

Cover the balls with some plain white icing, holding them on a fork or skewer while doing so. Then roll in desiccated coconut and castor sugar mixed. Allow the snowballs to dry, and serve them garnished with sprigs of holly.

Suggestions for Decoration

1. Coat the cake with pale pink icing and decorate the top with marzipan fruits.

2. Coat the top of the cake only with white icing, and when quite dry decorate with small sprigs of artificial holly. Put a Father Christmas or a robin in the centre, and tie round with a piece of white and a piece of scarlet ribbon, making a good bow at the side.

3. Colour the icing yellow and flavour with lemon. Coat the cake with this and decorate with crystallised orange slices and small green leaves.

4. Coat the cake with white icing, and with a forcing-bag and small pipe write "A Merry Christmas" across the top. Pipe the sides of the cake with more of the icing and decorate with silver dragées.

5. Make a coffee icing, cover the cake with this, and decorate with crystallised violets and leaves and stalks of angelica.

Did you know that,
owing to—

The Adulteration *of* Food

You have more than 1,000 chances of
being Poisoned each Year of your Life?

HELENA NORMANTON, B.A.

IF you like really exciting literature, and your stock of detective, cave-men, and desert sheik novels shows signs of giving out, let me suggest to you a study of the last three or four Annual Reports of the Ministry of Health. Turn to the sections in them dealing with the Inspection of Foods. After a perusal of these enthralling statements you will be stimulated right enough; and no doubt pleasantly surprised to find yourself alive at all. The dangers of the desert are mild to those of the dinner-table.

Let us turn, for instance, to the 1922–3 Report. There will you find the charming idyll of the Inedible Fat. The Manchester Port Sanitary Authority discovered and reported that inedible fat, derived from diseased American animals, had been released upon undertaking that the fat should be used for commercial purposes only. It was in fact sent to a factory, refined, and sold as " pure English lard." It is satisfactory to note that proceedings and fine followed upon the heels of this smart piece of commercial enterprise. But what of those who, prior to that punishment, had consumed that " pure English lard? " History is silent. Perhaps she had better be!

The 1919–20 Report regales us with the story of the great Tea Analysis which adorned that year. 12,117 samples were analysed; 5,533 were found to be unsatisfactory. The year 1919 also witnessed the Itchington arsenic poisoning story. A load of sugar was conveyed in the same railway-wagon with a load of weed-killer containing arsenic. Result—many arsenical poisoning cases at the destination. Such mixed transit has consequently been made illegal. As to coffee, the Report speaks with a classic calm of samples at St. Marylebone and Camberwell respectively which were proved to contain 59 per cent. of chicory in the first place, 37 per cent. in the latter. In St. Pancras, out of thirty-six samples of vinegar ten were adulterated.

Egg and custard powders are a fairly constant source of complaint by public analysts. The Durham analyst says: " There is occasion to draw attention to the way in which certain articles are described by label when exhibited for sale, and a particular instance is found in the misuse of the word ' custard.' One sample which was described as being ' Double Cup Cream Custard, Extra Delicious and Creamy,' proved to consist of 100 per cent of a tinted starch, without any trace of cream or eggs which might reasonably be expected in an article so described."

The Public Analyst for the County of Lancaster also says:

" Generally speaking, an egg powder is a coloured baking powder and a custard powder is a coloured and flavoured preparation of starch. A few brands of custard powder now contain a proportion (usually very small) of dried eggs. Owing to the present scarcity of eggs there is now a great sale for all these preparations, and a tendency exists in some quarters to exaggerate their qualities. For instance, a sample of egg powder devoid of egg was labelled, " One packet is equal to 2 or 3 eggs and contains the essential properties of new-laid eggs." A sample of custard powder devoid of egg was contained in a packet labelled " Double-yolk " and displaying a coloured picture of a broken egg with two yolks, which was more eloquent to the eye than any verbal statement. Another sample of custard powder labelled " Contains milk and eggs " was for all practical purposes devoid of the latter ingredient.

To continue the troubled story of eggs, one must recall that large quantities of liquid eggs are imported from abroad (China chiefly) and are preserved by means of boric acid. This chemical is not of itself poisonous, although it cannot be said to have a good effect upon the human frame, but it is a derivative from borax. Commercial borax practically always contains arsenic, which can only be dissociated by a highly costly process. Hence we find the liquid imported egg of commerce a purveyor of arsenic into the system. So evil were the results of this that the Bakery Allied Traders' Association has now promised the Ministry of Health that the quantity of preservative to be used in liquid eggs consumed in this country shall be limited, and that, as sponge cakes and fingers enter so largely into the dietary of infants and invalids, liquid egg shall not be used in their composition. *But what about other cakes?*

Boric acid as a preservative now enters into a formidably long list of foodstuffs—meat and fish pastes, cream, and many other things. In tiny letters at the foot of many restaurant menus you will find some small percentage of it stated to be used in cream or perhaps other articles. The amount seems so small a decimal percentage that it seems nothing to make a fuss about—if one considers only the one individual dose. But what of the accumulation of all these tiny doses, taken in many articles, in many meals throughout the year?

Fruit cordials are another vehicle of danger. A sample of lemon-squash analysed in Surrey proved to contain 13.1 grains of salicylic acid per pint and 1.20 per cent of phosphoric acid. The vendor, on being prosecuted under the Sale of Food and Drugs Acts, produced a warranty from the wholesaler, and thus was triumphantly acquitted. He was, however, presumably on account of a misleading label, convicted under the Merchandise Marks Act and fined. A sample of raspberry fruit juice from Durham turned out to be sugar solution coloured by coal dye and acidulated with phosphoric acid.

Fats are often profitably adulterated—one sample of dripping contained 40 per cent. of cotton-seed oil. Some chopped suet was, in fact, 15 per cent. rice flour. Preserved peas have an unenviable reputation. Of 168 samples examined in 1921–2, no fewer than 73 were found to contain copper salts for colouring purposes. Many of these hail from Italy. One begins to understand the inwardness of the proverb, " See Naples and die." Some spinach was preserved by the friendly aid of no less than 6.8 grains per pound of copper sulphate.

In 1922–3, out of 1,851 samples of cocoa, 26 contained arsenic. Rice was faced with talc; aerated waters contained copper, lead, or zinc. One sample of sausages contained only 42 per cent. of meat. Jams were dyed, " improved," had salicylic acid and apple pulp added. Coffee extracts had salicylic acid. Vinegar contained arsenic and acetic acid. One sample of dripping revealed itself as: 20.8 per cent. water, 4.9 per cent. organic impurities, 2.2 per cent. mineral matter! One would suppose that a community thus passively drenched with organic and mineral poisons would at least demand a high standard of purity in the drugs necessary to counteract all the effects of this adulteration. If so, one's expectation is frustrated. The report as to drugs is bad each year, and increasingly so. The percentage of adulteration increased from 6.7 in 1921 to 7.3 in 1922. Of 429 prescriptions in 1922, 22.4 per cent. *(Continued)*

The Adulteration of Food

were inaccurate, as against 16.3 per cent. in 1921.

All this is a loathsome story. And, bad as the official figures are, reflection shows things to be even worse. Take any Annual Report of the Ministry of Health, and it will be observed that the average number of analyses made for the whole country is just over a hundred thousand. At first sight this sounds a lot. But is it? Conjecture to yourself the enormous bulk of the millions of tons of foodstuffs a populace of some 40,000,000 must consume, and it will be realised that the sampling accomplished is the merest flea-bite. Read the Reports from another point of view, namely, the penalties inflicted. Imprisonment is exceedingly rare, fines not very crushing, and the law does not allow much imprisonment nor very heavy penalties even when guilt has been proved. The big trader can afford to laugh at all our penalties.

The root of all the difficulty seems to be that our law is outworn. In 1875 we were the pioneers in passing the first Sale of Food and Drugs Act; nowadays other countries, notably France, the United States, and our own more enlightened colonies, have far surpassed us. The administration of our Acts is vested in local authorities, with overlapping effects, as when County Councils take action in respect of adulteration and district councils act in the same way with food which has become unwholesome or bacteriologically unsound; whilst the Ministry of Health has inadequate powers of supervision over the work of the local authorities' work. Every authority (or group of authorities has its own analyst, and their work goes on in an unco-ordinated way. This produces the usual result—want of standardisation. Hence what passes muster in one place is counted as adulteration in another.

Our method of procedure is also probably the one calculated to produce the least efficiency in results. There is a passion in this country for entrusting duties of far too important and technical a nature to benches of untrained magistrates. This has been realised in France, and since 1905 the work of suppressing food adulteration has been taken away from local authorities and a Central Service (*Service de la Répression des Fraudes*) has been instituted at the Board of Agriculture. Fourteen superintending inspectors under it are stationed at different centres in France, and a separate service of minor officials. This *Service de la Répression* prescribes the number of samples to be taken in each district, and the conditions under which they are taken. Local authorities are never allowed to have anything to do with the institution of proceedings before the law. To those who know something of the so-called preliminary inquiries in small English places (with the door wide open for favouritism) this provision will appeal as being of enormous value. The *Service* also prescribes the analytical methods to be used and collates the results. There are thirty-nine splendidly equipped Government laboratories for the whole of France, instead of the two hundred odd private individual ones we have here. Four of the French laboratories are specialised for drugs, cereals, resins, and preserved meat-stuffs, etc. This means that a far greater degree of chemical skill is likely to be brought to bear upon each sample analysed than in this country. It is fair to ourselves to say that once proceedings have begun our law is stronger than the French because guilty knowledge of adulteration is not essential to procure conviction here, as it is in France. But probably neither system is ideal at this stage. It is worth while considering whether the official interrogation of France, and the criminal procedure under summary jurisdiction of England, might not profitably be replaced by a special procedure, proceedings being initiated by civil proceedings allowing scope for inquiry into all the circumstances; the Court being assisted by technical chemical assessors with power to remit to the Criminal Courts if criminality be an element. To make my meaning clear I will revert to the case of the sugar poisoned by the weed-killer in railway transit. Here the true culprit was the railway company, neither the vendor, who was as much deceived as anyone else, nor the innocent manufacturer of the sugar.

Further legislation is badly needed in the way of definition of foodstuffs. Until we have a settled standard as to whether golden syrup may or may not contain glucose, or how much cocoa-bean may be present in chocolate, it is idle for local authorities to institute proceedings. To leave these important scientific questions at the mercy of mere justices of the peace, as we do to-day, is simply to be farcical. There is no doubt the argument that to fix minimum standards of purity in foodstuffs is to court the practice of manufacturers vending stuffs of just that minimum standard, and no more. But could not manufacturers who sold goods higher than the legal minimum of purity be safely trusted to advertise the fact?

As far back as 1893 we managed to pass a very useful act obtaining for the soil and for cattle provisions as to fertilisers and foodstuffs of a standard much higher than we exact for ourselves, by enacting that every person who sells a fertiliser for the soil shall give to the purchaser an invoice stating:

(1) the name of the article;
(2) whether it is artificially compounded or not;
(3) what is at least the percentage of the nitrogen soluble and insoluble phosphates, and potash in it.

And a seller of a foodstuff for cattle must state:

(1) name of the article.
(2) whether prepared from one, or more than one, substance or seed.
(3) in either case, if no indication is given that it has been mixed with any other substance or seed, a warranty shall be implied that no other *unindicated* substance has been added.
(4) a warranty is also implied that the article is fit for feeding purposes.

And since 1893 this Act has been strengthened by a further Act.

It seems extraordinary that we cannot do as much for our children as we do for cattle and for the soil. We ought to have a standard of food, and are entitled to have those standards stated to us. Perhaps when our women Members of Parliament have eradicated their inferiority complex they will remember that 4 times 365 is 1,460—which is the number of times that most people take nourishment per annum—so that at present their constituents stand, on an average, more than a thousand chances of being poisoned every year. And men are supposed to be interested in food, too. Will they please do something about some Pure Food Laws, and do it soon?

The trained cook may lecture on cookery, apply her craft in her own home or make money journalistically by writing on her subject

Cookery as a Career for Women

By Florence B. Jack, M.C.A.

Director of the "Good Housekeeping" Cookery Department, Author of "Cookery for Every Household," etc. Editor of "The Woman's Book"

I T has been said that man is the only animal who cooks his food, and that the performance of this act differentiates him from the lower animals. True, there are a few cases where savage tribes live entirely on raw food, and the present century has introduced among us a group of faddists, who boast that their food is untouched by fire. These, however, are but a handful, and the majority of human beings have always cooked their food and will continue to do so, believing this to be a necessary preliminary to digestion.

Cooking serves the purpose of breaking up fibres and cells, of destroying micro-organisms and causing certain chemical changes in the food. It also makes animal food more agreeable to the eye, develops new flavours, and enables us to have more variety in the daily menu.

During the last few years scientists have been devoting much time to the study of foods, their necessary proportions, and the manner of serving them. They have urged that this knowledge be disseminated, with the result that cookery is included in the curriculum of many schools.

The work of catering and cooking should not be depreciated, for it is even more necessary to mankind than the housing and clothing trades, and as a profession it should stand on an equal footing with medicine. To prevent a body becoming diseased by feeding it properly is surely as advantageous to mankind as curing it with drugs.

There will always be a demand for cooks, and the skilled exponent of the gastronomic art will never lack employment. This statement does not apply, however, to the careless individual who

W E wonder if girls now choosing a career know that the really well-trained cook is one of the few women who need never fear unemployment. Cookery is a craft requiring a high degree of intelligence and one offering a variety of work, ranging from the lecture-room to authorship. When you have read this month's career article by Florence B. Jack, who has won conspicuous success in all the branches of her profession, you will, perhaps, decide *not* to go on to the stage after all !

is too ignorant and lazy to master her art, and who has no ambition to reach the topmost rung in the ladder of her profession.

Hitherto, it is the man *chef* who has been allowed to carry off the laurels and obtain the highest posts in the culinary world, his income sometimes running into four figures. But there is no reason why the woman cook should not reach the same heights of fame, now that the other professions have thrown open their doors to enfranchised womanhood, and the cry of "equal pay for equal work" is being endorsed by political economists. She must, however, take up the work seriously, put real devotion into it, and be prepared to go through the same arduous training as the man *chef,* if she wants to fit herself to supervise the cuisine and staff of a large hotel or club.

Sir William Orpen's picture of a *chef* in a recent Royal Academy Exhibition depicts on canvas the true spirit of the culinary artist. We see a man in *chef's* outfit, looking down thoughtfully on the materials which his hands are going to convert into some dainty and succulent dish. The face is that of one who regards his work as being of paramount importance and the well-shaped hands

are itching to begin their intricate and highly skilled task.

There is no doubt that the future will open up many opportunities for women in the higher branches of cookery, while there will always be plenty of more modest posts for the good but less skilled workers.

Cookery seems to be such an obvious career for a woman that it often attracts those who are unsuited to it. Many people have the idea that brains are not required for this kind of work—nothing could be more misguided. Brains are certainly essential, and the dull girl of the family, although she may make a good routine worker, will never go far in cookery. A creative brain and a fine imagination are necessary to the cook who wishes to invent new dishes and fabricate toothsome *plats* ; and a resourceful, orderly, and far-seeing mind is required by one who would manage a kitchen and its staff. Cookery also demands a great capacity for hard and serious work, calmness of temperament, and presence of mind in emergencies.

A special training in cookery is necessary to the would-be cook, and the nature and duration of this will vary according to the type of after-career. The woman who wants to make herself proficient in the art must first of all master the many methods of cooking, and the rules and principles underlying these methods. She must study food values, the amount and kind of food required, and the modifications made necessary by age, climate, occupation, etc., so that her menus may be suitable. She must then obtain as wide a knowledge of cookery as possible—that of other countries as well as her own—in order to keep up to date with changing fashions. She should also *(Continued)*

Cookery as a Career for Women

study the choice of food and economical buying, the management of a kitchen, and the storing and preservation of food.

There are different ways of training as a cook. A cook's certificate may be taken at a good school of cookery, a period of from six to twelve months being required at a cost of from £25 to £40 for a full course. Or the "Cordon Bleu" course may be taken at the National Training School of Cookery, London, entailing three terms' tuition for a fee of £60. During these courses she will learn to make hors-d'œuvre, stocks, soups, sauces, dressed fish and meat, hot and cold entrées, dressed vegetables and salads, hot and cold sweets, soufflés and omelets, ices, savouries, pastry, bread, biscuits and cakes.

Another way for a girl to get her training is to enter the kitchen of an hotel or restaurant and to work her way up, until she becomes highly skilled in all the different departments. The London County Council have established an excellent training school for boys who wish to become *chefs* and waiters, but so far there is nothing of a similar kind for girls. Let us hope that one will be inaugurated in the near future. It must be remembered that training, valuable as it is, must be supplemented by experience.

The openings for employment in cookery, pure and simple, are numerous and varied in character. A good cook can obtain employment in a private house, in the smaller clubs, hotels, restaurants and tea-rooms, in service-flats, schools, hospitals, University and other hostels. There is also work to be had in factory canteens and large business houses. Salaries range from £60 to £100 and upwards, with keep. There are also openings for peripatetic cooks, who will go to private houses to cook meals, or to supervise the arrangements for a dinner party, dance, or "At Home."

When cooking on a large scale is required, as in an institution or restaurant, special experience would be necessary to learn how to cope with large quantities. This can often be obtained by working as a pupil or probationer in a hospital or restaurant, or by going through a special course in Institution work, offered by some of the training schools. Posts of this kind can only be filled by one well versed in organisation as well as in the culinary art. The work is somewhat strenuous—it involves a great deal of standing, and should only be undertaken by those who are physically strong.

Tea-room work is much lighter, and here the skilled cook is much in demand. As a rule there will only be light luncheons and teas to serve, but she must be an adept in making bread, scones, and cakes, and possibly in sweetmaking as well.

Then, again, the woman who has a little capital at her disposal can often set up a tea-room or restaurant of her own. Many women have done this and are carrying on quite a profitable business. The furnishing and outfitting should be on artistic lines, with a touch of individuality, and a well-chosen name or signboard. Daintily cooked food and good service will often attract more clients than the stereotyped, luxurious restaurant. Needless to say, sound business capacity, organisation, management, and careful counting of costs are all necessary in a venture of this kind.

There are also openings for specialists in sweet-making, cake-making, fruit and vegetable bottling and preserving, invalid foods, etc. Sweet-making is particularly well-suited as an occupation for women wishing to add to their income without leaving their homes. It is not such arduous work as general cookery, and quite a fair amount can be made by the clever and artistic worker. A special course in sweet-making can be taken at most of the cookery schools (from 10s. to 12s. 6d. per lesson), and after a short course the worker can perfect herself by practice.

Another avenue of work for the lady cook is that of demonstrator on gas, electric, and other special stoves in showrooms or at exhibitions. This is quite a good opening for the enterprising woman who does not require regular employment. Sometimes she will be given a retaining salary by a good firm to demonstrate cooking apparatus and household equipment of various kinds, or to advertise proprietary articles at exhibitions and elsewhere.

The educational side of cookery now claims our attention. Should teaching appeal to the intending student, a thorough training is required in both the theoretical and practical side of the work. A good secondary education is necessary as a foundation, and for the more important posts, matriculation standard is advisable. A student in Domestic Science must be over 18 years of age, and in order to become a teacher she must work for her diploma at a training-school recognised by the Board of Education. These training-schools are established in most of the large towns—London, Liverpool, Leeds, Newcastle, Edinburgh, Glasgow, Dublin, etc. The training takes from two and a half to three years, and includes not only cookery, but at least

---

Our Shopping Service

In addition to the articles illustrated on pages 56, 57 of this number, any of which we will buy for you on receiving your order and cheque, our Shopping Service staff will gladly purchase for you any article shown in the advertisement columns of the magazine

---

two other domestic subjects as well.

Cookery training will include lessons in marketing, household accounts, dietetics, practice in working out food budgets, the physiology of nutrition, elementary chemistry, the theory of education, and the special problems of discipline, etc. The fees generally amount to from £25 to £50 per annum, according to the school chosen, but the expenses can be reduced by a maintenance grant offered by the Board of Education. Those who aspire to the higher posts in Domestic Science can widen their knowledge by taking a special course in the Women's Department of King's College, London University. This Department offers a three-years' course for a degree in Household and Social Science, or a one-year's course in Applied Science for those already holding a diploma in Domestic Arts. The fee for either course is 30 guineas per annum.

When first trained, the cookery teacher will probably begin her career by teaching elementary and secondary school children, or she may obtain work in a private school or college. There is also work in connection with the various County Councils, afternoon and evening lectures and practical lessons for adults in Polytechnics, Technical Schools, and Domestic Subjects Centres; for these more experience is required. Then again there are classes for Girl Guides, factory-girls, shop-girls, members of Women's Institutes, and occasionally special lessons are required in private houses by ladies and cooks.

If a *diplomée* attains the higher ranks of her profession she may become a staff teacher or principal in a training school. The salary of a qualified cookery teacher will vary according to the locality and status of her school; it may be anything from £150 to £350 and upwards per annum.

Some teachers, after years of experience, have started a private school of their own, and made quite good incomes in this way. A suitable locality must be chosen, preference being given to a large residential neighbourhood, where there is no competition. Of late years there has been rather a scarcity of posts in the teaching profession, but already there are signs of improvement in this direction.

The work is exacting, but it is very interesting, and there is always the compensation of long holidays. There are, too, always a certain number of higher posts which the ambitious woman can aim to fill, such as catering supervisor in a large institution or restaurant, inspector and

---

An Index to GOOD HOUSEKEEPING

READERS who wish to obtain an index to their volumes of GOOD HOUSEKEEPING may procure one, to the first four volumes, for threepence, post-free, from GOOD HOUSEKEEPING, 153 Queen Victoria Street, London, E.C.4. Separate indexes are being prepared for each additional volume (Volume V was completed by the August 1924 Number) and may be obtained for three-halfpence each, post-free. Kindly write "Index" on the envelope containing your order

---

examiner in cookery schools, organiser and superintendent of domestic subjects, etc. To these posts good salaries are usually attached.

Mention might also be made of laboratory work. A woman with a scientific turn of mind can sometimes take up research work, and carry out experiments in the interests of science and for the assistance of food-packers and manufacturers, but these posts are few and far between.

And, lastly, the woman with experience and a literary turn of mind may devote herself to writing on food and cookery subjects. This may take the form of books, or of articles, illustrated or otherwise, for newspapers or magazines. Women can also act as cookery advisers to newspaper or magazine inquirers, while broadcasting on domestic subjects is occasionally done and may be developed.

A training in cookery is never wasted. Should a girl relinquish her profession for marriage, she will find that the knowledge and skill she has acquired will stand her in good stead in her own home. She will be able to organise her domestic arrangements in the most approved fashion; or, if she goes abroad as a colonist, she will be able to adapt her knowledge to her new surroundings.

AND in every kick of those tiny pink feet you foresee the panting energy of the Prep. School playground . . . . He's worth building well . . . . Horlick's Malted Milk, containing all the good of fresh milk, malted barley and wheat flour, will help him towards the constitution you would wish him.

HORLICK'S
THE ORIGINAL
MALTED MILK
MADE IN ENGLAND

Ready in a moment with hot or cold water.
At all chemists, in four sizes, 2/-, 3/6, 8/6 and 15/-. The tablets also in flasks, 7½d. and 1/3.
Served in Restaurants and Cafés of standing.
A liberal sample for trial will be forwarded, post free, for 3d. in stamps.
HORLICK'S MALTED MILK COMPANY, SLOUGH, BUCKS.

"Let us partake of the good things which are set before us."—Charles Dickens

What Should a *Woman* Eat?

By Dr. Cecil Webb-Johnson

THE question of what to eat has always been a vexed one, and there are several different schools. The vegetarians, for instance, carry on their campaigns against the eating of flesh-food with an extraordinary bitterness and vehemence. We do not find the meat-eaters retorting to the vegetarians with like acrimony, which seems to indicate that they have broader minds and better tempers. Even among the objectors to flesh-food there are several sects. Some admit eggs, milk, and butter to their dietary; but the stricter sort rigidly bar such animal products.

It is difficult to lay down any hard-and-fast law, for people differ noticeably in their personal idiosyncrasy. We find a person sometimes with a natural distaste for meat, and another for whom very small quantities suffice. These individuals are ready-made vegetarians. Several extraordinary cases have come under the writer's notice. One was of a man who as a child disliked meat intensely, and lived upon the vegetable and "pudding" part of the family meals. But, on attaining man's estate, he took to meat, and now relishes a chop or a slice of succulent sirloin as much as anybody at the table. Another man can eat mutton or pork, and enjoy it, but sickens at the sight of roast beef. Another likes all kinds of meat, but cannot touch game or poultry.

The assertions of the strict vegetarian that man was never intended to eat meat at all, and that his natural food is of vegetable origin, are of course unsupported by any known facts and are, indeed, contradicted by the very structure of the human body. If a man were intended to eat like a horse or a cow, he would have a digestive apparatus like theirs, but it is notorious that he has not. We must therefore place human beings among the "mixed feeders," being neither purely carnivorous (like the lion and the tiger) nor purely herbivorous (like the sheep and the horse). A mixed diet is the natural one for the normal human being, though in various lands and climates the proportions of animal and vegetable foods vary. Thus we find in very hot countries, such as India, the natives eat a larger proportion of vegetable food, while in very cold countries the dietary is almost exclusively of animal origin.

The woman who lives in a temperate climate like ours should allow about a quarter of her dietary to consist of animal food. Meat should only be taken once a day, and preferably at dinner. We all eat too much animal food, and suffer for it accordingly. Consider the day's dietary of the average woman.

MOST women to-day share man's healthy interest in food. Some actually make a painstaking study of food values in planning the family's meals. Cookery, too, becomes daily less of an accident, and is more widely recognised as a craft, to be pursued with enthusiasm by the imaginative housewife. Such a woman will turn with keen interest to what Dr. Webb-Johnson says in his excellent article on wisely planned diet

She may have bacon or kidneys or a cutlet at breakfast, and then a meat dish at lunch, and more meat at the evening meal. This is, of course, a great excess of meat, and one that will have unpleasant consequences, for diseases of the kidneys and liver, cancer, and increased blood pressure await the incautious person who habitually devours too much flesh-food. To remain in good health, it is necessary to restrict the amount of animal food ingested to the extent which has already been indicated.

The function of flesh-food is to supply energy by means of the proteins which it contains; it is also a stimulant. Flesh-food is rich in albuminous and nitrogenous substances, also in fats; and it has one great advantage over foods of vegetable origin in that it is more easily assimilated. In vegetables we find both albumen and fat, but a smaller proportion of nitrogen. They are notably rich in the carbohydrates: wheat, for instance,

DIGESTIBILITY OF FOOD	
Beef, boiled . .	3 hours
Beef, roast . .	4 ,,
Bread . . .	$2\frac{1}{3}$,,
Eggs, boiled .	$1\frac{1}{4}$,,
,, poached .	$2\frac{1}{2}$,,
,, hard-boiled .	3 ,,
,, in an omelette	3 ,,
Fish . . .	$2\frac{1}{2}$,,
Apple . . .	$3\frac{1}{6}$,,
Cabbage . . .	3 ,,
Potatoes . . .	$2\frac{1}{2}$,,
Peas . . .	$4\frac{1}{4}$,,
Boiled rice . .	$3\frac{1}{2}$,,

containing 81.9 per cent. of carbohydrates against 16.6 per cent of nitrogenous constituents, with a trace of fat (0.4 per cent.) and water (0.6 per cent.). Wherefore we see that a mutton chop with potatoes forms a well-balanced meal, proteins and fat being present in the chop, and carbohydrates in the potatoes. If a green vegetable be added, there is the additional advantage of its valuable salts. The green vegetables—such as cabbage, spinach, or cauliflower —are not particularly nutritious, but contain the useful vitamines. At this

moment we know little about vitamines, but we are aware that roots and tubers do not contain so many as green vegetables and fruits.

Of all the animal foods, beef is the most nutritious and it is also the most digestible, though the digestibility of mutton is about the same. Pork is the least easily digested of the foods which are in popular parlance grouped as "butcher's meat," and veal, though more digestible than pork, is less so than beef or mutton. A table showing the relative digestibility of various foods is given on this page.

It is a curious fact that the flesh of young animals is less digestible than that of those fully-grown. Experiment has shown that veal is more indigestible than beef, and lamb than mutton. People of delicate digestions find fish, game, and the domestic poultry more suitable than butcher's meat. Fish is no doubt a most useful food; but the main objection to it is that it is so easily digested that the system soon requires another meal. Some fish, of course, are less digestible than others. Soles, plaice, whiting, turbot, and brill, for instance, are more easily assimilated than the fatty fish such as salmon, eels, herrings, sprats, pilchards, and sardines. The difference in the fat-contents of various fish is amazing: thus, sole contains 0.25 per cent. of fat, and eel 28.37, while the proportion of albuminates is 11.95 in the former fish and 12.98 in the latter. Cod and haddock are apt to be tough and difficult of digestion. Shellfish, besides being very popular on account of their flavour, are also highly nutritious. Lobsters and crabs contain the most nutriment, but are not easy of digestion. The much-praised oyster, though delicious eating, contains very little of a nutritious nature, and it has been estimated that ten dozen would be required to yield the nitrogenous substances needed in a day's ration. As a strengthening agent, therefore, the oyster has been very sadly overrated.

Poultry and game are more digestible than meat because they are more free from fat and connective tissue, thus being more readily attacked by the gastric juice. The flesh of a young chicken is the most digestible and tender of all; next to this comes the young partridge or pheasant. Quail, grouse, woodcock, and ptarmigan are not only delicious in flavour and esteemed a great delicacy by gourmets, but are very stimulating and also nutritious. Guinea-fowl is good eating, and is the most "gamey" of the poultry tribe; some people assert that its meat is comparable to that of the pheasant for flavour and delicacy.

HEINZ Tomato Chutney

The name "Heinz" on a bottle of Tomato Chutney means the most perfect, luscious, full-flavoured tomatoes that sun and soil can produce, the most savoury spices, the purest and most carefully selected ingredients throughout. And, finally, such skill and care in preparation as can be found only in Heinz spotless kitchens.

NO PRESERVATIVES — NO ARTIFICIAL COLOURING

Some of the **57** *Varieties*

Heinz Baked Beans   Heinz Cream of Tomato Soup

Heinz Tomato Ketchup

H. J. HEINZ COMPANY, LIMITED, LONDON.

The 20th century Health & Pure Food Crusade

White Bread danger exposed: adoption of Wholemeal advocated

Allinson's advice "Eat natural food" now the rallying-ground of medical opinion

Wholemeal for Health. Unanimity of experts

In the history of the development of medical knowledge as applied to the study of food-problems, no result has been so remarkable as the complete agreement of those best qualified to judge, as to the dangers of that apparently harmless article of diet, white bread.

During the present century there has been a continuous line of out-spoken attacks on the fetish of white bread, culminating in such emphatic utterances as the following:—

Sir Harry Baldwin, Surgeon-Dentist to H.M. the King: "White bread and white flour from which all the most valuable constituents have been removed . . . are an absolute fraud."

Sir Arthur Crosfield, Bt.: "Innutritious white bread, if persisted in for three generations, will, in the opinion of many medical men, turn us into a C3 nation."

Sir William Arbuthnot Lane, Consulting Surgeon to Guy's Hospital: "Instruct the public on the general use of whole-wheat flour, to the complete exclusion of white flour."

These eminent authorities and many others blame white bread for very many diseases and ailments and much of the physical weakness prevalent to-day. Moreover, they assert with equal confidence that "wholemeal bread is by far the most important and efficient food to ensure health and prevent disease."

In spite, however, of this clear lead in the matter of diet, there still remains a grave risk in the public's inability to distinguish genuine wholemeal bread from its many imitations. Allinson Limited, who are specialists in the milling of wholemeal flour, regard it as their special duty to instruct the public on this all-important matter.

Difference between Brown Bread and Allinson

Let it be clearly understood that while every wholemeal loaf is brown, not every brown loaf is wholemeal. A great deal of the brown bread sold is no better as a food—no better agent for promoting health and preventing disease—than white bread.

Readers who recollect the rubbish proffered by unscrupulous millers and indifferent bakers when the daily press was advocating the standardisation of bread must rid their minds of any confusion as to the identity of such chaff and genuine whole-wheat. Much of the Standard Bread then sold comes under one or another of the classes in the following Black List.

Black List of valueless or even harmful kinds of brown bread sometimes sold as Wholemeal:

1. Brown bread baked entirely from the refuse and by-products of white-flour milling.
2. Brown bread made from poor grades of wheat unfit for so important an item of human food.
3. Brown bread containing only 70 to 75% of wheat. (*Allinson Wholemeal is 100% wheat.*)
4. Brown bread containing malt, which negatives much of its value.
5. Brown bread containing over 90% of white flour, some bran and colouring matter.

All these kinds of bread are commonly offered for sale, and the public must be on their guard against them, for, in addition to their other several failings, they all lack the two outstanding virtues of genuine wholemeal:—
(a) the germ of the wheat-grain—the seat of the vitamines and of concentrated nutriment; (b) the outer layer of the wheat-grain — the seat of the mineral salts which promote good digestion and prevent constipation.

Registered   Trade Mark

Allinson Bread promotes health. Remarkable letter

Allinson Ltd. have never claimed medicinal properties for their Wholemeal Bread. They know that it has benefited the health of thousands of people, but it has done so solely by the virtue of wheat, which, when properly milled, is a perfect natural food.

Allinson Wholemeal Bread is not only rich in nourishment, but it also contains the means of enabling the system to absorb all that nourishment; it promotes a strong, healthy digestion by nature's own means. The following letter, which is only one of many such received by Allinson Ltd., shows one way in which this bread establishes healthy conditions :—

June 25th, 1924.

Dear Sirs,—I suffered from constipation for four years, having had to take numerous medicines to try and get relief, but without avail. A friend having recommended your bread to me, I gave it a trial, and was indeed surprised to find my constipation soon disappeared.

I am writing this to let you know what a lot of good your bread has done me, and I am recommending it to any of my friends who are in the same plight as I was.

Yours faithfully,
John Clark.

(*Original letter can be seen at offices of Allinson Ltd.*)

Other letters could be quoted to show how Allinson Wholemeal Bread helps to strengthen the nerves; how greatly it has helped in cases of anæmia, dyspepsia, and other complaints arising from malnutrition; how athletes have trained on it; how sturdy children, strong in bone and teeth, have been reared on it. All these letters substantiate the opinion of modern science that natural food, rather than medicine, provides the remedy for ills due to incorrect diet, and is the only true preventive of illness. "Natural food creates the strength to resist disease."

The watchword is "Wholemeal": the password—"Allinson"

Facts about Allinson Flour and Bread

1. Only the very finest grades of wheat (home-grown and colonial) are used for milling the Allinson Wholemeal Flour which is supplied to bakers for baking Allinson Wholemeal Bread.

2. This superb quality of wheat is ground direct into Wholemeal Flour; nothing is added, nothing is taken away. Allinson Flour is 100% wheat.

3. The milling of Allinson Wholemeal Flour is done, not under steel rollers, but between millstones, in the old-fashioned slow but highly efficient and cleanly way. Only thus can the exact degree of required fineness be attained.

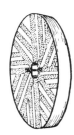

One of the many old-fashioned mill-stones used to grind the Allinson Flour to the ideal degree of fineness.

4. Every genuine loaf of Allinson Wholemeal Bread is encircled by a paper band which bears the portrait and signature of the founder and the well-known windmill trade mark. The loaf is also stamped ALLINSON on both sides.

5. Allinson Wholemeal Flour, identical with that sold to bakers for baking Allinson Bread, is supplied in 3½-lb., 7-lb., and 14-lb. sealed bags for home baking of cakes, pastries, etc.; every bag contains the new **80-recipe Cookery Book.** Obtainable from all grocers and cornchandlers, or direct from

ALLINSON LTD.
CAMBRIDGE ROAD, LONDON, E.2

See this paper band on every loaf.

Allinson UNADULTERATED WHOLEMEAL Bread

A delicacy always in season

HAPPILY, unlike such delicacies as plovers' eggs and oysters, St. Ivel Lactic Cheese is always with us.

If you have a palate for cheese you can tell St. Ivel with your eyes shut, by its cool creaminess, its smoothness, its clean Cheddar flavour.

Every day gallons of rich foaming milk from West Country cows are turned into these delicious little cheeses—in the spotless gleaming dairies at Yeovil.

But there is more than the mere richness of good things in St. Ivel Lactic Cheese. It abounds in that Lactic Culture—the wonderful Bacillus Bulgaricus—which is the keynote of Metchnikoff's famous life-prolonging treatment.

* * *

There are many delightful ways of serving St. Ivel. Spread it on biscuits or sandwiches (it spreads just like butter), adding, if you will, lettuce, cream, celery, or even jam. It is in itself the ideal light lunch or tea, and as a digestive, the perfect close of any meal.

No Nightmares

When you get home from a dance or theatre, St. Ivel sandwiches are just the thing. St. Ivel is so digestible—there's no fear of nightmares. It is delicious combined with lettuce, cress, tomatoes, or jam.

'Lucullus' Salad

On a foundation of young lettuce leaves or endive lay alternate sections of oranges with grapefruit and chopped apples with walnuts. In the middle place a square of St. Ivel Lactic Cheese. Serve this with a cream dressing.

Snatching a lunch

The "snatched meal" problem is solved delightfully. A St. Ivel "Minnie" (price 2d.) is just the right size for a quick lunch. Light —yes—but it really nourishes you and carries you on to your next meal. It's so clean on the palate, too. Try it to-morrow at lunchtime, and a cup of hot Ivelcon with it.

Metchnikoff at home

St. Ivel Lactic Cheese is a miniature Metchnikoff treatment in itself. Metchnikoff discovered that Lactic culture which wards off Old Age by keeping the internal organs in perfect health. St. Ivel Cheese is rich in this very Lactic culture.

St IVEL
LACTIC CHEESE

From your dairy or your grocer in 8½d. cartons, or a miniature form—called St. Ivel "Minnies"—for 2d.

ST IVEL LIMITED HEAD OFFICE YEOVIL SOMERSET

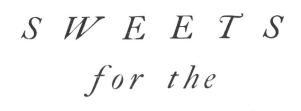

S W E E T S
for the
DANCE SUPPER

Rivals in popularity are Petits Gâteaux Chantilly and hot-house melon with fruit salad

SUGGESTIONS for some new and delicious sweet dishes, specially suitable for evening parties and dances, will not, perhaps, be inappropriate at this festive season. The illustrations and the recipes given are ample testimony to the fact that a successful sweet should always be decorative, delighting the eye as well as the palate.

Lemon Mousse

3 eggs	½ oz. gelatine
2 tablespoonfuls sugar	A little water
1 or 2 lemons	Cream

This sweet is very easy to make. Divide the yolks from the whites of the eggs, putting them into separate basins. Add the sugar and the grated rind of half a lemon to the yolks, and beat with a wooden spoon until light and creamy. Then add the strained juice of 1 or 2 lemons according to size and taste. Dissolve the gelatine in a small quantity of water and strain it into the egg mixture. Continue the beating until the mixture begins to set, then stir in very lightly and by degrees the whites of the eggs beaten to a stiff froth. Put the mousse into a glass or china bowl and keep in a cool place until required. Serve with a little whipped and sweetened cream on the top.

Peach Cream

½ pint peach purée	Castor sugar
1 gill custard or condensed milk	1 oz. gelatine
1 gill cream	Some clear jelly
	A few glacé cherries

Make the purée by rubbing some tinned peaches through a fine sieve. Use only a little of the syrup and do not make the purée too thin. Make also a gill of custard, using 2 yolks of eggs to 1 gill of milk; or condensed milk may be used, whipping it up as stiffly as possible. Add the custard or whipped milk to the purée, and strain in the gelatine which has been dissolved in some of the syrup from the tin. Sweeten to taste with fine castor sugar. Whip the cream and mix it lightly with the other ingredients, and add a few drops of carmine to make the mixture a peachy colour. Stir occasionally until beginning to set, then pour into a mould that has been previously prepared in the following manner:

To Prepare the Mould: Choose a mould that will hold 1½ pints, and of a pretty pattern. Rinse it out with cold water and leave it wet. Then dissolve a little clear jelly—orange, lemon, or wine—and cover the bottom of the mould with this. When set arrange on the top a few neatly cut pieces of peach, and small pieces of glacé cherry to give colour. Pour in more jelly to keep these in position and leave until firm before pouring in the cream mixture.

If preferred, the cream may be set in small individual moulds, decorating them in the same way with jelly and fruit.

Peach Cream

Other Fruit Creams can be made in the same way by using a different variety of tinned fruit, such as apricots, pears, grated pine-apple, gooseberries, etc. Or, fresh fruit may be used if it is first cooked until soft with sugar and a small quantity of water. Some of the soft fruits may be used without cooking, such as raspberries, strawberries, loganberries and bananas. The sieve used for the fruit must be very fine, and the pureé must not be too liquid.

Melon with Fruit Salad

1 melon	2 sheets of gelatine
1 tin of fruit salad	The juice of ½ lemon
1 glass red wine	A few drops of carmine

Choose a ripe hot-house melon or cantaloupe melon of medium size. Cut a slice off the top, and scoop out the inside without making the walls too thin. Remove the seeds and cut the pulp of the melon into small pieces. Turn the melon itself upside-down to drain whilst preparing the filling. Drain the syrup from the fruit salad. Put the fruit into a basin and add to it the cut melon. Pour the syrup into a small saucepan, add the gelatine and lemon-juice, and dissolve over the fire. A little sugar may also be added if necessary. Strain into a basin, add the wine and a few drops of colouring. Cool and pour over the fruit. A short time before the melon has to be served fill it with the fruit salad and replace the lid. Place the melon on a pretty dish and garnish it with vine leaves or sprigs of fern.

Petits Gâteaux Chantilly

These are easy to make and they always look attractive. Small round moulds with a hole in the middle or little savarin moulds are required. Grease these and dust them out with a coating of fine sugar. Then prepare a sponge cake or other white cake mixture, half fill the tins with this and bake in a moderate oven. When sufficiently cooked, turn out the cakes and let them cool. Spread the sides of the cakes with a little jam and sprinkle them with ground-nuts, browned coconut, or chopped pistachio nuts. A short time before serving sprinkle them with a little sherry or rum, and fill up the centres with whipped and sweetened cream, flavoured with a little vanilla. A few crystallised violets, or small pieces of glacé cherry may be used to decorate the top. Small pieces of fruit or preserved ginger may be mixed with the cream.

Kedgeree and Italian Turnovers are delicious dishes containing rice

Uncommon Ways of —

Serving Rice

By E. Edwards

First Class Diploma, Cookery, Laundrywork, Housewifery, and Needlework; King's College Certificate of Household and Social Science; Certificate of the London Sanitary Board

RICE is generally regarded as suitable for puddings and as an accompaniment to curry, but it is not always realised that there are many other dishes, both sweet and savoury, for which it is delicious. A well-balanced diet must include carbohydrates. Of these, white flour, potatoes and rice are perhaps the most typical examples. The use of whole rice and other grains will be discussed in a future article, polished rice being used for the recipes given below, which will appeal to those who enjoy well-flavoured and light yet nourishing dishes.

It is a well known fact that rice forms the staple diet of the inhabitants of many hot countries, but its composition renders it less suitable, if used alone, for the people of northern or temperate climes. This is due to the fact that it is very deficient in protein and fat and rich in carbohydrates, which must be borne in mind when preparing dishes composed largely of rice. Protein and fat must be added to make the food value more proportionate. Meat, bacon, eggs and cheese are all suitable, particularly as they give a definite flavour to the rice, which alone is lacking in flavour and somewhat insipid.

The two chief varieties of rice in common use in this country are Patna

To separate the grains run cold water through from the tap

and Carolina. The former can be distinguished by its long, narrow, polished grain and the latter by its more opaque, wider and less shapely appearance.

Patna rice should always be chosen as a border for curry or mince, or for any dish where a well finished appearance is essential. Provided that it is cooked correctly, each grain will be clearly defined and separate, whereas the grains of Carolina rice, owing to their glutinous nature, tend to bind together in an indistinct mass. This type of rice is therefore particularly suitable for milk puddings, crôquettes and rice fillings.

Boiling Rice for Curry

Wash the rice in a deep dish under the cold water tap until all the starch is washed from the outside of the grains and the water runs clear. Soak for 20 minutes, drain and put into a large pan of fast boiling salted water to which has been added a squeeze of lemon juice. Boil hard for 8 to 10 minutes. Remove a grain and test between the finger and thumb to see if it is tender and correctly cooked. Pour into a colander and run cold water through from the cold water tap. Put the colander over the pan, cover with a towel and stand for a few minutes or until required.

Kedgeree

12 oz. cooked smoked haddock or other white fish	3 oz. butter
	6 oz cooked Patna rice
1 or 2 hard boiled eggs	Salt
	Cayenne pepper
	Chopped parsley

Remove the bones and skin from the fish when it is hot. Flake it coarsely with a fork. Chop the whites and part of the yolk of egg, reserving a little of the latter for garnishing.

Uncommon Ways of Serving Rice

Melt the butter in a saucepan, add the fish, rice, chopped egg and seasonings. Stir thoroughly over a moderate heat until hot. Pile on a hot dish and garnish with lines of chopped parsley and a little sieved yolk of egg. A kedgeree should be fairly dry.

Egg and Rice Cutlets

½ pint milk	1 oz. flour
2 hard boiled eggs	1 oz. butter
1 tablespoonful white breadcrumbs	¼ teaspoonful chopped parsley
	Salt and pepper
2 oz. boiled Carolina rice	Tomato chutney or sauce
Grating of nutmeg or cayenne pepper	Egg and breadcrumbs for frying

Melt the butter, add the flour and cook for a few seconds. Add the milk, stir and boil for five minutes. Add the rice, chopped egg, seasonings, breadcrumbs and parsley and mix well. Spread on a floured plate and allow to cool. When cold, divide into even pieces and shape into cutlets, coat in egg and breadcrumbs and fry in hot fat from which a faint blue smoke is rising. Drain well and serve hot with tomato chutney or sauce.

Italian Turnovers

For the Pastry

4 oz. flour	Salt and cayenne
2 oz. butter	pepper
1 oz. grated cheese	Cold water to mix

For the Filling

½ pint milk and water	Cayenne pepper
	Salt
1½ oz. grated cheese	1½ oz. Carolina rice

Wash the rice and soak it for ½ hour. Strain and cook it in the milk and water with the seasoning until it is tender and thick, stirring occasionally as the rice is apt to stick. Add the cheese and allow the mixture to become cold.

Make a pastry by rubbing the butter into the flour, adding the cheese, seasonings, and sufficient water to mix. Roll this out very thinly and cut into 3-inch rounds with a fluted cutter. Moisten the edges with a little water or beaten egg and place a teaspoonful of the mixture on each. Fold over, press the edges together and brush with a beaten egg. Bake at 360° F. for a few minutes until golden brown in colour. Serve hot.

Rice Soup

2 pints stock and milk	½ oz. butter
	1 shallot
2 oz. Patna rice	A small piece of carrot and turnip
1 teaspoonful curry powder	A sprig of parsley
A pinch of salt	

Melt the butter and fry the sliced shallot in it to a golden brown. Remove the shallot and fry the curry powder. Pour the stock and milk into the pan and bring to the boil. Slice the vegetables, and then add to the contents in the pan, together with the fried shallot, washed rice, parsley and the salt. Simmer for 1½ hours, then rub through a sieve, re-heat and serve. This makes a fairly substantial soup and if preferred the amount of rice may be reduced to half.

Pilau of Rice and Cooked Meat

6 oz. Carolina rice	2 cloves
2 oz. butter	¼ teaspoonful cinnamon
1 small onion	
1 pint stock	Fried onion rings
2 oz. sultanas	6 oz. diced cold meat
Salt and pepper	2 oz. streaky bacon

Wash the rice in plenty of cold water. Put in a saucepan and cover with cold water, bring to the boil, strain and rinse in cold water. Return to the pan, pour on the stock and add the butter, seasonings, sultanas, cinnamon and the onion stuck with cloves. Stir constantly and cook gently until the rice is tender. This will take about 25 minutes.

Meanwhile, cut the bacon into small pieces and fry until golden brown. Then fry the onion rings, remove them, and fry the meat. Take out the onion and cloves and arrange the rice in a neat border. Put the meat and bacon in the centre and garnish with the onion rings.

Note.—Those who do not care for the combination of sultanas and cinnamon with meat can omit these when preparing the rice.

Savoury Rice and Tomato

6 oz. Carolina rice	2 oz. grated cheese
½ lb. tomatoes or 3 tablespoonfuls tomato sauce or chutney	¾ pint milk and water
	Crescents of fried bread
Salt and cayenne pepper	

Wash the rice thoroughly and soak it in the milk and water for 20 minutes. Bring to the boil, stirring occasionally, and simmer until tender and fairly thick. This will take about ¾ hour. Add the salt, cayenne pepper and the skinned and sliced tomatoes. Stir and cook gently until the mixture is thick. Stir in the cheese and serve garnished with crescents of fried bread.

Lenten MENUS

By Helen Clarke

First Class Diplomas, Cookery, Laundrywork, & Houswifery, N.T.S.C.; late Staff N.T.S.C.

EVERY housewife will agree that the regular planning of meals and drawing up of menus entails considerable thought and patience even if there be no need to practise strict economy. In offering the following Lenten menus for breakfast, lunch, and dinner for 2 complete weeks it is hoped that the difficult task of selecting appetising meatless dishes will be minimised.

In drawing up the detail of dishes (the literal meaning of menus), attention has been paid to the importance of food values, to which subject an article is devoted this month. When meat is omitted from a diet, either temporarily or permanently, it must be replaced by foods rich in nitrogen—thus eggs, cheese, nuts, and milk figure largely in the dishes selected.

With few exceptions the recipes are to be found in the *Good Housekeeping Cookery Book* or previous numbers of this magazine. Those not to be found there, and which have only recently been evolved in the Institute, are given below.

Salmon Cream Pie: 1 tin of salmon; ½ pint thick white sauce; seasoning; mashed potatoes; chopped parsley for garnish. Flake the salmon finely, mix with the sauce, heat this thoroughly, and season to taste. Dish up in a border of hot mashed potatoes, and sprinkle the potato with the parsley.

Teneriffe Mould combines bananas and prunes, and so is specially suitable for this season of the year, when there is little variety of fresh fruit obtainable. The ingredients required are: ½ lb. prunes; 1 pint water; 1 oz. sugar; the rind and juice of 1 lemon; ¼ pint cream; 3 bananas; 1 pint packet lemon jelly. Wash the prunes and soak them all night in 1 pint of water; next day turn them into a saucepan, and stew gently until tender. Strain from the liquid, remove the stones, and cut the prunes and bananas into small pieces. Measure the liquid, dissolve the jelly in this, making it up to ¾ pint with water, if necessary. Decorate a border mould with bananas or blanched almonds, setting the decorations with a little of the jelly. Pour the rest of the jelly over the prunes and bananas, mix well, and turn into the mould. When set turn on to a glass dish and pile the whipped cream in the centre.

Stuffed Apples are both nourishing and delicious. Take 3 lb. apples; 1 oz. almonds (blanched); ½ lb. dates; a little sugar. Wash and core the apples, carefully removing all the core, then cut the skin round the top of each. Stone the dates and blanch the almonds, chop both and mix them together. Half fill each apple with this mixture, then put in a little sugar, and fill them up with the date and almond stuffing. Place in a glass fireproof dish or pie-dish, and add sufficient water to cover ¼ inch up the side of the dish. Bake in a moderate oven till the apples are tender when tested with a skewer,

Walnut and Parsnip Croquettes make an excellent vegetarian entrée, suitable for either dinner or lunch. The ingredients needed are: 1 lb. parsnips; 2 oz. chopped walnuts; 1 oz. flour; 1 oz. butter; 1 gill milk. Cook the parsnips until quite tender, then rub them through a sieve. Melt the butter in a small saucepan and stir in the flour, then add the milk, and boil, stirring all the time. Season to taste. Add to this sauce the sieved parsnips and chopped walnuts, stir them well in, turn the mixture on to a plate, and spread into a flat cake. When this is cold, form into balls, egg and crumb them, and fry in very hot fat. Serve on a hot dish.

Haddock and Tomato on Toast: 1 small cooked dried haddock; 8 large tomatoes; bread for toast; ¼ pint milk; ½ oz. margarine. Cook the haddock in a flat tin with the milk and butter. Strain off the liquid and reduce. While the fish is still hot, flake it finely, removing all skin and bones, and mix with the liquid, seasoning to taste. With a plain cutter, the size of the tomatoes, cut 16 rounds of bread, and fry these in deep fat. Cut the tomatoes across, place one half on each round of fried bread. Cook in a slow oven, pile a little of the haddock mixture on each tomato, and sprinkle with chopped parsley.

Cheese Tartlets.—Line 12 patty-pans with trimmings of pastry. For the mixture take: 1 oz. cheese; 1 egg; seasoning; ½ oz. flour; ½ oz. butter; 1 gill milk. Melt the butter in a saucepan and stir in the flour, then add the milk and stir vigorously until the contents thicken, and boil well. When cool add the grated cheese, yolk of egg, and seasoning. Stir the stiffly beaten white of egg into this mixture, and half fill the lined patty-tins. Bake in a quick oven (390° F.) for about 20 minutes.

Lobster Cutlets are made in a similar way to fish cakes, except that lobster or tinned salmon is used, and the mixture is coloured pale pink with cochineal. Pat up into pear-shaped cutlets, and egg and crumb them.

Beetroot and Celery.—Cook the beetroot, cut into dice, and cut the celery into small pieces. Thoroughly blend both with dressing, and sprinkle with finely chopped parsley. For the dressing take: 2 tablespoonfuls salad oil; 1 tablespoonful vinegar; ⅛ teaspoonful pepper; ¼ teaspoonful salt; ¼ teaspoonful made mustard. Mix the salt, pepper, and mustard with the salad oil, then stir the vinegar in vigorously.

Curried Vegetables are prepared in the same way as curried meat. Any mixed vegetables can be used, but butter beans or lentils should be present to replace meat, and the water in which the beans have been soaked should be used as stock to make the curry sauce.

Teneriffe Mould is nourishing and of attractive appearance

Haddock and Tomato on Toast and Salmon Cream Pie are popular substitutes for meat

SUGGESTIONS for MEALS without MEAT

First Week's Menus

MONDAY

BREAKFAST
Fish Cakes. Boiled Eggs. Toast

———

LUNCH
Savoury Omelette
Pancakes
Cheese and Oatmeal Biscuits
Raisins and Almonds

———

DINNER
Green Pea and Celery Soup
Walnut and Parsnip Croquettes
Fried Plaice. Brussels Sprouts. Fried
Potatoes
Apricot Fool
Cheese Fritters

———

TUESDAY

BREAKFAST
Grape-fruit. Tomato and Haddock on
Toast

———

LUNCH
Bird's Nest with Cheese Sauce
Stuffed Apples. Corn Cake

———

DINNER
Bananas on Horseback
Rice Cream Soup
Salmon Cream Pie. Cauliflower
Primrose Pudding
Cheese Straws

WEDNESDAY

BREAKFAST
Potato Cakes. Scrambled Eggs

———

LUNCH
Stuffed Baked Herrings. Rye Bread
and Butter
Orange Tapioca

———

DINNER
Chestnut Soup
Egg en Petite Cocotte
Timbale of Fish in Aspic. Salad
Teneriffe Mould
Water-Lily Savoury

———

THURSDAY

BREAKFAST
Porridge. Sardines on Toast

———

LUNCH
Poached Eggs on Welsh Rarebit
Pop-overs with Jam Sauce

———

DINNER
Tomato Bisque
Bean Casserole
Raised Fish Pie. Celeriac. Potatoes
Orange Pudding
Sardines à la Tartare

FRIDAY

BREAKFAST
Kedgeree. Oatcakes. Toast

———

LUNCH
Tomato Dumplings
Nut and Date Bread. Bananas

———

DINNER
Puritan Soup
Whiting and Maître d'Hôtel Butter.
Chip Potatoes. Cauliflower
Chiffon Pie
Prunes à l'Indienne

———

SATURDAY

BREAKFAST
Waffles. Poached Eggs on Toast. Potted
Salmon

———

LUNCH
Shrimp Patties
Cheese Dreams
Spiced Nuts

———

DINNER
Hors-d'œuvres Various
Cucumber à la Poulette
East India Fish. Seakale. Potatoes
Prune Snowballs
Crôutes Almira

Lenten Menus

SUNDAY

BREAKFAST
Prepared Wheat and Hot Milk
Grilled Herrings

LUNCH
Cheese Apples. Raisin Bread
Semolina Caramel

DINNER
Cauliflower Soup
Gnocchi à la Romaine
Egg Cutlets. Potatoes à la Maître d'Hôtel
Orange and Banana Salad
Lobster Canapés

Second Week's Menus

MONDAY

BREAKFAST
Baked Apples
Fish Omelette
Rolls and Butter

LUNCH
Egg Darioles
Jam Tart
Cheese and Biscuits

DINNER
Spinach and Rice Soup
Shredded Cabbage with Tomato Sauce
Halibut Steaks in Milk. Spinach. Mashed Potatoes
Apple Fritters
Cheese Tartlets

TUESDAY

BREAKFAST
Girdle Cakes
Lobster Cutlets. Toast

LUNCH
Curried Vegetables
Stewed Figs and Custard

DINNER
Beetroot and Celery
Lentil Cream Soup
Baked Sliced Salmon. Potato Croquettes
Lemon Pie
Dessert

WEDNESDAY

BREAKFAST
Potato Cakes
Soused Herrings

LUNCH
Parsnip Soufflé
Baked Apple Pudding

DINNER
Fruit Soup
Brussels Sprouts and Chestnuts
Egg Fricassée. Potatoes. Sauté Butter Beans
Apple Cheese Cakes
Cheese Balls and Lettuce

THURSDAY

BREAKFAST
Barley Meal Scones
Herring Roe Savoury

LUNCH
Fish Baked in Custard
Spiced Apple Cake

DINNER
Alsatian Soup
Buttered Beetroot
Baked Sole and Italian Sauce. Stewed Celery. Potatoes
Lemon Jelly
Tomato Bonnes-Bouches

FRIDAY

BREAKFAST
Porridge
Scrambled Eggs

LUNCH
Egg sur le Plat
Folkestone Pie

DINNER
Prawns
Macaroni Soup
Ceylon Curry of Tomatoes. Parsnips
Pineapple Wheels
Egg Tartare

SATURDAY

BREAKFAST
Prepared Wheat and Milk
Poached Eggs on Haddock

LUNCH
Italian Macaroni and Tomato
Bottled Fruit and Custard

DINNER
Celery Cream Soup
Glazed Carrots
Fish and Potato Timbale. Cauliflower
Hawaian Delight
Sardine Eggs

SUNDAY

BREAKFAST
Rye and Corn Gems
Fish Savoury

LUNCH
Savoury Rice and Bananas
Rode Grœd

DINNER
Corn Soup
Scallops
Spaghetti en Casserole. Turnips and Sauce
Fruit Salad and Cream
Tomato Cocktail

and so - to Breakfast

A BREAKFAST like this is as good as a running start at the day's work. Moreover, it gives you momentum—power and vigour to carry on. Just begin your usual meal with a plate of these golden, crisp and crunchy Post Toasties. Tasty, Toasted flakes of nature's energy food—Indian Corn—made from highly-cultivated varieties of that same grain which for ages served as mainstay food of the American Redskin—most stalwart, most enduring of men.

NO COOKING—ready Toasted—ready to serve. The sweet, firm heart is taken—cooked—flaked—then crisp-toasted to a golden brown and sealed in airtight packages. You eat them just as they are—no cooking; no preparation. See how Post Toasties stay crisp in cream or milk (because each flake is Double Thick) and how the snap and flavour remain right up to the moment of eating.

Post Toasties

DOUBLE THICK INDIAN CORN FLAKES

INDIAN CORN · FOOD O' THE STALWART

52

The Housekeeper's Dictionary of Facts

Recommended by "Good Housekeeping" Institute

FOOD
Glorious
FOOD

1925

Protecting the House From Mice

The use of efficient mouse-traps is not the only means of exterminating this pest. The utmost care should be taken to prevent the entry of field mice. Damaged ventilating gratings should be renewed or covered with fine mesh wire netting, and any other possible means of entry looked for. Mice often come into the house by means of small holes in the larder or in cupboards, particularly those under the stairs. Holes too large to be repaired easily with cement should first be filled with corks and then cemented. Worn linoleum or floor-boards should be repaired or renewed.

Conditions are made unpleasant for mice if cayenne pepper is sprinkled on shelves and near food. Special precautions should be taken that no food is left uncovered, and in houses that tend to be overrun with mice all foods should be stored in tin or wood containers, not in sacks or bags.

To Untie Knots

Place the knot on a table and gently hammer with a wooden article for a second or two, reversing the knot as you do so. Then insert the closed points of a small pair of scissors, gradually open them, and the knot will come untied.

A Light Yorkshire Pudding

Mix the necessary flour, eggs, salt, and a small quantity of milk to a very thick, smooth paste, and then add the remainder of the milk made very hot in a saucepan. Bake the puddings, if possible, in fairly small round tins, and you will find they will puff up to the top of the tins and be delightfully crisp and light. By mixing in this manner less eggs are required.

Mending With Sealing-Wax

Sealing-wax can be used satisfactorily for effecting small repairs in enamel basins, jugs, etc., not used to contain hot liquids. By the following simple method tiny holes can be mended and the vessel given a new lease of life: Get a stick of sealing-wax the colour of the vessel to be repaired, cleanse and thoroughly dry the part to be made good, and apply the sealing-wax, melted, over the worn surface, pressing down firmly and neatly. Any leakage will be effectively stopped.

Boiling Cracked Eggs

Cracked eggs can be boiled without the loss of any of the egg if the following method is adopted: Add a tablespoonful of salt to the water in which the egg is boiled, rub the crack well with common salt, and put the egg at once into the fast-boiling salt water. The white of the egg will not ooze out nor the crack become larger.

Some Uses for Glycerine

A mixture of two parts glycerine and one part lemon-juice makes an excellent cleansing lotion for the skin. Apply it sparingly, and rub well into the hands. Glycerine may also be used for loosening round glass stoppers in bottles when they cannot be removed by any other means. Apply it with a paint brush around the top of the stopper. It will gradually soak between the two surfaces and facilitate the removal of the stopper. If this is very persistent, the bottle should be inverted and placed in a small egg-cup or jar of glycerine and left for several days. Patent leather shoes may also be cleaned with glycerine. Rub it well into the leather and polish with a soft cloth.

A Nursery Suggestion For Dull Days

The making of jigsaw puzzles is a fascinating amusement for dark days in the nursery. Select a pretty picture

A Lasting Joy—

That is the test which thoughtful donors apply when sifting through their list of possible Christmas gifts. The Christmas number of GOOD HOUSEKEEPING, with specially augmented Cookery, Household, Furnishing, and Shopping Service Sections, reaches the high-water mark of practical, literary, and artistic excellence, and will be hailed with delight by every reader. All the year round the magazine reacts to the pulse of women's interests and activities, and caters for miscellaneous moods as well. Therefore one of the most appreciated gifts you can possibly make to your friends at home or abroad is a year's subscription to

Good Housekeeping

and paste it on to a fairly thick piece of smooth cardboard. When quite dry, cut the picture into many pieces of different sizes and shapes, and shake these up in a box before trying to fit them together.

A Substitute For Ice.

It is often necessary to cool jellies, blancmanges, etc., quickly, and when ice is not available the mould or basin may be stood in water containing equal parts of common salt and washing soda in solution. Sufficient should be added so that just a little is left undissolved. Other chemicals which make a good freezing mixture are ammonium nitrate and washing soda, in equal parts.

Washing a Heavy Artificial Silk Jumper

Artificial silk jumpers require care in laundering to prevent undue stretching. If tacked flat on to a towel before being washed, a jumper will not lose its shape. When dry, it should be pressed with a warm iron before it is untacked from the towel.

A Portable Kitchen Range

A portable or self-setting range is so called because it requires no brick-setting. It is merely connected to the chimney by a short length of smoke-pipe. This pipe should pass at least one foot through the sheet iron register-plate which closes in the bottom of the chimney. A range should not, if possible, be placed directly opposite an outer door. This causes the fire to burn too rapidly, wasting fuel and burning away the fire-bricks. As sheet iron wears out after two or three years' use, it is advisable when buying a range to have one that is fitted with a cast-iron back and ends. It is also advisable to have the smoke-pipe of cast iron. This should be fitted with a loose door on the front to admit the flue brush.

A removable oven which can easily be renewed without removing the range for repairs is a distinct advantage.

Etceteras for Convenience

Other features which add to the convenience of a stove are a lifting fire, which also effects economy in fuel, and a pedal opener to the oven door, so that the latter can easily be opened with the foot, leaving both hands free to put the dish in the oven. A plate-rack is also very useful. It is often not supplied with the range, but may be obtained for a small extra charge. A side boiler fitted with a draw-off tap is not recommended in a range of this type, unless it is kept automatically supplied with water by a ball valve. A boiler of this kind holds very little water and has to be constantly filled by hand.

Getting the Best Results

If a false bottom is used, the space between the real bottom and the grating must be kept clear of ashes, or the fire will become clogged.

Fire-bricks should be renewed before they are burnt through or the ironwork will be burnt away as well, making much more expensive and extensive repairs necessary.

Before using a range for the first time, examine it to become thoroughly acquainted with the direction of the flues and the position of the soot or flue-cleaning doors. These doors must all be closed while the range is working. Clean the flues thoroughly at regular intervals, at least once a week when the fire is used daily. If there is a back boiler, the boiler flue must be cleaned every day.

Tea-Time *At*

Good Housekeeping Restaurant

449 Oxford Street, W.1
(Opposite Selfridge's)

It is not only for our real home-made cakes that so many people come to Good Housekeeping Restaurant, but also for the wonderfully refreshing tea that is served there

So many customers have asked if they can buy the tea itself, that we have had it put up in half-pound packets to take away, and also ready for posting.

½ lb. *Indian Tea* - 1/6
½ lb. *China Tea* - 2/-

Or Post Free U.K.:
2 lb. *Indian Tea* - 6/6
2 lb. *China Tea* - 8/6

GOOD HOUSEKEEPING
RESTAURANT
—
Special Fruit Teas
—
Pot of Tea
Roll and Butter
Fruit Salad
1/6

STRAWBERRIES

The Six Most Delicious Ways of Serving Fresh Straw-

berries and the Three Best Methods of Preserving

Strawberry Wafer Cream, shown above, is delicious

STRAWBERRIES need no recommendation, the only point which really troubles the housewife is their scarcity or profusion. Where choice can be exercised, medium-sized dark red fruit is to be preferred to large pale fruit. which is lacking in flavour. Small strawberries make excellent jam and the flavour is often superior to the larger specimens. For jam making the fruit may, with advantage, be slightly under-ripe.

Probably the majority of people agree that such a luscious and delicate fruit should be eaten only in its natural condition, as cooking or preparing it in any way is inclined to detract from rather than add to its delicacy of flavour. There is, however, one exception—that of jam making. This is undoubtedly the most satisfactory way of preserving the fruit for use during the eleven months of the year when fresh strawberries are not available.

Of all jams, strawberry is the one where housewives encounter the most difficulties. This is because the fruit is naturally deficient in pectin and acid, whilst the water content is very high, and therefore the jelling qualities are poor. To overcome this difficulty acid must be added, and either lemon juice, citric acid or tartaric acid, or, if preferred, gooseberry or red currant juice can be utilised.

The following recipes give excellent results. All have been tested in Good Housekeeping Institute. The fresh strawberry recipes are delicious and unusual.

Strawberry Jam, First Method

4 lb. strawberries (not over-ripe)	The juice of 4 lemons or ¼ oz.
3½ lb. sugar	citric or tartaric acid

Pick the strawberries. If the weather has been wet and the fruit appears to be gritty it should be washed and put into the preserving pan with the lemon juice, citric or tartaric acid. Boil the fruit slowly until it is tender. This extracts the pectin and also drives off surplus moisture. When the contents of the pan are thick and reduced, add the sugar, previously warmed in the oven, stir and bring to the boil. Continue stirring and test for jelling after boiling has continued over 10 to 15 minutes. When it sets firmly when tested on a cold plate or saucer turn out the gas, allow the contents of the pan to cool partly by stirring gently, and when half cold pot and tie down.

Note.—In order to preserve the bright colour and the flavour of the natural fruit it is important not to add the sugar until the pectin has been extracted from the fruit and the surplus moisture driven off in the form of steam.

Many housewives write to the Institute complaining that their strawberry jam, whilst wholesome, does not taste of fresh fruit and is brownish in colour. The reason is easy to explain—if the sugar is added with the fruit and the boiling occupies from 45 minutes to 1 hour, or even longer, the temperature of the contents of the pan rises above 212° F. and may even become as high as 220° F. with the result that changes take place in the sugar and both the flavour and colour of the preserve is impaired.

Strawberry Jam, Second Method

4 lb. strawberries
The juice of 1 large lemon
4 lb. sugar
½ pint red currant juice

Method as above. The fruit is boiled with the lemon juice and red currant juice for 45 to 60 minutes, or until tender, and the contents of the pan have evaporated considerably. The sugar is then added and the jam boiled until it jells.

Continued

Strawberries

Economical Strawberry Jam

| 8 lb. strawberries | 2 lb. minced goose- |
| 9 lb. sugar | berries |

Top, tail and wash the gooseberries. Pass through a mincing machine, put into a pan and cook for a few minutes, until they are tender. (If minced the fruit cooks very quickly.) Rub through a sieve to remove the seeds and cook the pulp with the strawberries before adding the sugar, then proceed as above.

Strawberry Dream

| 1 lb. strawberries | Sugar to taste |
| 2 whites of egg | Whipped cream |

Mash the strawberries and add sugar to taste. Many people consider the flavour to be superior if sugar is omitted. Whip the whites of egg to a stiff froth and cut or fold carefully into the mashed pulp. Fill individual glass with the mixture, chill and serve topped with cream.

Strawberry Pyramids

| Genoese pastry or | 1 gill cream |
| sponge cake | 1 lb. strawberries |

Cut the pastry or cake into 2 in. rounds, ½ in. in thickness. Hull the strawberries and slice with a silver or stainless knife. Whip the cream stiffly and sweeten to taste. Put the sliced strawberries and whipped cream in alternate layers on the rounds of pastry, topping with cream. Chill and serve on a silver entreé dish decorated with a few fresh strawberry leaves.

Strawberry Wafer Cream

1 sponge cake 5 in. to 6 in. across and 1 in. thick	2 oz. sponge cake crumbs
8 to 10 wafer biscuits	½ teaspoonful ratafia essence
1 lb. strawberries	1 pint cream or ½
Strawberry jam	pint custard, ¾ oz.
Royal Icing	gelatine, ½ gill
2 oz. sugar	water
	1 lemon

Trim the sponge cake to the correct size and thickness. Brush the sides with the jam. Stand on a flat glass or silver dish and arrange the wafer biscuits round, pressing them firmly against the sponge and piping a little Royal Icing behind each to keep it in place. Pipe the edges of the biscuits where they touch in order to make a firm join. Finally, decorate by piping round the top and bottom edge of the biscuits. By tying a wide band of ribbon round the wafer case it remains firm.

Wash and hull the strawberries reserving a few of the choicest for decorating the finished cream. Cut up the remainder and mix with the sponge cake crumbs, sugar and lemon juice. Stand for three-quarters of an hour. Meanwhile, whip the cream stiffly, add the essence, and stir in the fruit and crumbs. Pour into the case. Decorate with the strawberries.

Note.—If for reasons of economy the custard and cream filling is to be used, instead of cream, prepare it as follows. Dissolve the gelatine in the water and when it is hot, but not boiling, strain it into the warm custard. Allow to cool, stirring occasionally, and fold in the whipped cream, essence and fruit mixture lightly. When it is on the point of setting, pour into the prepared case.

Strawberry Salad

1 small tin of pineapple rings	A few green glacé cherries
1 lb. strawberries	1 flat teaspoonful powdered gelatine
1 gill pineapple syrup	

Drain the rings and fill the centres of each with a large strawberry. Arrange the remainder on the pineapple rings. Dissolve the gelatine in the syrup and when it is cold, but not set, pour over the piled fruit and put in a cold place to set. Decorate with the glacé cherries.

Strawberry Cream Ice

1 pint milk	2 oz. sugar
1 gill cream	Cochineal
2 eggs	Whipped cream and
4 oz. sugar	strawberries to
1 lb. sieved strawberries	finish

Heat the milk in a double pan and meanwhile beat the eggs and sugar together very thoroughly. When the milk is hot but not boiling, pour it on to the eggs and sugar, stirring rapidly. Return the liquid to the pan and stir over a gentle heat continuously until the custard coats the back of the spoon. Cool, stirring occasionally, and when almost cold fold in the lightly beaten cream. Whilst this is becoming quite cold, rub the strawberries through a sieve, add the 2 oz. sugar and stir the purée into the custard. Cochineal may be added to improve the colour. Freeze as usual for about 20 minutes. Serve topped with cream and fresh strawberries.

Strawberry Cream Boats

8 oz. flour	Yolk of egg for
6 oz. butter	mixing
1½ oz. ground almonds	Whipped cream and strawberries
4 oz. sugar	

Rub the butter into the flour. Add the ground almonds and sugar, mix to a soft dough with the egg yolk. Roll out the dough thinly and line several boat shaped tins. Fill with beans or peas to prevent the pastry rising during cooking. Bake in a quick oven until pale brown in colour. After baking allow the pastry case to cool before removing from the tins. Then fill the pastry with sweetened whipped cream and cover the top with strawberries.

THE FIRST CREAM CRACKER

WHO WAS IT first discovered that almonds and raisins go so well together that neither of them is really itself without the other? What remarkable man was it who first added red-currant jelly to mutton? Discoverers like these don't always get their due fame but we do know who was responsible for adding the Cream Cracker to cheese. It was the firm of Jacob. They made the first Cream Cracker. Jacob's still have a wonderful hand for Cream Crackers and the oven is still going beautifully, turning them out tinted brown, dimpled and done to a turn

JACOB'S

CREAM CRACKERS

IN DAINTY
½lb. PACKETS.

PER **1/-** LB.

30,000
GALLONS OF MILK
ARE USED EVERY WEEK IN THE PHEASANT DAIRY
PHEASANT
MARGARINE
Equals choicest butter

OBTAINABLE FROM
HIGH CLASS GROCERS
PROVISION MERCHANTS
AND DAIRYMEN
EVERYWHERE

JURGENS LTD.
DAIRIES:
PURFLEET. ESSEX.

Acids · Acids · Acids ·

Continually formed from the food we eat —

Delicious, tempting . . yet acid-forming

They upset the vital balance of the blood on which our health depends

THE foods on which we most rely for nourishment, meat, fish, eggs — even bread . . . all these are *acid-forming* foods.

You cannot live without them, yet the acids they produce in the process of digestion are a constant menace to your health.

Why? Because acids destroy alkalinity — and your blood is alkaline !

The least change in its composition, the least alteration in its vital alkaline balance, brings immediate penalties. Headaches, fatigue, a liverish feeling — all these and similar complaints arise from acid poisons in the system.

A natural safeguard

To guard against this, to keep the blood pure, the body has stored up within it a reserve of alkaline salts — " buffer " salts — whose function is to neutralise poisonous acids.

When this reserve weakens, when the buffer salts are unequal to performing their task, then at once our health suffers. Minor complaints at first, but finally more serious ills—perhaps liver trouble, kidney trouble, rheumatism. These, and maladies still worse, doctors have traced to the breaking down of the body's alkaline reserve.

Salts that protect the body from poison

Now, after years of research, a new, pleasant effervescent saline— Sal Hepatica—has been evolved, which combines in one pleasant drink the two most important of the buffer salts. These two vital salts — Sodium Phosphate and Sodium Bicarbonate—are not to be found together in any other saline.

Quickly, easily, surely, Sal Hepatica builds up the body's alkaline reserve. Take it directly you suffer from headache or tiredness. Take it at the first sign of unfitness, before the oncome of more serious ailments. Just a teaspoonful each morning, fizzing up in a glass of cool water.

* * *

BESIDES the two buffer salts, there are four others in Sal Hepatica. The function of these is to clear the system of poisonous waste and to stimulate the eliminating organs, such as the liver and kidneys, to a healthy, natural action. Your chemist has Sal Hepatica —1/9 a bottle.

Bristol-Myers Company, 112, Cheapside, London, E.C.

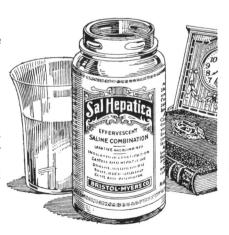

Savoury dressings add a touch of zest to an otherwise plain salad

Piquant Salad Dressings

All recipes serve six unless otherwise stated

THE best salad to serve at dinner is one which consists of plain salad greens alone or in combination. For variety, a touch of fresh tomato, cucumber, celery, or radish may be added, but it is better to keep the ingredients very simple.

It is in the dressings for these plain salads that it is possible to introduce just the individuality which adds the needed touch to the everyday meal.

For making successful dressings, be sure that the ingredients are very cold and of good quality. In very hot weather a lump of ice will facilitate the mixing of any dressing which contains oil.

To make *Savoury Salad Dressing,* mix together 4 tablespoonfuls salad oil, 1 tablespoonful tarragon vinegar, 1½ tablespoonfuls tomato ketchup, and ½ tablespoonful Worcester sauce. Season with salt, black pepper, and a few grains of cayenne. Beat well together until thoroughly blended and serve at once on a green salad.

Bloater Paste Salad Dressing: Work together 1 teaspoonful bloater paste, ¼ teaspoonful mustard, a pinch of salt, and pepper, and ¼ teaspoonful mustard, a pinch of salt, and pepper, and ¼ teaspoonful paprika. Add a few drops of Worcester sauce, 3 tablespoonfuls salad oil, and 1 tablespoonful vinegar. Mix thoroughly; then add 1 tablespoonful capers, ½ teaspoonful chopped chives, and ½ teaspoonful minced parsley. Pour over the salad. A salad finished with this dressing is excellent with cold fish.

For *Chives Salad Dressing,* mix together thoroughly 3 tablespoonfuls salad oil, 1 tablespoonful vinegar, 1 teaspoonful salt, ¼ teaspoonful of paprika, and a pinch of white pepper. Then add 1 teaspoonful minced chives and 1 hard-cooked egg finely chopped. Mix until smooth and serve on tomato or any green salad.

Spanish Salad Dressing makes a pleasing change for a dinner salad. Mix together in a bowl 1 teaspoonful castor sugar, ½ teaspoonful salt, ½ teaspoonful made mustard, and a pinch of paprika (a red pepper, which is much less pungent than cayenne). Moisten these with 1 tablespoonful lemon juice, 1 tablespoonful cold water, 1 teaspoonful Worcester sauce, 1 tablespoonful tomato ketchup, and 5 tablespoonfuls salad oil. Beat thoroughly and serve on any plain salad.

Creole Salad Dressing is especially good on asparagus, tomato, cucumber, or plain lettuce or romaine salad. Mix thoroughly ½ teacupful salad oil, 2 or 3 tablespoonfuls vinegar, ½ teaspoonful sugar, and a pinch of salt. Add 1 tablespoonful chopped pimientoes, 1 tablespoonful chopped green pepper, ½ tablespoonful minced onion, and 1 teaspoonful minced parsley. Beat until thoroughly blended. Chill well and beat again before using.

To make *Curry Salad Dressing,* mix thoroughly ½ teaspoonful curry powder, ¼ teaspoonful salt, a pinch of pepper, and a little finely minced onion. Add gradually 3 tablespoonfuls salad oil and 1 tablespoonful tarragon vinegar. This is very good with plain salads, and also as a dressing for fish.

Pot-pourri Salad Dressing: Beat together 4 tablespoonfuls salad oil and 2 tablespoonfuls vinegar with a little pepper and salt. Add one green pepper seeded and chopped, 1 small orange peeled and chopped fine, using all the juice, and ½ dozen chopped olives. Mix all the ingredients and serve the dressing with lettuce or other green salad.

Russian Salad Dressing: Mix together ½ teaspoonful dry mustard, ½ teaspoonful salt, a pinch of white pepper, and a pinch of paprika. Pour on gradually to these dry ingredients 1 tablespoonful vinegar, 1 teaspoonful lemon juice, 1 teaspoonful Worcester sauce, and 1 tablespoonful chili sauce. Add 1 teaspoonful grated onion, 1 teaspoonful minced green pepper, and 2 teaspoonfuls chopped parsley. Mix thoroughly and add slowly ½ teacupful best salad oil. Chill before using.

The *Literary Salad* published here is sufficiently interesting to reprint, and here is a practical interpretation of the recipe: Boil 2 large potatoes until tender and put them through a sieve or vegetable presser. Add 1 teaspoonful of mustard and 2 scant teaspoonfuls of salt. Stir in 3 tablespoonfuls of olive or other salad oil and 1 tablespoonful of vinegar, tarragon preferred. To this add the yolks of 3 hard-cooked eggs put through a sieve and 1 small onion grated. Mix all together well and add 1 teaspoonful of anchovy sauce. Chill and serve with any good salad.

Remember that the success of your Salad Dressing will depend very much on the quality of the materials employed. Use pure and fresh olive oil, bright and golden in colour and delicate in taste, and the finest malt vinegar, or, better still, a good French wine vinegar. See also that the dressing is served as cold as possible, using ice if necessary.

A Literary Salad

TWO large potatoes passed through kitchen sieve,
Unwonted softness to the salad give;
Of ardent mustard add a single spoon,
Distrust the condiment which bites so soon;
But deem it not, thou man of herbs, a fault
To add a double quantity of salt;
Three times the spoon with oil of Lucca crown,
And once with vinegar, procured from town,
True flavour needs it, and your poet begs
The pounded yellow of three hard-boiled eggs;
Let onion atoms lurk within the bowl,
And scarce suspected animate the whole;
And, lastly, on the flavoured compound toss
A magic teaspoon of anchovy sauce.
Then, though green turtle fail, though venison's tough,
And ham and turkey are not boiled enough,
Serenely full, the epicure may say—
" Fate can not harm me—I have dined to-day."

—Ingoldsby Legends

Nerka Norka

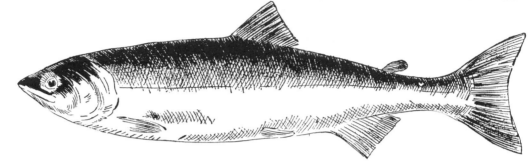

**IMPORTANT
FREE OFFER.**

A 1/- illustrated Recipe Book of dainty dishes prepared with a minimum of cooking, *FREE.* Contains a complete week's menus and details of valuable Gifts. Mention your grocer's name and address.

The finest salmon from the flavour point of view is the *Nerka Norka.* This is the only kind of Salmon that is good enough for SAILOR SALMON SLICE. *And* the best slice at that. If you want a real luxury for tea or dinner, ask your grocer for SAILOR SALMON SLICE.

**The Best Cut
from
the Best Fish.**

The name Angus Watson on any ready - to - serve food means the best of its kind.

ANGUS WATSON & Co., Limited, 76, Sailor Gardens, Newcastle-upon-Tyne.

The Secret of Good Housekeeping — is Good Food

Good Housekeeping is something more than the efficient management of your home, or the balancing of your family budget. Far more important than these is the maintenance of the health, vigour, and physical fitness of your whole family.

FOOD AND ITS FUNCTIONS

Health depends upon proper nourishment. Proper nourishment is governed not by the *amount* of food taken, but upon the selection of *the right kind* of food. Every morsel we eat should impart to the system positive nutrient —proteins to replace wasted tissues, carbohydrates to promote energy, mineral salts to encourage elimination. Most important of all, our food should include those vital food elements known as vitamins; for without vitamins no living organism can thrive.

THE VITAL IMPORTANCE OF BREAD

Consider the importance of the bread you and your family eat. It forms the basis of practically every meal, every day of the week, every week of the year. To millions of young and growing children bread is the staple article of diet. It is obvious, then, that every particle of bread eaten should not merely satisfy the appetite, but nourish the system as well. Our bread supply ought to be as far above suspicion as our water supply. Yet almost daily our most trusted medical men condemn the craze for whiteness in modern milling methods (to meet the craze for whiteness) discard the vital parts of the wheat grain, and render the resulting white bread not only innutritious, but indigestible.

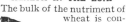

REGD. TRADE MARK

HEALTH IN THE LOAF

The bulk of the nutriment of wheat is contained in the "seed" and the "outer-layer." In the "seed" of the wheat Nature stores all its energy-producing, bone-and-body-building properties. It also contains the vitamins. The "outer-layer" is the repository of those mineral salts which act as a natural stimulant to the entire digestive system. Unless bread contains these vital constituents it cannot be regarded as a nourishing food. Here, then, is the difference between Allinson Bread and white bread. Allinson contains the *whole* of the wheat's nutriment exactly as Nature gave it; white bread does not contain any, and relies for its colour on chemical treating and bleaching.

SCIENTIFIC GRINDING METHODS

Allinson Ltd. not only preserve the valuable properties of the wheat, but they present the whole in a form which can be easily assimilated. For that purpose, old-fashioned millstone grinding methods are still retained which gently and naturally reduce the grain to a precise texture—fine enough to admit of complete digestion, yet coarse enough to persuade the bowels to natural activity.

ALLINSON BREAD ASSISTS DIGESTION

Allinson Wholemeal does something more than provide the body with adequate nutriment. In many thousands of cases a change over to Allinson Bread has resulted in an improved digestion, and has altogether banished constipation and the ills attendant upon it. Complete explanation of this is to be found in an address to the Royal Society of Medicine given by Dr. Aslett Baldwin. He said, "*Modern constipation is due to the removal of the aperient properties of the grain from flour, which should be retained.*"

PUT ALLINSON BREAD TO A TEST

As a final proof of the superiority of Allinson over all other breads we urge you to give it a month's conscientious trial. Without any artificial aids, "tonics," "restoratives," and the like, Allinson will nourish and strengthen you in Nature's way—the best way. Without any daily dosing and purging, Allinson will tone up your system and once more place you in possession of complete internal cleanliness. Once you have eaten Allinson you will prefer it ever afterwards for its wholesome, natural flavour alone.

NOT ALL BROWN LOAVES ARE WHOLEMEAL

Do not be satisfied with anything less than *guaranteed* wholemeal. There are many imitations, some of which are made from nothing more than inferior white meal, chemically coloured. See the Allinson Band around every loaf you purchase; you can then be *certain* of getting true and genuine stone-ground wholemeal bread.

ALLINSON BREAD FROM YOUR BAKER
ALLINSON FLOUR FROM YOUR GROCER

You can place your order for Allinson Wholemeal Bread with your baker. If you prefer it, you can get Allinson Wholemeal Flour for home baking from your grocer. Allinson Flour is sold in 3½-lb., 7-lb., and 14-lb. sealed cotton bags. In case of difficulty in obtaining either Allinson Bread or Flour, please communicate with Allinson Ltd., Cambridge Road, London, E.2.

ALLINSON WHOLEMEAL FOR HOME BAKING

To assist housewives to plan the family's dietary on more healthful lines, we include in every bag of Allinson Flour a useful Recipe Book. This little book shows you how to make a variety of delectable dishes, using Allinson Wholemeal in place of ordinary white flour. For just as Allinson Wholemeal makes better, more nourishing bread, so it makes better, more nourishing cakes, scones, biscuits, puddings, sauces, soups, etc. The recipes, which number 101, have all been thoroughly tested. They are free from fads and fancies, and do not involve the use of special cooking utensils. Here are a few examples chosen at random :—

SULTANA CAKE

Ingredients.—12 ozs. Allinson's Wholemeal, 1 teaspoonful baking-powder, mix together; 6 ozs. margarine, 6 ozs. castor sugar, 2 eggs, 1½ gills milk, 8 ozs. sultanas, essence to suit taste.
Method.—Cream margarine and sugar by beating together for some minutes. Add essence. Beat in eggs one at a time. Place wholemeal and mix lightly. Add sultanas and milk and mix thoroughly. Place into papered cake hoop (6 to 7 inches across is suitable size). Some blanched and split almonds placed on top of the cake is a great improvement. Bake in sound heat 1½ hours.

SCOTCH SCONES

Ingredients.—1 lb. Allinson's Wholemeal, 2 ozs. lard, 1 small teaspoonful carbonate of soda, 2 teaspoonfuls cream of tartar, ½ pint milk.
Method.—Place the wholemeal and lard in a basin, rub them together with the fingers until the lard is thoroughly mixed in. Rub the soda and cream of tartar through a sieve, add them and mix together with a spoon. Pour in the milk, again stir together. Turn the mixture out on a board and knead lightly. Roll out half an inch in thickness. Bake in a moderate oven for 25 minutes.

DUNDEE CAKE

Ingredients.—½ lb. sugar, 5 eggs, ½ lb. butter, 12 ozs. meal, ½ teaspoonful baking-powder, ¼ lb. peel (cut fine), ½ lb. sultanas, ¼ lb. blanched almonds, essence of vanilla, ½ gill milk.
Method.—Cream up butter and sugar in a bowl. Beat in the eggs, one by one. Add baking-powder to the meal and mix together with essence and milk. Then add fruit and almonds and finish mixing into a smooth batter. Place into papered cake hoop and bake in moderate oven 2 hours. If desired, some caraway comfits may be placed on top of cake before baking.

CANARY PUDDING

Ingredients.—8 ozs. Allinson's Wholemeal, 4 ozs. chopped suet, 3 ozs. sugar, 1 large tablespoonful apricot jam, 1 teaspoonful baking-powder, 6 drops saffron, ½ pint milk, 2 eggs.
Method.—Place the wholemeal in a mixing bowl, stir in the sugar and suet, add the baking-powder, and mix all well together. Place the eggs in a basin, beat them to a light froth, stir into them the jam. Drop in the saffron, pour in the milk. Pour the contents of the basin into the ingredients in the mixing bowl, and stir for three or four minutes. Pour the mixture into a greased mould and steam for two hours and a quarter. Turn out on a hot dish and pour round a lemon sauce.

Good Housekeeping Institute

Director, D. D.

Certificate Household and Social
London ; First Class Diplomas
Laundrywork, House

We Wish to
Apologise to those Readers

who were unable to obtain admittance to the lectures given at the Institute during October and November, and also to those who had not made previous application for a ticket and were obliged to stand. Owing to the great interest shown in these lectures we have decided to give a series of four Cookery Demonstrations on January 19th and 26th, and February 2nd and 9th, at 3 p.m., particulars of which will be found on page 78. For the comfort of the audience it has been decided to limit the number of tickets issued. Will those wishing to attend, therefore, please apply to The Director, Good Housekeeping Institute, 49 Wellington Street, London, W.C.2 ?

The Institute is able to send fully qualified members of the Staff to give lectures and demonstrations at girls' schools, Women's Institutes, etc. Private tuition can also be given in all branches of Cookery, Housecraft, and Laundry-work at the Institute. As only a few students can be accommodated, those wishing to attend are asked to make application as far in advance as possible

So many readers have asked us to give particulars of catering for a dance that we propose to devote the third and last article in our short catering series to dance suppers and refreshments.

Under normal conditions the work entailed in catering for, say 50 guests, is as much as can be undertaken in a private house. When larger numbers are invited, it is advisable to entrust the work to a reliable firm of caterers, first getting estimates from two or more firms so that the menus submitted at a given price per head may be compared.

The first thing to be considered is the particular type of meal—whether light refreshments are to be served at a buffet and handed round, or whether a sit-down supper is to be provided.

When arranging menus of any description, something quite plain in each course—e.g. tongue sandwiches, plain biscuits, etc.—should be available for any guest who may prefer it.

The following menus are suggested for light refreshments and the quantities required for 50 guests are given. We have included methods for preparing certain of the dishes mentioned. Many people will prefer to order the ices from a reliable confectioner's as this saves time and trouble.

The cost per head of the first menu, which is especially suitable for young people, works out at between 3s. and 3s. 6d. per head according to the quality of the food, while the slightly more elaborate menu on page 73 costs approximately 5s. per head, excluding drinks.

Catering for

The Institute gives MENUS

DANCE MENU and QUANTITIES REQUIRED

Tea Coffee Fruit Punch Cider Cup Orangeade Lemonade	½ lb. tea; 1½ lb. coffee; 4 qts. of milk (3 hot 1 cold); 10 qts. mixed drinks—lemonade, orangeade, and punch; 6 qts. cider cup. 50 chicken patties; 40 anchovy eggs; 35 plates salmon mayonnaise (4 lb. salmon).

Sandwiches

Chicken Patties Anchovy Eggs Salmon Mayonnaise	Sardine, Crab and Cress Ham and Cress Cucumber and Tongue Cream Cheese and Celery	150 mixed sandwiches: 75 bridge rolls (for sardines); brown bread for cress and crab: white bread and butter.

Macedoine of Fruit Coffee and Chocolate Cream Buns and Eclairs Fruit Salad	4 quarts of jelly for macedoine of fruit; ¾ pint cream; 6 quarts fruit salad.
Cake—Fruit, Madeira, Cherry Mixed Biscuits Mixed Chocolates and Sweets	40 cream buns and éclairs (20 coffee and 20 chocolate); 2 lb. fruit cake; 1 lb. Madeira cake; 1 lb. cherry cake; 3 lb. biscuits (chocolate, shortbread, and mixed fancy): 2 lb. chocolates; 1 lb. cream fondants.
Vanilla and Strawberry Ices Coupes Jacques Ice Wafers	40 vanilla ices; 40 strawberry ices; 20 coupes jacques; 1 lb. ice wafers.

Clear soup or broth should be served to the guests on their departure.

8 quarts clear soup or broth.

Department of Cookery

Cottington Taylor

*Science, King's College for Women,
in Cookery, High Class Cookery,
wifery, A.R.S.I.*

a DANCE

and Suggests Quantities

ALTERNATIVE MENU with QUANTITIES

Tea	½ lb. tea; 1½ lb. coffee; 4 qts.
Coffee	milk (3 hot, 1 cold); 10 qts.
Ginger Beer	mixed drinks—lemonade, ginger-
Claret Cup	beer, claret cup, cider cup.
Cider Cup	
Lemonade	

	25 eggs in aspic
Eggs in Aspic	30 sausage rolls
Sausage Rolls	25 lobster cutlets
Lobster Cutlets	50 bouchées à la reine
Bouchées à la Reine	50 galantine of chicken sand-
Galantine of Chicken Sandwiches	wiches
Vol-au-vent of Veal	50 vols-au-vent of veal
Bridge Rolls spread with	50 bridge rolls with gentle-
Gentlemen's Relish	men's relish

Royal Trifles	25 royal trifles
Charlotte Russes	25 charlotte russes
Cold Caramel Creams	25 cold caramel creams
Ginger Creams	25 ginger creams
Jellies à la Suisse	25 jellies à la Suisse
Babas au Rhum	25 babas au rhum

Cheese Creams	50 cheese creams

Neapolitan Ices	150 mixed ices
Praline Ices	
Pineapple water Ices	

Lemonade.—2 lemons; 1 oz. sugar; 1 pint of boiling water.

Peel the lemons thinly and remove all pith. Cut in half and squeeze out all the juice with a glass squeezer, then put the juice, rind and sugar into a porcelain jug or basin. Pour on boiling water. Cover and allow to cool. Ice, when cold, if preferred. One or two thin slices of lemon should be reserved and placed on the top of each glass jug in which the lemonade is served.

Orangeade.—2 oranges; 1 lemon; 1 pint boiling water; 4 oz. sugar.

Prepare in the same way as for lemonade, except that the mixture is improved by simmering for 8–10 mins.

Sandwiches.—The labour involved in the preparation of sandwiches is halved by ordering sandwich loaves cut into slices from the baker. By mixing 1 lb. butter with ½ pint of boiling milk, and whisking vigorously till they blend, a considerable economy is effected. It may be necessary to whisk for as long as ¼ hour.

For the crab and cress sandwiches it is advisable to order dressed crab. All the meat can then be pounded up together and seasoned with salt, cayenne, a very little vinegar and some made mustard. Spread on the cut bread and butter and cover with a little cress which should be well washed and then dried.

For the sardines, split the bridge rolls and butter them. Remove the skin and bones of the sardines, and place one in the middle of each roll, sprinkling with paprika.

Seville Orange Marmalade

9 Seville oranges   2 sweet oranges
2 lemons   8 lb. loaf sugar
         9 pints cold water

Cut the oranges and lemons across in thin slices, take out all the pips, and add the cold water. Allow to stand 24 hours. Tie the pips in a muslin bag and boil gently with the pulp for about 1 hour, or until it has reduced by half. Stand aside till cold, then add sugar and boil again until it jellies.

Grapefruit Marmalade

4 grapefruit   4 lemons
Sugar   2 quarts cold water

Put the grapefruit into a large saucepan with enough water to cover them, and boil slowly until the fruit is quite tender and can be pierced easily with a fork. Then remove from the gas and leave untouched overnight. Wash the lemons and cut them in half, squeeze out the juice and strain into a basin, then tie the pips in a muslin bag and put them with the lemon juice. Slice the lemon rind thinly and add it to the juice in the basin. Add the cold water and allow to stand overnight.

Next day, remove from the saucepan and throw the water away. Cut the grapefruit in half; scoop out the pulp from each portion and put into a pointed strainer or muslin bag. Squeeze out all the juice, discarding the pips and pulp as they would give a very bitter flavour. Slice the rind of the grapefruit and put into a preserving pan with the lemons and the juice. Boil this slowly until reduced to half. Measure the fruit and to each pint allow 1½ lb. of sugar. Re-boil and add the sugar. Stir constantly until it has dissolved, then boil until the marmalade will set when tested on a cold plate.

To Make Sour Milk

It occasionally happens that prepared sour milk is ordered in the diet and no local dairy supplies it. It is, however, quite possible to make this at home. Pure cultures of the lactic acid bacilli are required. If any difficulty is experienced in obtaining these, the Institute will be pleased to supply the name and address of a London firm from whom this culture can be obtained. The correct quantity of culture is added to the milk, which must then be kept at a temperature of 108° F. for 10 hours.

To Clean Light Shoes

Beige shoes can be cleaned quite successfully at home by rubbing over with a clean cloth moistened with carbon tetrachloride. When all the grease has been removed apply a little white cream and polish well with a soft duster.

Hints for Marmalade Making

Use oranges as soon as possible after purchase.
Although the juice of bitter oranges contains nearly 5 per cent. acid, it is considerably diluted with water when making marmalade. For this reason it is sometimes necessary to add lemon juice, as otherwise the marmalade is not likely to set satisfactorily. When using sweet oranges, add two lemons, and at least two bitter oranges, to twelve sweet oranges.

To Obtain a Good Colour

Do not boil for too long after adding the sugar as over-boiling at this stage invariably results in a preserve of a poor colour. It is therefore advisable to evaporate most of the water before adding the sugar so that the preserve jellies in less than half an hour's boiling afterwards.

Saving Time when Cutting Up the Fruit

Use a marmalade shredder when a large quantity of fruit has to be cut up. Ordinary steel knives should be frequently wiped to prevent discoloration, as the acid contained in the fruit stains the steel badly.
The proportion of pectin present in fruit is all-important in connection with its jellying properties. Even in the same type of fruit the proportion varies considerably with the degree of ripeness of the fruit. Some idea of the amount present can be gauged by the following simple test :

A Pectin Test

After boiling the fruit and water for about half an hour, a tablespoonful of the mixture should be strained and squeezed through a cloth. When quite cold, add three teaspoonfuls of methylated spirit to one teaspoonful of the strained juice. The mixture should be shaken, and the pectin, being insoluble in spirit, forms a clot of jelly-like consistency. The spirit should be poured off and the clot examined. If it can be poured from the cup without breaking up into separate lumps, the mixture is rich in pectin, if, however, it breaks up the proportion present is smaller. If plenty of pectin is present a satisfactory preserve can be made with a smaller proportion of sugar than is possible with one containing only a comparatively small percentage.

A Winter Jam

1 lb. figs, ½ lb. apples, juice of 3 lemons and grated rind of 1 lemon, 1 lb. sugar, ⅛ teaspoonful powdered cinnamon, 2½ gills cold water. Chop figs or pass through a mincing machine. Peel and slice apples. Put figs, apples, grated lemon rind, sugar, cinnamon and water into a pan, and when half-cooked strain in the lemon juice. Boil until the jam sets when tested on a cold plate ; approximately 50 minutes to 1 hour. A gill in this recipe is an Imperial quarter of pint.

Cleansing Badly Soiled Rubber

If white mackintoshes and hot water bottles become badly soiled it is possible to restore them to their almost white colour with soft soap. Rub a little soft soap over the article or garment to be cleaned. Leave for a few minutes and then scrub gently with a fairly soft nail brush, moistened in warm water. Rinse in warm water and dry with a clean cloth.

Save the Hands

A large glove made of thick, dark material, preferably black or navy velvet, with one compartment for the fingers and one for the thumb should be kept near or just inside the coal scuttle. It may easily be slipped on and saves soiling the hands and frequent washing after handling the poker, tongs and coal shovel. The glove is specially welcome when light needlework is in progress.

The Care of a Wringer

The rubber rollers of a wringing machine are apt to become soiled and corroded with soap, particularly in hard water districts. The rollers should be revolved slowly, at the same time being rubbed with a rag well moistened with turpentine, and afterwards washed with warm soap and water. To keep the metal parts in good condition remove any dust and soil by washing them with soap and water. To improve the appearance and protect the metal apply a little home-made furniture cream and wax polish, while the working parts should be lubricated with suitable machine oil from time to time. If the parts are of varnished wood they only require wiping with a soapy cloth : if all white wood, they must be scrubbed each time after use. As great heat perishes rubber, clothes should not be passed through the wringer straight from the clothes boiler, and rubber rollers should not be washed with very hot water. Lessen the tension when the wringer is not in use.

Dry Cleaning

When dry cleaning is done at home success depends largely on the use of a suitable type of soap. Small quantities of special dry cleaning soap, as little as a quarter of a pound, can now be purchased.

"IN THE INTERESTS OF NATIONAL HEALTH"

LORD KELVIN,
As the name acknowledges, Kelvination is based upon the discovery of the thermo-dynamic principles governing refrigeration, made by the famous scientist, Lord Kelvin.

Send to-day for the beautifully illustrated booklet "The Heart of the Home," which tells how easily you can avoid food waste and gain complete assurance of food safety.

4.—(1) No person shall manufacture for sale or sell any article of food which contains any added preservative or any of the colouring matters specified in Part II of the First Schedule to these Regulations :

From the Public Health (Preservatives, &c., in Food) Regulations, 1925, effective January 1st, 1927.

—by act of Parliament"

After January 1st, 1927, the use of any chemical preservative in food offered for sale is made illegal.

The few exceptions mentioned in the Act must be labelled plainly as a general warning to the public.

Thus warned, no housewife will choose to feed her family on adulterated products containing benzoic acid or other metallic poisons, recognized as injurious by the Government.

But food will spoil unless protected. Spoiled food is dangerous. And often food becomes unfit for use before taste or odour gives warning of danger.

Some method of food preservation which will keep food safe and avoid all waste must now be adopted by every housewife.

The best way is the Kelvinator way —modern Automatic Electric Refrigeration—low in first cost, economical in operation, cleanly, convenient, and absolutely safe.

Why not investigate, at least? Learn why Kelvinator has been selected for 2,500 ideal modern homes on one estate alone : why you will finally choose Kelvinator for sake of the health and safety of all the family.

"I am pleased to state that I am now installing 'Kelvinator' Automatic Electric Refrigerators as standard equipment in my modern homes now being erected on the Eden Park Estates, Beckenham. When completed this estate will comprise approximately 2,500 residences all equipped with many modern unique labour-saving appliances and fittings. I have come to this decision believing that 'Kelvinator' is the best obtainable for modern homes."
(*Signed*) W. Godfrey Gratten,

Estate Offices,
Croydon Road,
Beckenham, Kent.

Kelvinator preserves food without ice,
but makes all the ice you want.

Kelvinator
— the Larder that Saves your Food

If you are buying or building, insist that your new home must be equipped with a Kelvinator.

Kelvinator Ltd.,
30-35 Drury Lane,
Kingsway, London, W.C.2

Please send me your booklet, "The Heart of the Home," which tells how to keep food safe.

Name....................

Address....................

CLIP THIS SLIP—POST TO-DAY
Add note in margin if interested in Commercial Refrigeration.　G.H.1

The BRIDE'S Primer of

Selecting and Purchasing

By The Director

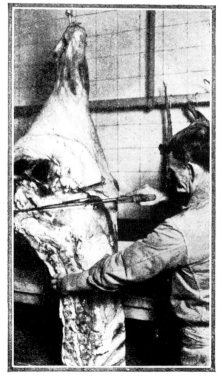

A quarter of beef showing the positions of the principal joints

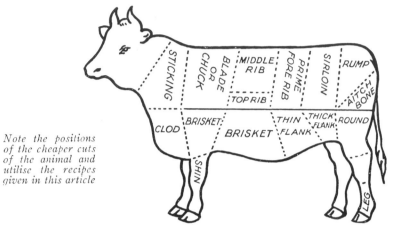

Note the positions of the cheaper cuts of the animal and utilise the recipes given in this article

Of all shopping expeditions, that of purchasing meat appeals least and presents the most difficulties even to an experienced housewife, whether she has to cater for a small or a large family. For this reason many hesitate to vary their order from sirloin, chops, steaks, shoulder and leg. Needless to say, this proves not only unnecessarily extravagant, as these are the primest and most expensive joints, but leads to lack of variety in the meat course.

This, and the next Primer article, will therefore be devoted to a careful study of the choice and usefulness of joints and cuts of meat, particular attention being paid to the cheaper cuts. In order that the article may contain reliable and up-to-date information, both from the butcher's and housewife's point of view, the matter has been discussed fully with the Institute butcher, and we are glad to acknowledge the help he has afforded us.

Among the foodstuffs which became costly during the war, meat shows the least tendency to come down in price. Many of our readers find it difficult to arrange economical meat meals for large hungry families and we have had many letters asking us to suggest ways of reducing the meat bill. This can be accomplished in two ways.

First, by choosing cheaper cuts and by cooking them in such a way that they are as tender and tasty as the more expensive ones. Cheap meat does not lack nourishment, as many people suppose, in fact, stews and broths made from bones and the cheaper parts contain the full food value of the meat used.

Secondly, by reducing the quantity of meat consumed — the amount actually required per day being less than the large majority of people imagine.

There is no doubt that the high price of meat is largely the fault of the housewife, for meat, no less than any other commodity, is governed by

the law of supply and demand, and if the absurdly disproportionate demand for prime cuts did not exist the average price per lb. could be reduced.

Beef, being a typical English food stuff and less expensive than veal or mutton, enjoys a greater popularity. In this article the method of cutting up a carcase of beef will be discussed and recipes given for dishes which utilise the cheaper cuts and which rarely appear on the table.

Meat prices vary in different parts of the country, and even in the same town. The detailed price list, at the end of this article, is given more as a guide, and shows the comparative prices, ruling at the time of writing, of both the cheaper and more expensive cuts of meat. At the same time, the list will also be helpful in that it shows the comparative prices of the best English and Scotch beef, and imported, both chilled and frozen. For the following recipes the less expen-

Showing the first division of a side of beef

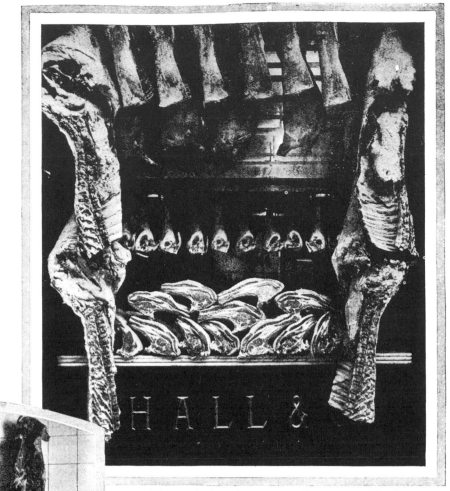

The purchasing of meat generally presents difficulties to the inexperienced housewife

sive parts of meat can be utilised.

Collared Beef.—5 lb. salted flank of beef; 3 crushed blades of mace; 2 cloves; 1 bay leaf; 24 allspice; 12 peppercorns; 1 shallot; 1 teaspoonful celery seeds; parsley, thyme, marjoram and a little sage.

Wipe the meat, removing any bones and gristle. Sprinkle sparingly with a little of the chopped parsley and thyme, roll up tightly to form a round, and tie securely in an old pudding cloth or piece of muslin. Simmer gently for four hours with the remainder of

Left: the principal joints of beef have been clearly labelled so that readers can distinguish each at a glance

the herbs and spices, in just sufficient water to cover. The celery seeds and peppercorns should be tied in a small muslin bag so that they can be removed from the saucepan if necessary. When cooked, dish the joint and put into a meat press. If a press is not available use a cake tin of suitable size and press with a heavy weight. Next day remove the cloth, glaze, decorate and serve with parsley.

Note.—This dish, if carefully prepared and seasoned, makes delicious pressed beef, and may be served for breakfast, lunch or supper.

Galantine of Beef.—2 lb. gravy beef, cut from top part of leg; ½ pint stock; 1 lb. lean bacon; 4 eggs; 12 oz. fresh

Right: two sirloins, from one the surplus fat and under-cut have been removed

breadcrumbs; pepper and salt.

Mince the bacon and beef, removing the gristle, place in a basin with the breadcrumbs, salt, and pepper. Add stock and the beaten eggs, and mix all well together. Turn on to a floured board and form into a short roll, tie tightly in a pudding-cloth, and place in a pan containing enough boiling water to cover. Allow to boil for 15 minutes, and then simmer gently for 2½ hours. Without removing the cloth,

press the roll between two tins or dishes, with a heavy weight on top. The cloth may be removed the next day, and the galantine coated with glaze.

Ragoût of Beef.—1½ lb. beef, flank or beefsteak; pepper and salt; 1½ oz. dripping; a pinch of herbs; 1½ oz. flour; 2 onions, carrots and turnips; 1 pint stock.

Melt the fat, chop the onions finely, and fry golden brown. Remove the onion from the saucepan, then fry the meat, cut into pieces of equal size. Remove from the saucepan and strain the fat. Add the flour to the fat in the saucepan and cook over a gentle heat until brown in colour, then add the stock and stir until it comes to the boil. Add the meat, seasoning, and pinch of herbs, and allow to simmer gently for 1 hour. Slice and cut the carrots and turnips into dice, add these to the stew, and continue to cook for about another hour. Arrange the meat and vegetables around the outside of the dish, pouring the gravy over. If liked, dice of carrot, which have been boiled in salt and water, may be used for a garnish, placing them in the middle of the dish.

(Continued)

Selecting and Purchasing Beef

Oxtail Soup.—1 oxtail; 2 rashers of bacon; 1½ oz. dripping; 1 carrot; 1 small turnip; 2 onions of medium size; 1 small head of celery; 1 small blade of mace; 3 cloves and 9 peppercorns; 1 small bouquet garni; ½ dessertspoonful Worcester sauce; salt; 2 quarts of stock or water; 2 oz. flour.

Wash and joint the tail, slice the vegetables and fry the bacon. Melt half the dripping, fry the piece of tail until brown, remove from the pan and fry the vegetables. Pour on the stock, return the meat to the pan, add spices, salt, etc. Boil gently for four hours, strain and allow to get cold. Melt the remainder of the dripping, fry the flour until brown, pour on the soup from which the fat has been removed. Cook for ten minutes.

Add the pieces of oxtail, Worcester sauce and salt if necessary.

A GUIDE FOR THE PURCHASER OF BEEF

	English or Scotch per lb.	Imported Chilled	Imported Frozen
Best Joints for Roasting			
Sirloin	1/8	11d.	8d.
Prime fore ribs	1/6	9d.	6d.
Prime wing ribs	1/8	10d.	7d.
Second Best Joints for Roasting			
Round, including topside and silverside	1/4	10d.	8d.
Rump	1/6	11d.	8d.
Middle ribs, top and back	1/-	9d.	7d.
Boned shoulder or blade	10d.	8d.	6d.
Aitch bone	10d.	7d.	6d.
Prime Pieces for Grilling and Frying			
Fillet	2/6	1/8	1/6
Rump steak	2/6	1/8	1/6
Second Best Pieces for Grilling			
Buttock steak	1/8	1/-	8d.
First cut of rump	1/8	10d.	8d.
Principal Joints for Boiling and Salting			
Silverside	1/2	10d.	8d.
Aitch bone	10d.	7d.	6d.
Brisket	8d.	6d.	5d.
Thick flank	9d.	8d.	7d.
Thin flank	7d.	5d.	4d.
Ox tongue	1/-	1/-	1/-
Prime Cuts for Stewing			
Beefsteak, cut from topside	1/4	10d.	8d.
Silverside	10d.	9d.	7d.
Kidney	1/-	1/-	1/-
Oxtail	1/4	10d.	10d.
Top and back ribs (boned)	10d.	9d.	8d.
Shoulder or blade	10d.	8d.	8d.
Cow heel	10d. each	10d. ea.	10d. ea.
Thick flank. (See p. 76)	9d.	8d.	7d.
Gravy beef, cut from top part of leg	1/4	10d.	8d.
Cheap Cuts for Soup, Stock and Stews			
Shin	8d.	5d.	3d.
Leg	8d.	5d.	3d.
Thin flank. (See p. 76.)	7d.	5d.	4d.
Neck or sticking	6d.	5d.	4d.
Clod	8d.	5d.	4d.
Cheek	5d.	4d.	3d.
Brisket, thin. (See p. 76.)	8d.	6d.	5d.
Meat Suitable for Meat Pies and Pudding			
Steak, blade and chuck steak	10d.	8d.	6d.
Skirt	10d.	8d.	6d.
Brisket, thick. (See p. 76.)	8d.	6d.	5d.
Boned shoulder. (See p. 76.)	8d.	7d.	6d.
Boned clod	8d.	7d.	6d.

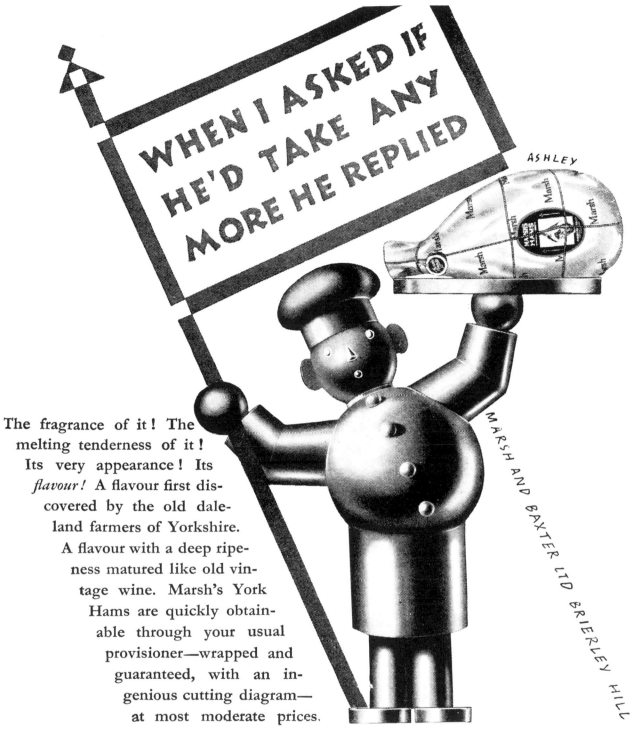

WHEN I ASKED IF HE'D TAKE ANY MORE HE REPLIED

ASHLEY

MARSH AND BAXTER LTD BRIERLEY HILL

The fragrance of it! The melting tenderness of it! Its very appearance! Its *flavour!* A flavour first discovered by the old daleland farmers of Yorkshire. A flavour with a deep ripeness matured like old vintage wine. Marsh's York Hams are quickly obtainable through your usual provisioner—wrapped and guaranteed, with an ingenious cutting diagram—at most moderate prices.

I'D LIKE SOME MORE MARSH'S YORK HAM!

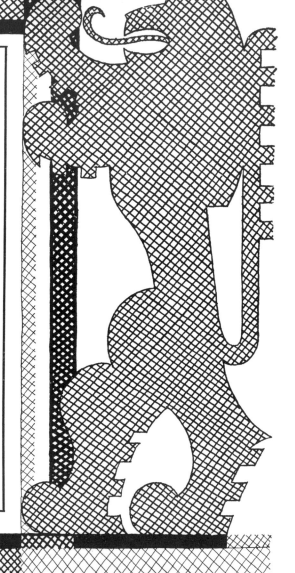

D5

'THE WIFE'S OUT EMPIRE BUILDING'

"Has she taken up politics?"

"No; she's buying food."

"Don't follow you."

"It's simple enough: she says women who buy Empire produce are doing a big thing for the country."

"Well—it's good food, right enough."

"Yes, but there's more than that. After all, our own folk come first, and it's wonderful what a lot of people you can put in work by a nod across a counter. If ten million women did that every day—"

"I see your point. That's *their* contribution to Empire-building."

BUY EMPIRE PRODUCE

from Home and Overseas

ISSUED BY THE EMPIRE MARKETING BOARD

Fresh fruits, soda water, cider, tea and coffee are among the simple ingredients required for cooling drinks

Cooling Drinks

for the

PARTY

ONE PART SALT

THREE PARTS ICE

COARSE SALT

Left: this strainer clips firmly on to the glass after the punch is poured in and keeps back the fruit. Right: beverages can be chilled with very simple equipment

ICED drinks can be prepared at home with an ease that is surprising to many housewives. Very little equipment is required, and if the mixtures are prepared well in advance so that they are quite cold before being placed in the refrigerator, the amount of ice and salt used will be quite modest.

The number of guests and the variety of beverages to be served must be considered beforehand and a pint should be allowed per head, exclusive of tea or coffee. Once the drinks are prepared they should be put into either ordinary bottles or fruit bottles with screw caps; the latter are particularly suitable for punches or other drinks containing pieces of fruit.

The method of chilling or icing is the same for all drinks, and if you are not fortunate enough to possess an ice-making refrigerator a small wooden tub or bucket will be required. A piece of old felt or flannel, news-paper or brown paper can be used for covering the outside of the receptacle, for like wood they are poor conductors of heat and prevent rapid loss of heat. A freezing mixture of ice and coarse salt, in the proportion of three parts ice to one part salt, should be put in in layers and the bottles packed well up to the shoulder. Care must be taken to prevent salt entering and it is not advisable to cover the bottles except with the ice. Finally, a piece of old blanket on the top will complete the packing.

The ice should be broken into pieces about the size of a walnut, with an ice needle. If one is not available, a hammer and a thick nail can be used quite successfully. If attempts are made to break the ice with a hammer or other heavy implement, it chips and breaks into thin pieces which rapidly melt.

Glasses and straws will be required for serving the drinks, and, although not essential, ice can be added if liked.

The novel strainer shown is particularly useful when beverages containing whole fruits are served.

Orangeade

| 6 oranges | 1¼ lb. sugar |
| 4 lemons | 2 quarts water |

Wash and peel the fruit thinly and put the rinds, sugar and water to boil. Boil for ten minutes, then strain through muslin. When cold add the strained juice of all the fruit. Chill before serving.

(Continued)

Fruit Punch is one of the many refreshing drinks that can be quickly prepared at home

Make these original St. Ivel sandwiches for your party

WHEN it comes to making sandwiches for a party St. Ivel Cheese simply radiates inspiration. There really seems nothing that won't combine deliciously with its fresh creaminess. Things as far apart as marmalade and smoked haddock, pineapple and ginger, raisins and chopped olives, make the happiest alliance with

'Open Face' Sandwiches

St. Ivel. You can serve St. Ivel sandwiches even at a children's party, for this creamy cheese is so digestible and the phosphates in it are very, very good for you. The St. Ivel Book, compiled by Miss Florence B. Jack, the well-known cookery expert, tells you how to make all kinds of original sandwiches. It also gives you new and attractive ideas for cutting and garnishing them.

Harlequin Sandwiches

Send a card to-day for your free copy of 'St. Ivel Cheese Recipes' to St. Ivel Ltd., 56 Newton Road, Yeovil, Somerset.

Harlequin sandwiches of brown and white bread and 'open face' sandwiches spread with St. Ivel and chopped radish are as decorative as they're delicious

Cooling Drinks for the Party

Lemon Syrup

10 lemons	1 heaped teaspoonful tartaric acid
3 lb. sugar	
1½ pints water	

Boil the sugar, water, and thinly peeled rinds together for 20 minutes. Strain through muslin on to the tartaric acid and stir well. When cold, add the strained juice and bottle. Put about two tablespoonfuls of the syrup into a tumbler and fill up with iced water.

Cider Cup

1 pt. cider	½ wineglass sherry
1 syphon soda water (1½ pts.)	½ lb. sugar
Rind of 1 lemon	Grapes and slices of lemon for serving
Nutmeg	

Chill the cider, sugar, lemon rind and nutmeg for 2 hours. Strain and add the soda water, fruit and sherry.

A 100 Year old Recipe for Cider Cup

1 qt. cider	Bunch of borage
1 pt. soda water	1 sliced orange
1 small glass brandy	1 oz. bruised sugar candy
Bunch of balm	

Put all the ingredients into a covered jug. Chill 2 hours, then decant free from herbs. Omit the soda water if preferred.

Champagne Cup

1 bottle champagne	Bunch of balm
1 qt. bottle of soda water	Bunch of borage
2 sliced oranges	1 oz. bruised ginger candy

Proceed as for Cider Cup.

Barbary Ale

The juice of 8 oranges	½ teaspoonful grated nutmeg
1 pt. water	½ teaspoonful ground cinnamon
6 oz. loaf sugar	
The rind and juice of 2 lemons	¼ teaspoonful mixed spice
6 bottles ginger beer	

Let all the ingredients stand 3 hours, then strain and add chilled ginger beer. Serve iced. To remove all trace of the grated spices it is necessary to strain through two thicknesses of fine muslin.

Ginger Punch

1 lb. sugar	6 oz. chopped preserved ginger
1 pt. water	
6 lemons	½ pt. bottle ginger beer
2 oranges	

Put the water, sugar and the finely peeled rinds of two lemons on to boil. Boil hard for 10 minutes, then cool. Add the orange and lemon juice strained through muslin and the preserved ginger. Put into the refrigerator on ice for two hours. Add the chilled ginger beer just before serving.

Raspberry Punch

4 oranges	4 lemons
Cochineal	1 syphon soda water
2 lb. bottle raspberries or 1 pt. fruit and juice	

Squeeze the juice from the oranges and lemons and strain on to the raspberries. (If the raspberries are bottled in water add

Ready for more, Mother!

AND—joy!—Kellogg's Corn Flakes need no cooking. Just add a little cold milk or cream or fruits, and you have a dish for all the family, as delicious, as appetising, as nourishing as any in the world!

Kiddies clamour for it. Watch the bowlfuls go. Let them have all they want. Health and vitality abound in the delightfully-flavoured golden-brown flakes—ideal food for growing youngsters.

Give your digestion a chance, too! Try a bowl of Kellogg's instead of the usual bacon and eggs. You'll be surprised at the goodness in this energy-giving cereal food—so simple to prepare, so easy to digest.

Insist on Kellogg's—the original Corn Flakes. Made by Kellogg in Canada, comes to you fresh and crisp in the Red and Green inner-sealed wax-wrapped packet.

Sold by all grocers—price 9^{D.} *per packet.*

Also makers of Kellogg's ALL-BRAN —*a laxative food.*

KELLOGG COMPANY *of* **GREAT BRITAIN,** *Ltd.*
329, High Holborn, London, W. C. 1

D.A.

Schweppes
LEMON SQUASH
Made from the finest Messina lemons

IN FLAGONS & BOTTLES
2/-

THE HUMANE GARDEN GUIDE

Herbaceous Borders

The greatest care should be exercised in planting these. Success in garden enjoyment depends upon full meditation in order to secure the expression of personal tastes. The process should be unhurried, considerate and calm.

176

Three-decker Tea Wagon, 2 ft. 4 ins. by 1 ft. 4 ins. by 3 ft. high. With 4 Brass Rubber-tyred Swivel Wheels, as shown, £4-15-0, or with Two Fixed Wheels and Two Swivel Wheels.

Can also be had with two decks. Prices range from £3-7-6

A handy Tea Wagon

Just the thing for the garden ....

.... a tea wagon that enables you to dispense with the troublesome "fetch-and-carry" process. Built on staunch, sturdy lines from seasoned teakwood that formed part of one of those famous battleships, H.M.S. "Thunderer" and H.M.S. "Lion," its life is almost interminable, even if left outdoors all the year round.

Write to-day for catalogue of all types of "Battleship" Garden Furniture—seats, chairs, etc.—to THE HUGHES BOLCKOW SHIP-BREAKING CO., LTD., Renown Wharf, Blyth, Northumberland.

"Battleship"
GARDEN FURNITURE

"BATTLESHIP" Garden Furniture can be had from the makers, or can be seen at the following addresses. Immediate deliveries. Catalogue FREE.

LONDON—*Maple & Co., Tottenham Court Road, N.W.1.*
ABERDEEN—*W.J. Anderson, 253 Union Road.*
BRADFORD—*Brown, Muff & Co., Ltd.*
CHESTER—*Brown & Co., 34-40 Eastgate Row.*
EDINBURGH—*James Gray & Sons, 89 George Street.*
GLASGOW—*R. Wylie Hill & Co., Ltd., 20 Buchanan Street.*
HARROGATE—*England, Robinson & Co.*
LEAMINGTON SPA—*Burgis & Colbourne, Ltd. | St.*
LEEDS—*C. W. Fillie, Albion*
LUTON, Beds.—*T. P. Vaughan & Sons, Leagrave.*
MARSKE-BY-THE-SEA, Yorks—*Hughes Bolckow & Co., Ltd., The Aerodrome.*
NOTTINGHAM—*Pearson Bros., Long Row.*
SHEFFIELD—*John Walsh, Ltd., 44-64 High Street.*
SOUTHPORT—*C. F. Chinery, Lord Street.*

A FINE TURN OUT

These moulds are made in a special way that enables a jelly to be turned out easily and whole. The even thickness of the pottery all over the patterned decoration ensures this. Shelley moulds are made in 14 distinct shapes. There are also the small individual moulds; from these, perfectly shaped jellies can be turned out for each person.

Write to Shelley, Dept. "G," Potters, Longton, for Coloured Illustrations of Shelley Tea Sets, Shelley Dainty White China, Domestic Pottery and Children's Ware, also name of nearest supplier.

Shelley.
MOULDS

There are 50 different Moulds to choose from and 14 distinct shapes

Look for the name "Shelley" on each piece of China.

¼ lb. sugar.) Chill and stand for two hours, stirring occasionally. Add the chilled soda water and a little cochineal. Strain before serving.

Fruit Punch

2 grapefruit	1 syphon soda water
5 oranges	(1½ pts.)
2 lemons	½ lb. sugar
1 gill crushed pine-apple	¼ pt. water

Boil the sugar and water together for 5 minutes; add to it the juice of the grapefruit, oranges, lemons and crushed pineapple. Stand and chill 2 hours. Add iced soda water before serving, and serve with thin slices of cut lemon.

A variety of drinks of which soda water is the principal ingredient may be made thus:

Lemon Soda

Squeeze the juice of one lemon and strain into a tumbler. Add a tablespoonful of sugar and stir well until dissolved. Fill up with soda water and chill.

Orange Soda

As for Lemon Soda but omit the sugar and add two teaspoonfuls of lemon juice. Sugar may also be added if liked.

Fruit Sodas

Half fill tumblers with pineapple, apricot, or raspberry syrup, then fill up with soda water.

Iced ginger ale or any bottled mineral water is of course delicious and requires no preparation beyond chilling.

Ice-Cream Ambrosias

Iced drinks and ice-cream can be combined with great success. A plain vanilla ice-cream can be added to any beverage, or if time and equipment permit, the ice-cream can be varied according to the beverage. Thus, lemon cream could be served on the top of iced lemonade, and coffee cream on iced coffee. Iced chocolate, orangeade, raspberryade, ginger beer, pineapple, and apricot drinks can all be served with the corresponding ice-cream.

Fruit Cocktail

1 grapefruit	1 tablespoonful brandy
1 banana	
The juice of 1 orange	The juice of ½ lemon
2 oz. sugar	
Glacé or maraschino cherries	

Halve the grapefruit and remove the pulp carefully with a grapefruit knife. Squeeze out any remaining juice, take out the pips and the pithy centre, and cut the pulp into small pieces. Mix the juice and pulp, the strained orange and lemon juice, thinly sliced banana and sugar in a jug and chill for one hour. Add the brandy and serve in small cocktail glasses, topped with a maraschino cherry. Glacé cherries should be soaked in the brandy to improve the flavour.

Crosse & Blackwell's

ESTD. 1706

BY APPOINTMENT

Other Crosse & Blackwell Soups include:

MOCK TURTLE

CONSOMMÉ

MUTTON BROTH

KIDNEY

GREEN PEA

VEGETABLE

HARE

JULIENNE

CHICKEN BROTH

CREAM OF TOMATO

GRAVY

REAL TURTLE

PALESTINE

MULLIGATAWNY

Fit for an Alderman!

A steaming plate of rich soup is a meal in itself. But in how many homes are there ready to hand all the different ingredients that go to make a really soul-satisfying soup?

Let Crosse & Blackwell provide your soup. All *you* have to provide is the heat. One of the most popular of their thirty different kinds is Thick Ox-Tail—a generous soup fit for an alderman's table. If you could see the good meats and vegetables that go into Crosse & Blackwell's giant stock-pots, you would say, "Let's have soup every day!"

Oxtail Soup

10 oz. tin 9½d.

1 lb. tin 1/3

AND 29 OTHER GOODLY KINDS

The Housekeeper's Dictionary *of* Facts

Early Autumn Preserves

During September it is possible to make some of the very cheapest although none the less excellent preserves. Blackberries and elderberries are all obtainable, and in most parts of the country they can be had for the picking. As with other fruit, it is important to avoid using blackberries for jam and jelly when rather over-ripe, for as the fruit becomes over-ripe the pectin, which is the constituent concerned with setting, becomes broken down. If, however, for any reason, the making of such preserves is attempted rather late in the season, it is particularly advisable to add a proportion of lemon juice or other acid as this helps to extract the pectin and render it soluble.

Blackberry Jam

As in the case of Blackberry Jelly, it is wise to add a proportion of acid such as lemon juice or tartaric acid, and although it is possible for an experienced cook to make this preserve by testing in the ordinary way, success is made almost a certainty for the mere amateur if the following method is adopted. Weigh the preserving pan and place 6 lb. fruit, $\frac{1}{2}$ pint water, and either 4 tablespoonfuls lemon juice or 3 level teaspoonfuls tartaric acid in it. The jam should then be cooked until quite tender and until the weight of the fruit pulp in the pan is $4\frac{3}{4}$ lb. The sugar should now be added—1 lb. 2 oz. to each 1 lb. of fruit—and the mixture cooked until the weight of jam in the pan is $11\frac{1}{4}$ lb. It should then be skimmed, poured into jars, covered with waxed paper circles and firmly tied down.

Blackberry Jelly

This is one of the most popular of blackberry preserves and by many is preferred to jam made from the same fruit on account of the absence of pips. After washing and looking over the fruit, one pint of water should be added to every 6 lb. fruit and then simmered gently until thoroughly cooked. The addition of 3 lemons to every 6 lb. fruit is specially desirable if the fruit is at all over-ripe, and in any case aids the setting considerably. When cooked, the fruit should be strained through a jelly bag and 1 lb. preserving sugar added to every 1 lb. juice. The mixture should then be brought to boiling point and boiled until it sets, being tested by pouring a few drops on to a cold plate. The jelly should be poured into clean, sterilised pots, covered with waxed paper circles and firmly tied down.

Blackberry and Damson Cheese

6 lb. blackberries. Sugar.
2 lb. damsons. 1 gill water.

The fruit should be weighed, water added, and the fruit cooked until tender. Now pass through a hair sieve and weigh the pulp. 1 lb. sugar should then be added to every 1 lb. of pulp and the mixture brought to boiling point, and tested after about 10 minutes.

A Useful Cleaning Device

A special scrubbing brush designed for use with a broom-handle is an almost invaluable possession to the housewife who does her own housework. The handle can be fixed into either side of the brush which ensures even wearing of the bristles.

A September Sweet
HOT BLACKBERRY MOUSSE

1 oz. crushed Savoy biscuits	$\frac{1}{4}$ lb. whole ripe blackberries
2 oz. butter	$\frac{1}{4}$ gill blackberry syrup (made by stewing $\frac{1}{2}$ lb. blackberries in syrup and afterwards straining)
Rind of 1 lemon	
2 oz. castor sugar	
$\frac{3}{4}$ oz. flour	
1 teaspoonful lemon juice	
	3 eggs

Cream the butter and sugar together until it is white and soft. Separate the yolks from the whites of the eggs and beat them in to the mixture one at a time. Add the crushed Savoy biscuits, grated lemon rind, lemon juice and sifted flour, blackberries and syrup. Beat the whites of eggs to a stiff froth and carefully fold into the mixture. Add sufficient carmine to improve the colour, steam in a lined, buttered soufflé mould for 1 hour. Turn out in a hot dish and serve with hot blackberry syrup or purée.

Removing a Stain

A reader from Glasgow has written to the Institute asking for advice as to the best way of removing a dark stain from a biscuit-coloured and rather valuable Wilton carpet. Some ink was spilt a few months ago and salt and lemon juice were applied immediately. This successfully removed the stain but the much rubbed in salt remained embedded in the pile, and makes a damp patch with the least appearance of rain.

The Institute, while realising the tremendous difficulty of the task, wrote suggesting that the carpet be taken into the garden and cold water poured through the affected spot with some little force, say, from a can with a fairly wide spout. This in time would dissolve and wash out the salt though the treatment would have to be carried out many times. The carpet should be pile downwards and raised from the ground.

A Kitchen Aid

The handle of an ordinary all-metal kettle is very liable, especially when placed on a fire, to become extremely hot. The simple and cheap addition of asbestos rope or string provides a covering for the handle which is both a poor conductor of heat and is non-inflammable. Procure some asbestos rope or string and wind it over the curved handle as tightly as the material permits, the asbestos being pressed firmly into place while being wound. The ends should be secured to the handle by wire. The lid can also be treated, the knob being covered by splaying a couple of short pieces of asbestos rope over it and securing these at the curved-in base of knob by wire. The handles of other domestic appliances, such as flat irons, can with advantage be dealt with in a similar way.

Cooking and Cleaning Hints

Tough meat will become tender if soaked in vinegar before it is cooked. When boiling rice for curries or to serve as a vegetable, a little vinegar in the water will make the rice whiter and keep the grains separate. A teaspoonful of vinegar is sometimes added to the water when poaching eggs or boiling fish as it aids in the coagulation of the proteins. It will also help to take away all smell when washing plates that have been used for fish, onions or cabbage. Vinegar and salt will remove stains on china and will cleanse glass flower-vases, water bottles and tumblers.

Blacklead mixed with vinegar gives a brighter and more lasting polish to the grate, and hot vinegar will remove paint from windows. Vinegar effectually preserves vegetables from putrefaction and fermentation and is therefore employed for pickling. It is said to aid the digestion of crude vegetables, and is appropriately used for salads.

More Uses for Vinegar

Vinegar has been known from the earliest times, and was formerly much used for medicinal purposes. The vapour, simple or aromatised, is a powerful restorative in cases of fainting, and as a means of relieving headache.

Vinegar is also invaluable for the toilet in the summer; nothing is so refreshing for sponging the face and temples to allay heat. Two tablespoonfuls poured into a bath of warm water is most refreshing for a tired person, especially after walking on a hot day.

POST

appeals to thinking mothers

The modern mother — above all people — is the family health specialist. *She* knows that happiness in the home largely depends upon what she gives her family to eat and drink.

Her man comes home tired. She gives him Postum with his evening meal—and at bed-time. He drinks it because he likes it. She —tactfully—doesn't rub in the fact that it is good for him.

The kiddies won't drink milk . . . A new drink appears on the table—a warm, golden-brown fluid which tastes like creamy toffee. Gorgeous stuff! Postum again—made with hot milk.

Often during the day she feels she needs something to set her up. So she makes herself a cup of Postum —it's so quick and easy to prepare—made in a cup in a moment.

Postum is a delicious drink in its own right. But, unlike most good drinks, it doesn't bring the reaction of nerves, sleeplessness and indigestion. It is nothing but wheat sweetened a trifle and transmuted into tiny sparkling granules, instantly soluble in boiling water or hot milk. Try giving your family Postum for thirty days. Then see how much healthier and happier they are. We will give you the first week's supply free.

Most grocers sell Postum in two sizes —1/7 tin, sufficient for 45 cups. 2/8 tin, sufficient for 90 cups. Postum is one of the Post Health Products which include Grape Nuts, Post Toasties and Post's Bran Flakes.

FREE—Post this coupon (or copy it out on a postcard) to-day!

THE GRAPE NUTS CO., LTD., Dept.-B.E.7
5, CHANCERY LANE, LONDON, W.C.2

I should like my family to make a thirty-day test of Postum. Please send me, without cost or obligation, one week's supply.

NAME ....

ADDRESS...

....
(Please write VERY plainly!)

U M

By *Lady Violet Bonham Carter*

Are YOU a GOOD Housekeeper?

The mechanism of a house well kept should be silent and absolutely invisible. Really good housekeeping is neither seen nor heard. It is only deeply and gratefully felt

IT seems an act of almost mad temerity to choose this theme to write upon between these covers, and I want in my first sentence to ward off (if at all possible) the inevitable misunderstanding which such a choice must bring crashing down upon my head. If I venture to write about housekeeping at all, it is not vaingloriously, dogmatically, helpfully—as one who knows her first job, and wants to let others know it. It is in a humble, a groping, almost a broken spirit.

I am not going to say, " But it's all *so* easy! Don't you know how to make new pitch pine look like old walnut? Why, just take two old banana skins, dip them in the tea-pot (after you've finished tea, of course) pass them lightly two or three times over the surface of the wood—and there you are "; or give an equally painless, economical and impossible receipt for wringing out flannels with button-hooks, making omelettes out of egg-shells or persuading last winter's cabbage-stalks to taste like next spring's asparagus. . . .

No, that, alas! is not my line of business. (Would that it were!) I want on my own behalf to explore, I want, if I can, to discover by what mysterious method, trick, knack, science or inspiration that miracle, good housekeeping, is achieved.

Though we may not know how it is brought about, yet how unmistakably we recognise it, how joyfully we hail it directly we come up against it. On crossing the threshold of a well-" kept " house we are immediately enfolded by an atmosphere of comfort and well-being which it seems almost irreverent to dissect and analyse.

What are the ingredients that go to make up this perfection? How are they put together? Coldly summed up, they will be as useless to us as a friend's receipt of her own ambrosial dish is to our own fumbling cook. We find that the prescribed proportions do not really vitally matter. It is the spell one mutters over them. Some people come into the world knowing the spell, others die without having learnt it. A little greed, and much kindness, an inventive appetite, an imaginative sense of comfort, linked with a Permanent Under-Secretary's power of running a

machine, these all play their part, but in the main good housekeepers are born and not made. But I hope (sometimes against hope) that bad ones may be improved.

Let us, starting at the wrong end, first consider " effects," coming to causes later. What are a few of the symptoms of a really well-kept house?

First and foremost it is important that the door should be opened to us by a familiar figure, one whom we have learnt to regard as an integral part of the human structure of the household, and who welcomes us as a host and a friend. A sense of personal responsibility on the part of the servants towards the guests of the house is the lynch-pin of the comfort and well-being of both, mental as well as physical.

One of the next things one notices on entering the house is that it *smells* good, though one can't quite say of what. Wood fires? Pot-pourri? Lavender in linen cupboards? No—it is more subtle—mixed—pervasive and inexplicable. It is simply the smell of a nice house.

Upstairs in the bedroom there is a fire burning—a *real* fire of coal or wood. Not gas peering luridly through skulls or licking the lichen off a sham log, not even (to my mind) electricity glowing through large blocks of amber and coffee-sugar (though both these devices are great time- and labour-savers). There are dark blinds to pull down over the windows and wedges to stick in the sashes in case they rattle, for a bedroom *must* be " a chamber deaf to noise and blind to light." A reading-lamp, a bell and a pencil and paper are within reach of the bed, perhaps even a good novel as well.

The bed itself and particularly the pillow should be exquisitely comfortable. When one considers that we spend nearly half our lives in beds, the mattresses which the majority of human beings, quite gratuitously and of their own free will, elect to sleep on, are amazing. I have a fairly wide experience of " taken " houses in various parts of England and it is the rarest thing in the world to find an even tolerably comfortable bed. There are infinite varieties of discomfort, ranging from mild malaise to torture.

There is the soft lumpy and springless kind in which one sinks deeper and deeper into a suffocating grave, dug by one's first unwary wriggle. There is the hard ditto, in which one tosses, bruised and aching, making not the smallest dint by one's most convulsive effort at adjustment.

There is the bare, lean, springy mattress of wafer thinness, sagging in the middle almost to floor level.

Good mattresses are expensive no doubt, but there are few things I would not forgo by day in order that my nights might be spent on the exquisite surface of a best hair or (still better) best white hair mattress.

In the well-kept house nothing is tepid. The bath-water is always boiling, and the drinking water icy. The bath-towels are enormous. (The luxury of a hot bath is more than half undone if, on getting out, one is received by a meagre pocket-handkerchief which barely covers one to the waist, instead of in the all-enfolding embrace of a bath-sheet.) The bath-soap also is large and smells delicious, with no suggestion of disinfectant properties to produce the illusion of being treated like a dog.

But let us leave washing and sleep on one side for a moment and turn to food. And here I long not for the tongues of men and of angels but for the pen of one woman—Lady Jekyll—who has shown us in her masterly book. *Kitchen Essays*, how food can be treated lyrically. Only a poet who was (incidentally) also a millionaire could aspire to her great efforts, the joints rinsed in the best burgundy, the birds studded with truffles and bathed in cream, the jellies like " an emerald green pool set in a flat glass bowl. reminiscent of Sabrina fair in her home below translucent waves, or of Capri caverns, cool and deep." . . . But what we all ought to be able to achieve (and it really is the thing most worth achieving) is to make the ordinary, everyday food of life not a banal, wearisome treadmill of the jaws, but a constant surprise and delight.

That bacon should be crisp, brittle and curly instead of pink and limp that toast (most difficult and testing of all feats) should not be a flabby sandwich stuffed

Are You a Good Housekeeper ?

with cotton-wool; that hot milk should have foam and bubbles instead of skin on the top of it; that bread should be new; jam a delicious *compote* in which real fruit floats as units, instead of an anonymous and undiagnosable amalgam of dull red slush; that beef should be red and mutton brown, not *vice versa*; that vegetables should be cooked in butter and cream rather than tepid water; that the soup should not have floating in it the alphabet carved out of custard; that elaborate arrangements of parsley, cherries and lemon peel should be rigidly eschewed (it matters so much more what food looks like even than how it tastes)—these are things that really cost little but count infinitely much.

Nice food need not be any more expensive than nasty food.

Oysters, caviare and *foie gras* are treats, of course, once in a way, but they are not things it occurs to us to miss from the menu of our daily lives. It is humiliating to reflect that it is not to want of money but to want of skill, taste, intelligence and resource that we owe our nasty or our dreary fare. We are food-bores, food-Philistines, where we might be food-wits, food-artists, food-poets. We try to avoid platitudes—we do our best not to sing flat, but do we ever reflect how many old threadbare tags and *clichés* we utter, how many false notes we sing in terms of food?

Men are as a rule far better hands at ordering a meal than women. In fact it is quite arguable (if one rules out extravagance as a disqualification) that they are better housekeepers. They are either superlatively good at planning comfort or else quite helpless. In a bachelor's household one touches top or bottom. One suffers the extreme of hardship or enjoys the highest degree of luxury. Both are to be explained by the fact that in household matters men rule by abdication. They make one crucial decision when they choose their servants. Then they hand over completely, delegating all detail. There is a great deal to be said for this system. People naturally work better when they are given responsibility and opportunities for initiative, and every servant must feel a flood-tide of energy released by serving a man who is busy and absent all day, rather than a woman who is always about the house telephoning, ringing bells and generally giving trouble.

For the same reason good house-keeping, even for a woman, is child's play in a house in which no nursery exists. No one who has not experienced it can guess at the strain imposed by constant diplomatic missions between nursery and kitchen, the difficulties of conveying tactfully to the cook that "grease" was again detected on the top of the children's chicken-tea and had to be removed with tissue-paper, that the "twice-cooked meat" which is gratefully received by the dining-room is regarded in the nursery as a con-

fection planned by the Borgias, that the Yorkshire pudding was fried in fat, that there was pepper *and* onions in the Irish stew, and that they had again sent up (or failed to send up) tomatoes for Nannie's supper.

Then the perambulator scratches off the paint in the hall, the children fall down and hurt themselves on linoleum that the housemaids have overpolished. . . . Above all the nursery is seldom away and never "out." A nursery is in the words of Sherlock Holmes (applied by him to love) "sand in the clockwork, a fly in the amber, iron near the magnet."

I have said nothing about economy because that is a dragon which every one of us must wrestle with single handed and in our own way. We each have a separate scale of values as to what are and what are not essential extravagances. With some of us it is the fruit-bill, with others the laundry; to others again warmth comes before dessert or washing, and they would sacrifice all for the sake of a fire (even in the dining-room) or hot pipes at full blast throughout the winter. Sometimes one puts a thing so high in the scale that one dare not indulge in it at all for fear of going too far. I have a passion for flowers, and realising that if I bought them at all I should go to dangerous lengths I made it a rule when I married to give them up altogether and this I found easier and less painful than having too few.

I regretfully admit that I think one ought to "do" weekly books if one wants to learn anything at all about one's household expenditure. None of them present any difficulties at all except the grocer's; and that after ten years' baffled perusal floors me completely to this very day. The grocer's book is a nightmare. To begin with it is always enormous. And why? There's the rub. One knows so well as one glances through the butcher's (for instance) whether one has or has not had several more legs of mutton or shins of beef this week than usual, and if so why one has had them. But when one sees mixed up with macaroni and currants, and Demerara, Demerara (a recurring rhythmic wail that seems to have come straight from Synge), quite arbitrary quantities of cleaning materials and incredible numbers of bundles of sticks, one's power to check and still more to criticise dwindles to vanishing point.

My advice to would-be economists is: "Conquer the grocer's book." Once you have laid that many-headed hydra low the game is yours with the reluctant respect of your cook thrown in.

One last warning. The mechanism of a house well kept should be silent and absolutely invisible. There should be no sense of strain or hustle anywhere and nothing should be or appear difficult or inconvenient. Really good housekeeping is neither seen nor heard. It is only deeply and gratefully felt.

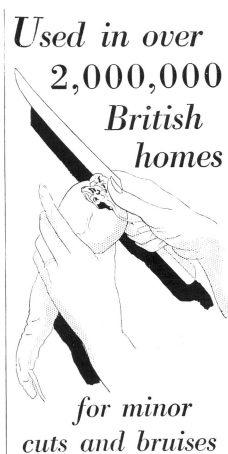

For size and flavour !

If when you open a new bag of sultanas you taste some because they are so silky and smooth, and you find they've far more flavour and far tenderer flesh than usual, then you may know that your grocer has given you Australian Sultanas.

No other country has the soil or the sunshine to grow sultanas like those of Australia; and the sultanas are dried and mellowed in the vitalising sunlight until perfect in taste and food value.

Value for value Australian Sultanas cost no more and they are always just a little more pleasing than the best sultanas from other countries.   Best and cleanest, too, for they are never touched by hand from the moment they're picked till they reach the shop.

Now wouldn't it be wise when you're shopping in future to say :
"I want Australian Sultanas, please" ?

Australian Sultanas

Issued by the Director of Australian Trade Publicity, Australia House, Strand, London, W.C.2.

Wayside Berries
for WINTER PRESERVES

By E. Edwards

First Class Diploma, Cookery, Laundry-work, Housewifery, and Needlework; King's College Certificate of Household and Social Science; Certificate of the London Sanitary Board

AUTUMN'S glowing fruits and berries not only please the eye with their beauty but appeal also to the practical, minded as possible material for preserves. Elderberries, crab apples, damsons and blackberries are now fairly plentiful and when the seeds and stones, etc., are rejected, prove the basis of many delicious jams and jellies.

Elderberries, which in many districts can be had for the picking, have a distinct and somewhat acrid flavour which is pleasing when blended with other fruits. The following recipes suggest ways of using them to the very best advantage. The Elderberry Syrup will be found a soothing hot drink for persons suffering from a cold.

Elderberry Jelly

3½ lb. elderberries	2 lemons
1½ lb. apples or crab apples	2 pints water Sugar

Wash the elderberries and stew together with one pint of water and the juice of the two lemons for half an hour. Wash and cut up the apples and stew with the other pint of water for half an hour. Combine the contents of the pans, mash well and stew for a further half-hour. Strain through a scalded jelly bag and allow to drip overnight. Weigh the extract and allow 1 lb. sugar to 1 lb. extract. Bring the extract to the boil, add the sugar, previously warmed, stir and boil. Test as usual after 5 minutes' boiling. Skim, pot and cover as usual.

Elderberry Syrup

1 lb. elderberries	1 lb. sugar
1 gill cold water	

Wash the elderberries and put into a double saucepan with the sugar and water. Cook without the lid, stirring occasionally, for two hours or until the liquid becomes syrupy. Cool a little then strain into clean dry bottles. Cork and store in a cool place.

When required, measure a table-spoonful of the syrup into a tumbler and fill up with hot water.

Blackberry and Apple Jam

8 lb. blackberries	1 pint water
3 lb. sour apples	Sugar

Place the blackberries in a pan over a low heat. Stew until tender and sieve in order to remove the seeds. Peel, core and slice the apples, add the water and cook until tender. Add the sieved blackberries and cook all together until thick. Weigh the pulp and add an equal weight of sugar, previously warmed. Stir, boil, test and pot as usual.

Note.—If the preserving pan is weighed before cooking is commenced, the weight of the pulp can easily be calculated.

Blackberry and Damson Cheese

8 lb. blackberries	½ pint water
3 lb. damsons	Sugar

Wash the fruit well and add the water. Simmer in a covered pan, stirring occasionally until the fruit is tender. Sieve and weigh the pulp, bring to the boil and add an equal weight of sugar. Boil, test, and pot as usual.

Bramble Jelly

4 lb. blackberries	¼ oz. tartaric acid
¾ pint water	Sugar

Put the berries, acid and water into a preserving pan and bring to the boil. Cook slowly for one hour, or until the fruit is quite tender. The slow cooking in the presence of the acid helps to bring the pectin into solution. During the cooking, the fruit must be stirred from time to time. Pour through a jelly cloth and allow to drip several hours. Weigh the extract and allow 1 lb. sugar to 1 lb. extract. Put the extract in a jelly pan, bring to the boil and add the sugar, previously warmed. Allow to boil briskly for about 5 minutes, then test for jelling. When the jelly sets when tested on a cold plate, it is ready to be potted.

Crab Apple Jelly

6 lb. crab apples	A few cloves or root ginger if liked
3 pints water	
Sugar	

Wash the crab apples and cut them in half without peeling or coring. Add the water and simmer until tender. If the crab apples are lacking in flavour, a few cloves or a little bruised ginger may be stewed with them. Stir and mash the contents of the pan from time to time, and when the fruit is tender strain through a scalded jelly bag. Weigh the extract and add an equal weight of sugar. Stir, boil, and test as usual.

Barberry Jam

6 lb. barberries	6 lb. sugar

Wash the berries and put them into the pan with the sugar. Stir and bring slowly to the boil. Boil gently for 15-20 minutes, stirring meanwhile. Pot and cover as usual.

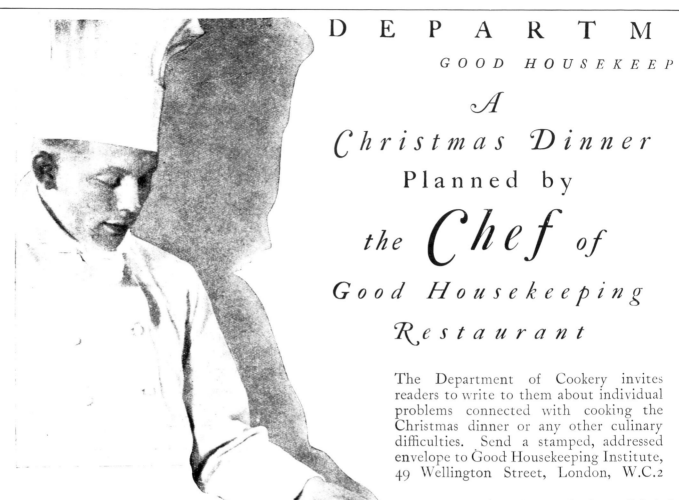

A Christmas Dinner Planned by the *Chef* of Good Housekeeping Restaurant

The Department of Cookery invites readers to write to them about individual problems connected with cooking the Christmas dinner or any other culinary difficulties. Send a stamped, addressed envelope to Good Housekeeping Institute, 49 Wellington Street, London, W.C.2

THOUGH children look forward to Christmas Day with unalloyed joy, for adults this joy is tinged with some anxiety; fathers, perhaps, pondering whimsically and a little sadly on the increase in financial expenditure, and mothers regarding with some dread the heavy increase in catering and cooking which is inevitable over the Christmas festivities.

To relieve that work, the Chef at the Good Housekeeping Restaurant has planned a menu, and gives recipes and helpful suggestions as to the way in which it may be cooked with the minimum of work and worry. Though it is sufficiently elaborate when entertaining on a lavish scale, it can easily be adapted for smaller households and smaller appetites by omitting hors d'œuvre and perhaps fish.

In order that the suggestions given on the planning of the work may be clear and definite, the time has been fixed for the meal as 1 p.m. Christmas Day. This has been chosen as being the most probable hour, especially for a household in which there are children.

Hors d'Œuvre Variés

A selection, or all the following, may be served:—Potato Salad, Iced Olives, Sardines, Russian Salad, Egg and Tomato Mayonnaise, Fillets of Anchovy, Pimentos Stuffed with Rice, Tomato Salad.

Hors-d'Œuvre Variés

Consommé Printanière

Filet de Sole Bercy

Dindonneau de Norfolk farci aux Marrons

Pommes Frites

Choux de Bruxelles

Mince Pies

Pouding de Noël

Mandarine Blidah

Mixed Vegetable Clear Soup. (*Consommé Printanière.*)—½ lb. lean shin of beef, 2 whites of egg, 1 quart white stock (free from fat), browning.

Garnish.—1 carrot, onion, turnip, leek (diced); 18 French beans cut in diamond shapes, salt and pepper, sugar, 1 oz. butter.

To Clarify Stock.—Remove all fat and sinew from the shin of beef and pass through a mincing machine two or three times; make into a paste (using a wooden spoon) with the whites of egg, and gradually add the stock. Stir over the fire until it boils and then allow to simmer 1½ to 2 hours with lid on. Strain through double muslin, re-boil, and remove any scum or fat. Add seasonings and garnish and a little browning.

To Prepare the Garnish.—Place diced vegetables in a thick saucepan, add just enough water to cover, a pinch of salt, sugar and butter and cover with a buttered paper. Heat gently until the liquid is reduced to a glaze.

White Stock.—2 lb. knuckle of veal, 2 quarts cold water, 4 oz. onion, 3 oz. celery, 1 clove, 6 or 8 peppercorns, ½ teaspoonful salt.

Cut any meat off the knuckle, chop

Mandarine Blidah makes a pleasant alternative to the heavier Christmas fare

the bone into small pieces. Add cold water, salt, vegetables and flavourings, bring to the boil and allow to simmer gently for 6 hours, removing the scum as it rises. Allow to cool, then strain through a hair sieve.

Fillets of Sole Bercy Sauce (*Filet de Sole Bercy*).—4 fillets of sole, 1 gill

Director
D. D. Cottington Taylor

Certificate Household and Social Science, King's College for Women; First Class Teaching Diplomas, Cookery, Laundrywork, Housewifery, High Class Cookery, N.T.S.C., London, A.R.S.I.

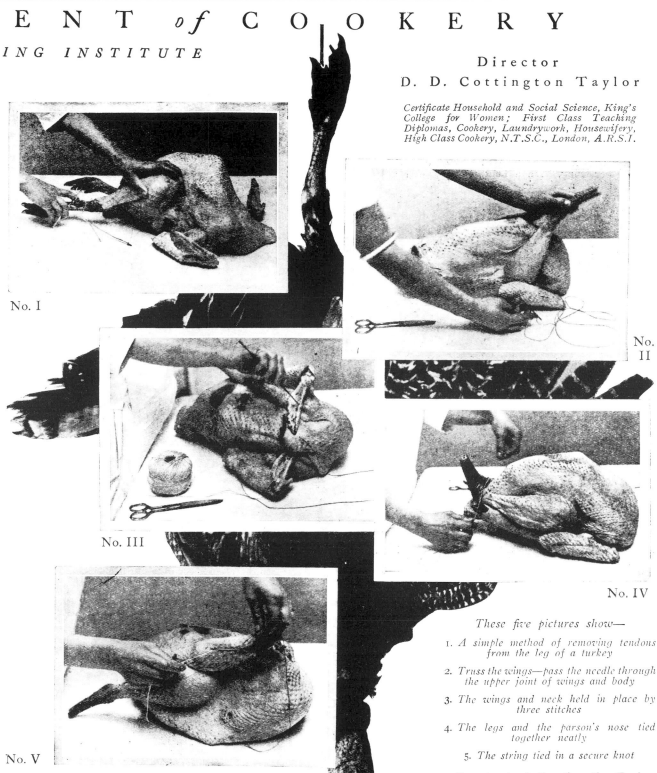

No. I

No. II

No. III

No. IV

No. V

These five pictures show—

1. *A simple method of removing tendons from the leg of a turkey*

2. *Truss the wings—pass the needle through the upper joint of wings and body*

3. *The wings and neck held in place by three stitches*

4. *The legs and the parson's nose tied together neatly*

5. *The string tied in a secure knot*

fish stock, ½ gill Fish Velouté Sauce, 2 oz. butter, ¼ gill cream, salt, cayenne, ¼ teaspoonful blanched and chopped taragon, ½ teaspoonful chevril, ½ teaspoonful parsley.

Trim the fillets, and place in a greased sauté pan. Sprinkle with a pinch of salt and add enough stock to cover. Place greased paper over the fish and bring to the boil. Lower heat and poach until cooked (5 to 10 mins.) Remove the fillets and add Fish Velouté to liquor in sauté pan. Boil until it forms a paste, stirring meanwhile. Work the remainder of the butter into it, adding a small piece at a time. Add sufficient cream or milk to make sauce of good coating consistency, salt and cayenne. Strain and pour over fillets and garnish with taragon, chevril and chopped parsley.

Fish Velouté Sauce.—½ pint fish stock, 2½ oz. butter, 2 oz. flour, 1 carrot, 1 onion.

Melt the butter in a saucepan, add the flour, cook for 10 minutes and gradually pour in the stock. Add onion and carrot, cut in small pieces, cook for half an hour and strain.

Trussing and Roasting the Turkey (Dindonneau de Norfolk Farci aux Marrons).—Trim and singe the turkey if this has not already been done. Remove the tendons (photo 1) by cutting through the skin between the knuckle bones, then inserting skewer under each tendon separately, twisting and pulling it out. To make the carving easier and more economical remove the wishbone. Insert stuffing, beginning at neck end, and truss.

Trussing.—As the trussing is likely to present difficulties, each step in the process has been photographed. Arrange wings as in photo 3. Turn bird over as in photo 2, and holding legs towards neck end pass needle through

*The first step in carving a turkey
is to remove the legs*

upper joint of wing through body
and out on the other side. Then
turn bird over again and inserting needle an inch or so lower on
the upper joint of wing, pass it
through terminal joint, through
the flap of skin on neck, similarly
through terminal and upper joint
of the other wing. Tie a knot,
giving string a double twist.
Pass parson's nose through vent.
Press legs together (photo 4) and
tie string tightly around them and
the parson's nose with a double
twist.

Place turkey on its side on a
baking tin. Sprinkle with salt
and cover with a little butter or
dripping. Bake in a hot oven
(450° F.) for 20 minutes. Reduce the heat, and after roasting
the other side of
the bird for 20
minutes turn on its
back and continue
r o a s t i n g i n a
moderate   o v e n
(350° F.) u n t i l
cooked (1–2 hours)
according to the
size of the bird.
Baste frequently—
about every 10
minutes. Place on
serving dish.

Gravy

Pour fat out of
tin, and rinse with
stock made from
giblets which have
been boiled for
2–3 hours. Bring
to the boil, remove
any scum, season,
and colour. Pass
through a f i n e
strainer.

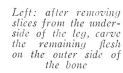

*Left: after removing
slices from the under-
side of the leg, carve
the remaining flesh
on the outer side of
the bone*

Carving the Turkey

The legs should be pointing away
from the carver. Remove the legs by
cutting through the film of skin between the breast and top of leg. These
should be carved separately, a few slices
being served with portions of the breast.
Rest the leg on joint of drumstick and
carve downwards in slices. (See illustration.) Then reverse the position,
and cut further slices from the fleshy
part on opposite side of bone. Remove
both wings with lower part of breast
and then carve the breast in slices,
from this point getting the slices gradually longer until the whole length of
the bird is being carved.

When only a few persons are dining
it is advisable to remove the leg and
wing from one side only, leaving an
entire half-carcase for a future occasion.

There is an alternative method of
carving a turkey (as shown in the illustration). In order to steady the bird
the wings are left on until all the breast
has been removed.

Chestnut Stuffing

1 lb. chestnuts
White stock
Salt
2 teaspoonfuls sugar
1 oz. butter
Celery seed or fresh celery
1 lb. pork sausage meat

Bake the chestnuts until
half-cooked. Peel them, removing brown u n d e r s k i n
while hot. Put in a saucepan
with sufficient stock to cover,
add salt, also the sugar, butter,
and celery seed, tied in muslin.
Cook until liquor is reduced
to a glaze, then mix them with
sausage meat.

Fresh celery gives a better
flavour than celery seed.

Fried Potatoes

(*Pommes Frites*)

Wash, peel and cut some
large potatoes into cylinder
shapes about 1¼ in. in diameter.
After slicing very finely place
in water. Wash, dry, and
place in a frying basket.
Plunge into fat when smoking
hot, and cook until bubbling
subsides. Remove them and
place on a clean cloth to drain.
Sprinkle with salt, and serve.

Mincemeat

1 lb. currants	1 lb. sugar
1 lb. sultanas	1½ tablespoonfuls mixed spices
1 lb. mixed peel	
1 lb. chopped apples	2 lemons (juice and rind)
1 lb. chopped suet	½ teacupful brandy

Mix the ingredients together and allow to stand
at least 15 days before using.

(*Continued*)

*Holding the meat in position with the fork, the breast
should be carved in long thin slices*

Your health—Your home— and Frigidaire

THE primary consideration of every home should be Health—and nothing so vitally influences the health as the food you eat. But the health of the home to-day is assailed by a greater danger than ever before, because since chemical preservatives in food are now prohibited, food will not keep.

This new housekeeping problem can fortunately be overcome because the safety of the food you eat can be assured by proper provision being

made for its preservation in the home. Frigidaire Automatic Electrical Refrigeration is the solution to this problem, for in the automatically maintained, dry, crisp cold of Frigidaire food stays fresh. There can be no risk to your *Health* if *Frigidaire* is installed in your *Home*.

Frigidaire is air-cooled, self-starting, self-stopping, self-oiling and needs no water.

Send coupon for full particulars and details of deferred payments.

London Showrooms :
Frigidaire House, Chapter Street,
Vauxhall Bridge Road, S.W.1, and
Imperial House, Kingsway, W.C.2.

Frigidaire
Automatic Electrical Refrigeration

Branches at :

Birmingham, Manchester, Leeds,

Brighton, Glasgow and Edinburgh.

FRIGIDAIRE LIMITED (*Incorporated in Canada*).

Dept. A-602, Frigidaire House, Chapter Street,
Vauxhall Bridge Road, S.W.1.

Please send me, without obligation, complete information about Frigidaire.

Name..

Address ....

No. in Family ....

A Christmas Dinner

Christmas Pudding
(Pouding de Noël)

1 lb. currants	1 tablespoonful
1 lb. sultanas	mixed spice
1 lb. mixed peel	1 lb. raisins
1 lb. chopped apples	1 lb. breadcrumbs
1 lb. chopped suet	16 eggs
	1 lb. brown sugar

Mix all together; place in a buttered and sugared basin, cover with a cloth, and steam or boil for about 7 hours.

Those who find Christmas pudding and mince pies too heavy for them will probably prefer a lighter dish, such as the following:

Glazed Tangerines and Rice
(Mandarin Blidah)

1 pint milk	Apricot sauce
2 oz. sugar	Angelica
3 oz. rice flour	Glazed cherries
7 or 8 tangerines	Whipped cream

Boil the milk, add the sugar and stir in the rice flour. Allow to cook for 30 minutes without further stirring. Stir, re-boil and continue stirring. Pour into a greased and sugared border mould, and allow to set in a cold place. Peel and remove pith in hot water from tangerines, and glaze with Apricot Sauce. Turn the rice mould out on to a dish. Arrange the tangerines on rice and garnish with angelica, cherries and whipped cream.

Apricot Sauce

1 pint apricot jam	2 oz. sugar
(2 heaped table-spoonfuls)	2 teaspoonfuls cornflour
	1½ gills water

Boil the jam with 1 gill water and the sugar, stir in the cornflour which has been blended with the remainder of the water. Bring to the boil, and allow to simmer for 20 minutes. Pass through a fine strainer. If liked add a little yellow colouring, and then allow to cool.

Order of Work and Time-Table for Christmas Dinner

To be cooked and served by 1 p.m.

Saturday, December 22nd.

Make stock.

Monday, December 24th

Make Consommé, without garnish.
Stuff and truss turkey.
Make Mince Pies.
Make Mandarin Blidah.
Prepare breadcrumbs for Bread Sauce.
Make Fish Velouté Sauce for Sole Bercy.

Tuesday, December 25th

9.30 a.m.
Put giblets on to cook for gravy.
Prepare Hors d'Œuvre and put aside in a cool place.
10.30 a.m.
Light oven.
Prepare garnish for soup.
10.45 a.m.
Prepare Brussels Sprouts and potatoes.
11 a.m.
Put turkey in oven (time will vary according to size).
11.15 a.m.
Put saucepan on for heating Christmas Pudding.
11.30 a.m.
Put Christmas Pudding in saucepan.
11.45 a.m.
Begin Bread Sauce.
Put water on for sprouts.
12 noon.
Put sole on to poach and make Bercy Sauce.
12.15 p.m.
Put sprouts on to cook.
Fry potatoes.
12.30 p.m.
Finish Bread Sauce.
Heat Consommé and add garnish.
Finish the Sole Bercy.
12.45 p.m.
Dish up the turkey.
Make gravy.
Dish up the sprouts.
Put Mince Pies in oven to warm.
12.55 p.m.
Place Hors d'Œuvre on the table.
1.5 p.m.
Serve soup.
1.10 p.m.
Serve fish.
1.20 p.m.
Serve turkey, vegetables and sauce.
1.35 p.m.
Serve Christmas Pudding and Mince Pies.

The Christmas pudding and mincemeat should be prepared some weeks beforehand.

Here are some of the " sweet seventeen " in " P.F. Assorted " Biscuits.

*Y*OU MAY think you know your favourite biscuit—till you meet "P.F. Assorted." There are seventeen different Peek Frean kinds there—creamy kinds, shortcake kinds, fruity kinds, wafer kinds, and what not—and they're *all* favourites !

Whenever you buy biscuits, it's important to say "Peek Frean's." For if anybody knows how to make better biscuits than they do—if anybody puts purer ingredients into them, or bakes them to a more beautiful crispness—then every one of Peek Frean's bakers will eat his snow-white hat.

Can you say:

'BRITAIN'S CRISPEST BISCUITS'?

It's easier to say—

Peek Frean's

The Institute Suggests uses for
Oatmeal
&
Prepared Oats

Oatmeal and Cheese Biscuits are a delicious accompaniment to celery

THE average household is rather inclined to regard oatmeal as the "Cinderella" among the cereals; prepared oats and various patent cereals have, to a large extent, usurped the place oatmeal porridge formerly filled in the breakfast menu. For reasons both of health and of economy, however, it is a good plan to serve it fairly frequently, but not sufficiently often for it to become unpopular with the younger members of the family.

Oats are one of the most complete grain foods, containing as they do about 10·5 per cent. protein, 5·5 per cent. fat, 58·5 per cent. carbohydrate, 3·1 per cent.

Prepared oats and oatmeal can be used in a variety of ways

ash, 9·6 per cent. fibre, and 12·9 per cent. water. Combined with milk, oatmeal becomes an almost perfectly balanced food.

The grain must be carefully prepared, as the bran sometimes proves slightly irritant. For this reason it is always advisable to cook oatmeal very slowly. It is, of course, an excellent laxative on account of the large proportion of cellulose present.

Oatmeal is obtainable in three grades —coarse, medium, and fine—and various forms of prepared oats are now manufactured. These are treated by rolling under steam pressure, which not only flattens the grain, but alters its

flavour and shortens the time required for cooking. Prepared oats are useful for quick breakfast porridge, and are delicious for milk puddings and as an addition to various sweet cakes.

Ordinary oatmeal has a noticeable lack of gluten and is therefore unsuitable for using alone in cooking, other than for dishes such as oatcakes or porridge. A proportion of wheat-flour is necessary to provide the gluten and give firmness to the bread or biscuits when baked.

The following recipes suggest some methods of using oatmeal in its various forms:

Oat Cinnamon Bread

6 oz. butter	Pinch of salt
4 oz. brown sugar	6 oz. raisins
12 oz. syrup	1 teaspoonful cinnamon
1 lb. flour	namon
6 oz. rolled oats	½ pint milk
1 teaspoonful bi-carbonate of soda	

Melt the syrup, sugar, and butter without heating. Sieve the flour, salt, and cinnamon together and add the oats and then the raisins. Dissolve the bicarbonate of soda in the milk. Combine all the ingredients and beat thoroughly until well mixed. Put into four greased sandwich tins measuring about 7 inches across or bake in one large tin at a temperature of 340° F., for half an hour or until brown and firm. Allow to cool a little before turning out.

Oatmeal and Cheese Biscuits

4 oz. fine oatmeal	¼ teaspoonful salt
2 oz. flour	3 oz. butter
3 oz. grated cheese	Yolk of egg and
Cayenne pepper	water to bind

Grate the cheese, separate the yolk from the white of egg, and beat up the yolk with a little water. Mix the oatmeal, salt, and flour, rub in the butter, add the cheese and cayenne pepper to taste. Mix to a stiff paste with the yolk of egg and water. Roll out ⅛ in. thick, cut into small biscuits and place on a greased baking sheet. Bake in a moderate oven until pale brown. Allow to become quite cold before lifting from the baking sheet. Store in an airtight tin. These biscuits are delicious with celery.

(Continued)

Well Cooked Meals

A Second Well-balanced Menu
Cressy Soup
Sole au gratin
Surprise Salad
Cold Roast Mutton
Stuffed Apples

Cressy Soup

4 large carrots	1 onion
Little celery or celery salt	2 oz. raw bacon or ham
2 oz. butter	2 pints stock or water
¼ oz. flour	

Scrape and slice the carrots and slice the onion. Fry the bacon, then add one ounce of the butter, the carrot, onion and celery and allow to cook slowly over a low heat for 8 minutes, stirring occasionally. Then add the stock and simmer slowly until the vegetables are tender. Rub through a sieve. Melt the remaining ounce of butter in a saucepan, stir in the flour, add the sieved soup, bring to the boil, stirring to prevent lumps forming, and boil 8 minutes. Serve with croûtes of fried bread.

Sole au Gratin

1 sole	Mashed potatoes
1 small shallot	½ oz. butter
½ teaspoonful Worcester sauce	Brown sauce
A few mushrooms	Juice of one lemon
Parsley	Pepper and salt
	Brown crumbs

Wash, skin and trim the sole; grease a gratin dish. Chop the shallot, mushrooms and parsley and put some in a layer at the bottom of the dish, on which place the sole. Cover the fish with the remainder of the chopped mushrooms, etc., and a few pieces of butter, a sprinkling of lemon juice, the Worcester sauce and a little pepper and salt. Cover with greased paper and cook in the oven. When nearly done, remove the paper and cover with brown crumbs. Heat the brown sauce, pour round the fish, and garnish with mashed potatoes passed through a rose forcer.

Surprise Salad

1 crisp cabbage	2 apples
1 tablespoonful diced celery	Mayonnaise
2 oz. hazel nuts or walnuts	1 tablespoonful capers
	A little lemon juice

Take off the outer leaves of an average sized cabbage and reserve for boiling. Put the others to soak in cold, salted water, for half an hour or so, then drain. Take a quarter of the heart, fold up the leaves and pass through a food chopper, or shred finely with a knife. Peel and core the apples, cut into quarters and slice thinly. To prevent the sliced apples from discolouring, dip into lemon juice or into equal parts of lemon juice and water. Grind or chop the nuts, reserving a few for garnishing. Mix the shredded cabbage, apple, nuts, celery and most of the capers with enough mayonnaise sauce to mask lightly. Arrange on a bed of thin cabbage leaves, pour thick mayonnaise sauce over and garnish with capers and nuts. Serve immediately.

Stuffed Apples

3 lb. apples	½ lb. dates
1 oz. almonds	A little sugar

Wash and core the apples, then cut out the skin round the top of each. Stone the dates and blanch the almonds, chop both and mix them together. Half fill each apple with this mixture, then put in a little sugar, and fill them up with the date and almond stuffing. Place in a glass fireproof dish or piedish and add sufficient water to cover ¼ inch up the side of the dish. Bake in a moderate oven till the apples are tender when tested with a skewer.

Oatmeal and Prepared Oats

Oatmeal Soup

3 pints good brown stock	1 onion
1 oz. butter or dripping	Stick of celery
	Blade of mace
	Seasoning
2 oz. coarse oatmeal	

Put the dripping into a pan and allow it to become smoking hot. Fry the sliced onions and celery in it until brown. Drain away any surplus fat. Add the stock, seasoning and mace, cover and simmer for one hour. Strain on to the oatmeal. Return to the pan, stir and simmer gently for one hour. Serve with small sticks of celery as an accompaniment.

Oatcakes

6 oz. medium oatmeal	1 gill water
1 oz. fine oatmeal	Pinch of salt
¼ oz. dripping or bacon fat	¼ teaspoonful bicarbonate of soda

Mix the oatmeals, salt and bicarbonate of soda. Bring the dripping and water to the boil and pour quickly on to the oatmeal, stirring with a knife. Turn on to a board thickly dusted with oatmeal. Divide in half and roll out each half very thinly. Dust well with oatmeal and dry on a warm girdle. Put into a moderate oven to curl. Store in an airtight tin and re-heat if necessary to crisp the oatcakes before serving.

Wheat or Oatmeal Porridge

2 oz. crushed wheat or oatmeal	1 pint milk and water
	Salt to taste

Blend the cereal to a smooth paste with a little of the cold liquid. Boil the rest and pour on to the blended cereal. Return to the pan, stir and boil for ten minutes, add the salt and continue cooking in a double saucepan or in a covered stone jam jar standing in a pan of boiling water. Serve with demerara sugar and milk.

Sweet Oatmeal Bread

1 lb. wholemeal flour	2 teaspoonfuls baking powder
10 oz. cooked oatmeal porridge	4 oz. syrup
1 teaspoonful salt	2 oz. margarine
	1 egg

Mix the wholemeal, salt, and baking powder together, melt the syrup and margarine together. Beat the egg, and add it and the rest of the ingredients to the mixed wholemeal. If the porridge is stiff, add a little milk to bring the mixture to a moist dough. Beat thoroughly, turn into a greased loaf tin and bake at 370° F., for about one hour or until brown and firm. Cool before storing.

Oatmeal and Prepared Oats

Home-made Scotch Haggis

1 sheep's pluck	1 oz. suet
1 cup oatmeal	Pinch of powdered
1 onion of medium	herbs
size	Pepper and salt

Procure a sheep's bag (any butcher will supply one very cheaply), and plunge it into boiling water in which a generous amount of washing soda has been dissolved. Rinse in several lots of cold, salted water, then place in a large pot with plenty of water and bring to the boil. Remove from the pot, scrape the bag carefully with a blunt knife, steep again in cold salted water and leave till next day. Wash the pluck in cold, salted water, and boil for two hours in the pot in which the bag was put, care being taken that the windpipe is left hanging out of the pot, to allow all impurities to escape. Pass the heart and part of the liver through a mincer, then toast one cupful of oatmeal and shred one ounce of suet. Peel and cut a medium-sized onion into small pieces, mix with the heart, liver, oatmeal, and suet, together with a generous pinch of salt, pepper, and a tiny pinch of powdered herbs. Pack into the bag, taking care that it is only half full, to allow for expansion. Sew up carefully, then place in the pot and boil steadily for three hours, pricking the bag from time to time to allow the steam to escape. Serve as hot as possible with mashed potatoes.

Oatmeal Bread

1 lb. oat flour	¾ pint milk
1 lb. household flour	1 oz. fresh yeast
2 oz. sugar	1½ oz. salt

Mix the two flours and salt well together, then warm the milk and dissolve the sugar in it. Allow the sweetened milk to cool, then stir into it a little flour and the yeast, taking care that there are no lumps. Make a hole in the centre of the flour and pour in the milk mixture. Sprinkle a little flour on top, cover with a cloth and leave in a warm place until the yeast has risen, after which knead well. Place the dough in two floured tins, and set in a warm place to rise until it is double its size. Bake in a hot oven for one hour.

Oatmeal Biscuits

¼ lb. fine oatmeal	½ teaspoonful baking powder
5 oz. flour	
4 oz. butter	½ teaspoonful salt
1 egg	Water

Rub the butter into the flour with the tips of the fingers, then add all the other ingredients, excepting the egg. Mix to a stiff dough with the egg, well beaten, and a little water, turn on to a floured board, roll out to ½ in. thickness and prick well with the point of a fork. Cut into rounds or squares, place on a greased tin and bake in a moderate oven for 20 minutes.

He says: "It's good"

and YOU know these jolly grains help him grow big and bonny

SMALL bonny boys, lively as crickets, and their mothers' worry and joy, need good food — nourishing, appetizing, easily assimilated food — that they may grow big and strong and healthy.

Not a little man but loves Quaker Puffed Wheat and Puffed Rice. He just says "It's good!" and loudly calls for more. You tell him little boys should eat nicely — but in your heart you're delighted that such wholesome food is fun to eat as well as so good for little people.

Quaker Puffed Wheat and Puffed Rice are so good to eat because they are rich grains, containing abundantly the precious carbohydrates which are so easy to assimilate. Puffed Wheat has also the bran to keep little organs

working healthily. Each grain of wheat and rice is *steam-exploded to 8 times normal size*, so that every cell is broken, every atom made easy to digest.

Children and grown-ups alike— everyone loves the crisp, toasty deliciousness of Puffed Wheat and Puffed Rice. Serve these delicious nut-flavoured cereals often. Puffed Rice, heaped in a fluffy pile with cream for lunch — and either of these delicious foods taken with hot milk, as a light, nourishing supper.

Ask your grocer for Puffed Wheat and Puffed Rice to-day. Each full-size packet is only 8d. Send a post-card for samples to Quaker Oats Limited (Dept. P1), 11, Finsbury Sq., London, E.C.2.

Steam-exploded to 8 times normal size

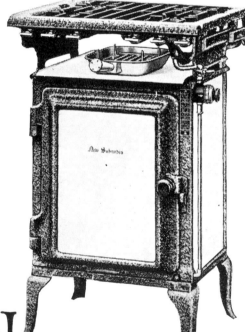

WHY CHANGE YOUR BUTCHER?

"Have you changed the Butcher, Mother? This is the nicest meat I have tasted for a long time, so tender and juicy."

"No, my dear, but I have changed our Gas Cooker for a PARKINSON NEW SUBURBIA, fitted with the PARKINSON Oven Heat Control. You can only get this Oven Control on the PARKINSON Cookers, and it saves me a lot of time, watching and standing over the Cooker these warm days. It cooks by itself and, as you say, improves the flavour of the meat."

See this wonderful Cooker at the local Gas Company's Showrooms, or write for illustrated Catalogue "G."

The PARKINSON NEW SUBURBIA GAS COOKER

THE PARKINSON STOVE CO., LTD., STECHFORD, BIRMINGHAM
London Showrooms : **8 & 10 GROSVENOR GARDENS, S.W.1**
and at **GLASGOW, MANCHESTER, BELFAST, DUBLIN**

Canned Foods are Safe Foods

THE average housewife relies to an ever-increasing extent on canned foods—meat, fish, fruit, and vegetables—as an easy way of relieving the monotony of her menu, but chiefly she regards them as an invaluable stand-by in any of the hundred and one crises in culinary affairs which are liable to crop up in the best regulated households.

She can, with the utmost confidence and assurance, use these concentrated harvests of land and sea as integral items in her daily catering because

Recent Scientific Research proves conclusively that :

(1) CANNED FOODS, such as salmon, herrings, sardines, lobster and meats, etc., far from suffering diminution of food value, are for the most part actually superior to their fresh prototypes in body-building and heat-producing elements, and digestible constituents. This statement is evident when it is realised that waste parts such as bone, shell, etc., are entirely eliminated and only the best of the food is preserved.

(2) CANNED FRUITS of all kinds possess the full food value of fresh fruit. The valuable natural fruit acids and salts are not deteriorated by the heating process, while—a most important point—the flavour is fully conserved.

(3) CANNED VEGETABLES, such as tomatoes, peas, beans, spinach and asparagus, etc., retain their vitamin content intact.

Experience proves that Modern Meticulous Methods of Harvesting, Selection, Preparation, and Canning guarantee absolute safety.

It is interesting to note that in an address to the Provision and Canned Goods Trade Sections of the London Chamber of Commerce in 1922, Sir William Willcox stated that in the provisioning, during the War, of five million troops over a period of four years, not one single case of poisoning occurred from food being infected in the unopened tin.

Common Sense Approves the Economy

of time and labour in preparation, storage space, and time and bother in shopping, as well as commending the fact that the canning principle brings foodstuffs to the larder *in season and out of season*.

Canned Foods are foods in their best condition preserved so that they may be available at all times and in all seasons. It goes without saying that if these foods could be obtained by the consumer in their fresh state in perfect condition, and could be handled by him so that no deterioration took place before being eaten, this would be preferable, but it is precisely because the above ideal conditions are only attainable to a comparatively small extent, that the consumer is so much indebted to, and

in fact, dependent upon the preserving of foods.

FINALLY, THESE FACTS ARE SUPPORTED IN A REPORT BY THE FOOD COMMITTEE OF THE NEW HEALTH SOCIETY, which consists of the following members :

S. Henning Belfrage, Esq., M.D. (Chairman).

Sir Bruce Bruce-Porter, K.B.E., C.M.G., M.D.

John Campbell, Esq., D.Sc.

Harold M. Chapple, Esq., M.Ch., F.R.C.S.

Ivo Geikie Cobb, Esq., M.D., M.R.C.S., L.R.C.P.

Mrs. D. D. Cottington Taylor, Director, Good Housekeeping Institute.

Sir Kenneth Goadby, K.B.E., M.R.C.S., L.R.C.P., D.P.H.

Sir W. Arbuthnot Lane, Bart., C.B., M.S., F.R.C.S.

Lady Arbuthnot Lane.

Nathan Mutch, Esq., M.D., F.R.C.P.

Professor R. H. A. Plimmer, D.Sc. (Professor of Chemistry in the University of London at St. Thomas's Hospital Medical School).

Sir William Willcox, K.C.I.E., C.B., C.M.G., M.D.

Copies of the Report can be obtained on application either to the Secretary, New Health Society, 39 Bedford Square, W.C.1, or to the Secretary, Canned Goods Trade Section, The London Chamber of Commerce, Inc., 97 Cannon Street, London, E.C.4, 3*d.* each post free.

The Consumption of Canned Foods in the United Kingdom during the year 1928 was upwards of One Thousand Million Tins

ON CHOPS

" Tell me what you eat, and I will tell you what you are."
Brillat Savarin

Here's comfort to newly married men, lodgers, pressmen on night duty, aldermen in reduced circumstances, and all others who have hitherto regarded chops as the British equivalent of chewing gum.

Here's the whole secret of the **chop** superlative!

With this secret even boarding-house keepers can serve a chop as tender, as juicily succulent as the **chef** d'oeuvre of a Cordon Bleu.

Just keep them in Frigidaire's dry, frosty **cold** 2 *days* before cooking —that's all.

But your humble mutton chop shall cut like a pheasant's breast and eat as tenderly. A rich content shall enter in and possess your soul. For in your menage, at any rate, the problem of the chop has been solved —once and for all.

A Frigidaire—the last word in automatic electrical refrigeration—can be installed for a small first payment. Fitted with the exclusive Frigidaire Cold Control, which enables you to make ice cubes, freeze sweets, etc., as quickly as you like. Needs less attention than your wife's vacuum cleaner. Fully automatic. Starts itself, stops itself, oils itself. Costs only a few pence a week to run. But what food! Pure, fresh, appetising, with all the flavour *kept* that "keeping" used to lose! Send in the coupon.

FRIGIDAIRE LIMITED.
(Incorporated in Canada)
Dept. B12, Frigidaire House, Chapter Street, S.W.1

Please send me, without obligation, complete information about Frigidaire.

Name...

Address...

No. in Family...

Offices in all principal towns.

Frigidaire
THE QUIET AUTOMATIC REFRIGERATOR

OVER ONE MILLION FRIGIDAIRES IN USE

Advertising is the consumer's guarantee of merit.

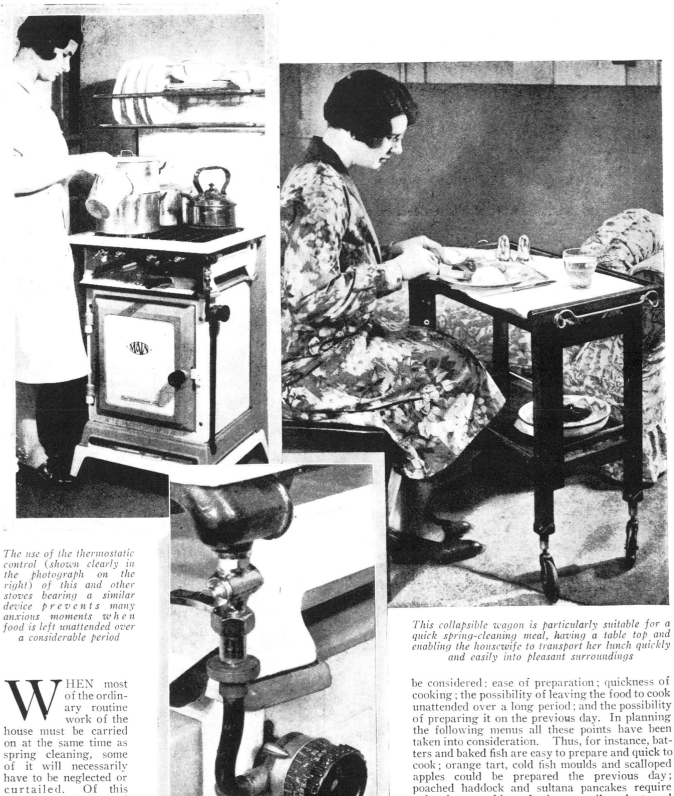

The use of the thermostatic control (shown clearly in the photograph on the right) of this and other stoves bearing a similar device prevents many anxious moments when food is left unattended over a considerable period

This collapsible wagon is particularly suitable for a quick spring-cleaning meal, having a table top and enabling the housewife to transport her lunch quickly and easily into pleasant surroundings

WHEN most of the ordinary routine work of the house must be carried on at the same time as spring cleaning, some of it will necessarily have to be neglected or curtailed. Of this routine, the cooking of meals, although a duty which must not be entirely neglected, can, by careful choice of dishes, be so arranged that much of the time usually spent on it is saved.

In choosing these dishes, four possible ways of effecting the saving of time and labour on the day of spring cleaning should be considered: ease of preparation; quickness of cooking; the possibility of leaving the food to cook unattended over a long period; and the possibility of preparing it on the previous day. In planning the following menus all these points have been taken into consideration. Thus, for instance, batters and baked fish are easy to prepare and quick to cook; orange tart, cold fish moulds and scalloped apples could be prepared the previous day; poached haddock and sultana pancakes require only short cooking; haricot oxtail and stewed kidneys and other dishes can be left unattended over a long period. It would be tedious to mention the category into which each dish in the menus falls, but it will be obvious in glancing at the recipes given at the end of this article how saving of time and labour is effected in each case.

If food is to be given little attention whilst cooking, some special form of equipment is advisable. Many anxious moments will be experienced by the housewife who deposits her lunch in the oven to cook unattended unless she has some indication that the temperature is the one required and that it will remain steady.

Pineapple rice is quickly made
and appetising in appearance

FOOD
Glorious
FOOD

1930

Quick Lunches *for* Spring-Cleaning Time

There are two ways of ensuring this. The first is by using a thermometer and only putting the dishes in when the correct temperature has been registered twice with a lapse of five minutes between the two readings. Thus, supposing a moderate oven of 350° F. is required and the thermometer registers this at 10 a.m., another reading should be taken at 10.5 to ensure that it is going to remain steady at 350° and is not a rising temperature. The alternative method of controlling the temperature of the oven, much in vogue at present, consists of a thermostatic control which is attached to the side of the stove and adjusts the flow of gas into the oven. When the indicator is at "hot," the gas flows freely until a hot temperature is reached and then remains steady. At "slow," the temperature will not rise above that given for a slow oven. This device obviously has great advantages, providing that the person using the stove understands how to adjust the control. The adjustment required varies according to the pressure of gas and other conditions.

There are many other special devices which enable food to "cook by itself" and which have been described in previous numbers of GOOD HOUSEKEEPING; for example, thick-based saucepans which require little or no stirring to prevent burning on the bottom, suitable for stews, milk puddings, and similar dishes; waterless cookers in which the cooking of simple but complete meals can also be carried out over a low gas flame without danger of burning; hay boxes, casseroles, double saucepans, and steamers, all too well known to require extra mention.

In planning the work of a spring-cleaning day, it is usually easier to prepare the food for lunch directly after breakfast, even though it will not be cooked until later. This leaves the morning free to deal with the repairs and renovations and removal of dirt which become necessary yearly.

A Short Course *in* Sweet- & Cake-Making

A short, three-day course in sweet-making and cake-icing will be given at Good Housekeeping Institute, commencing Wednesday, April 23rd.

The course, which should appeal to Domestic Science teachers and others interested in this branch of Cookery, will consist of demonstrations and practical work, the latter being carried out by the students themselves.

The fee for the complete course is £2 2s.

SYLLABUS

The principles of sugar boiling illustrated by the making of a variety of sweets, including fondants, toffees, caramels, candies and fudges, etc.

Soft sweets having a gelatine and starch basis will also be made, e.g. Turkish delight, marshmallow, creams, chocolate centres, and others.

The principles of chocolate-making and dipping.

The icing, frosting and decorating of large and small cakes. The making of Royal, Fondant, American and Glacé icings. Piping and the making of flowers will be demonstrated.

Arrangements can be made for students requiring further tuition, either to have a lesson on Saturday morning, April 26th, or during the following week.

Menus for Spring-Cleaning Lunches

1. Haricot oxtail and macaroni. Pineapple rice.
2. Liver and kidney hot pot. Orange tart.
3. Baked stuffed hake and tomatoes and baked potatoes. Adam's pudding.
4. Vegetable and rice soup. Moulded fish with salad. Steamed raisin pudding.
5. Veal and bacon savoury casserole. Scalloped apples.
6. Poached haddock. Sauté potatoes. Grilled tomatoes. Sultana pancakes.

Haricot Oxtail

1 oxtail	1 pint stock
2 oz. fat	3 oz. macaroni
1 carrot	1 oz. flour
1 turnip	2 oz. haricot beans
1 onion	Seasoning

Soak haricot beans overnight. Cut tail into joints and fry in smoking hot fat. Remove and fry the vegetables. Brown the flour in the fat, and add the stock gradually and bring to the boil. Return the meat, add the haricot beans, season, and continue to simmer very gently on the stove or in a casserole in a moderate oven of 330° F. for 4 to 5 hours. Add macaroni to salted boiling water and cook until tender (about 40 minutes). This can be used as a border if the oxtail is stewed and served on a dish, or arranged on top of the casserole.

Time to prepare oxtail .	20 mins.
Time to cook . .	5 hours.

(Continued)

THE CREAM OF THE MILK
for
Coffee and Cocoa

COFFEE and Cocoa demand the luxury of cream to enrich them and add its mellow flavour to their own.
Serve them with Libby's Milk and its rich creamy consistency will please the most delicate palate.

Cream is at its best IN Libby's Milk, not separated from the other vital substances which make WHOLE MILK the best food in the world.

Libby's Milk has the richness, consistency, flavour and smoothness which make cream so tempting to the appetite.

Use Libby's Milk for every milk and cream purpose; with stewed fruit, for cooking, with coffee and cocoa, and for infant feeding.

Libby's EVAPORATED Milk

LM 5-367

Libby, McNeill & Libby, Ltd.
London

Established 1868

Libby's Milk is recommended as a safe, pure, and easily digestible milk for infant feeding. Thousands of happy mothers praise it.

Write for Pamphlet.

Quick Lunches for Spring-Cleaning Time

Pineapple Rice

2½ oz. rice
1 pint milk
1 egg
½ oz. sugar
1 small tin pineapple chunks

Boil milk in upper part of a double saucepan. Add the rice and sugar. Cook until creamy and soft (about 2 hours over boiling water). Allow to cool slightly, stir in beaten egg and cook for a few minutes longer. Pour into a glass dish and serve hot with pineapple.

Time to prepare . . 10 mins.
Time to cook . . . 2 hours.

Liver and Kidney Hot Pot

2 sheep's kidneys
¼ lb. liver
¼ lb. rashers
1 oz. fat
1 oz. flour
Seasoning
½ pint stock

Wash kidneys and liver and prepare by removing skin and inedible parts. Fry in smoking hot fat. Remove, and brown flour in fat. Gradually add the stock and bring to the boil. Return meat to the pan, add seasoning, and simmer gently or bake in a casserole for 1½ hours or until cooked. Roll the bacon and bake on a skewer in the oven (about 8 minutes) or under a grill. Serve either on a dish or in casserole, garnished with bacon.

Time to prepare hot pot . 10 mins.
Time to cook . . . 1½ hours.
Time to prepare bacon . 5 mins.
Time to cook . . . 8 mins.
(in oven)

Orange Tart

Crust

3 oz. flour
1½ oz. margarine
Salt
Water

Filling

1 yolk egg
4 oz. sugar
2 oz. margarine
Rind and juice of 2 oranges
4 oz. crumbs
Desiccated cocoanut for garnish

Prepare short crust pastry by rubbing fat into flour. Add water until of a stiff consistency. Roll out and line a round plate or small sandwich tin. Mark the edges and prick the bottom. Bake in a hot oven 450° F. with a few beans or rice on greaseproof paper to prevent the bottom from rising unevenly. Remove beans and return the pastry to the oven for a few minutes to dry.

For the filling, put all the ingredients except the egg in a saucepan and heat together. Cool slightly, then beat in the egg and cook gently for about 5 minutes. Put filling in the case and sprinkle with cocoanut.

Time to prepare pastry . 6 mins.
Time to cook pastry . . 15 mins.
Time to prepare filling . 9 mins.
Time to finish tart . . 5 mins.

Baked Stuffed Hake and Tomatoes

½ lb. hake
½ lb. tomatoes
1 oz. dripping

Stuffing

1 teaspoonful crumbs
Egg to bind
1 teaspoonful suet
1 teaspoonful parsley
Grated lemon rind
½ teaspoonful herbs
Seasoning

Make stuffing on the previous day by mixing all the ingredients together and binding with egg. Wash the fish and place in a fireproof dish. Place stuffing on top and put cut slices of tomato around and dot dripping over the top. Bake in a very moderate oven at 320° F. until tender (about 35 minutes).

Time to prepare . . 10 mins.
Time to cook . . . 35 mins.

Adam's Pudding

1 lb. apples
1 egg
2 oz. margarine
2 oz. sugar
2 oz. flour
¼ teaspoonful baking powder
Rind of lemon

Peel, core and chop the apples. Add half the sugar and the lemon rind. Place in a fireproof dish. Then cream margarine and sugar, and add the beaten egg, sieved flour, and baking powder alternately. Place the mixture on top of the apple and bake in a moderate oven 350° F. until well risen and firm. Dredge with sugar and serve hot.

Time to prepare . . 10 mins.
Time to cook . . . 35 mins.

Vegetable and Rice Soup

½ lb. potatoes
1 small onion
1 stick celery
1 small carrot
1 teaspoonful herbs
Parsley
2 pints milk or stock
1 oz. rice

Prepare and cut up vegetables very small and neatly. Sauté them in the fat. Add the stock and milk and bring to the boil. Season and add herbs and parsley, tied in muslin. Add washed rice, and allow to simmer gently until cooked (about 1¾ hours). Remove herb bag, and serve the soup very hot.

Time to prepare . . 10 mins.
Time to cook . . . 2 hours.

Scalloped Apples

½ lb. apples
3 tablespoonfuls white crumbs
1 oz. sugar
Juice and rind of lemon
¼ teaspoonful grated nutmeg
Brown crumbs
1 tablespoonful golden syrup
1 tablespoonful water

Grease a pie dish and line with brown crumbs. Cut the apples in very thin slices and place in a dish alternately with white crumbs, sugar and lemon and nutmeg. Cover with a syrup made from the golden syrup, water and lemon juice. Bake slowly in moderate oven 350° F. about 1 to 1½ hours according to shape of dish and ripeness of apples.

Time to prepare . . 20 mins.
Time to cook . . 1 hour (approx.)

Veal and Bacon Savoury Casserole

½ lb. veal
¼ lb. bacon
1 small turnip
½ lb. potatoes
4 leeks or ¼ bundle celery
1 oz. fat
1 oz. flour
1 pint milk and stock

Cut meat and vegetables in small pieces. Melt the fat in the saucepan, add the flour and seasoning and gradually pour on the stock and milk. Place this sauce, meat and vegetables in a casserole and bake in a moderate oven 350° F. until the meat is tender (about 2 to 2¾ hours), or if preferred, simmer gently on a hot plate.

Time to prepare . . 20 mins.
Time to cook . . . 2¾ hours.

DIPLOMA "RAREBITS"

This wondrous Cheese, beyond compare,
That's honoured in select Mayfair,
Is relished, too, in other scenes
By people of quite modest means!

The 'richer you are the better you fare' can never apply to 'Diploma.' Riches cannot buy better cheese, yet modest purses can afford it because of its economy.

CHEDDAR **DIPLOMA**
The **ENGLISH**
CRUSTLESS CHEESE CHESHIRE

Cheddar or Cheshire. Box of 6, 8 or 12 portions, 1/4½

D 113. Clowes A.A.

1 9 3 0

The Theory of Bottling and Canning

The equipment desirable for home use when preserving fruit and vegetables is discussed on page 42 of the Household Engineering section of this number. Readers who may be experienced in the art of jam making but have not yet attempted home bottling or canning of fruit and vegetables will welcome brief instruction for this. If the work is to be done intelligently the reason for each operation should be known and understood, as otherwise it is apt to become mechanical and insufficient care may be given to some important point.

Everyone is aware that unless they are sterilised, fruits and most vegetables deteriorate comparatively rapidly. This deterioration is due to the action of various micro-organisms, including yeasts, moulds, bacteria, and also ferment or enzyme action. All of these are destroyed by subjecting to heat, but the time and temperature required for complete destruction naturally vary with the different organisms. When bottling and canning, the heat to which the food is subjected not only cooks it but destroys at the same time any bacteria, moulds, etc., which may be associated with it.

In the case of fruits, most of which contain an appreciable percentage of acid and sugar, sterilisation or destruction of these organisms is usually comparatively simple, but vegetables are more difficult to preserve satisfactorily, few of them containing much acid or sugar. Great care and attention to details is therefore essential if the latter are to be bottled satisfactorily. With both, of course, care must be taken to ensure that after sterilisation precautions are taken against the entry of any fresh organisms. This is ensured by seeing that the covers are all air-tight.

The Method of Bottling

Details of the methods advocated for bottling various fruits vary slightly, but in most cases they are sterilised satisfactorily if heated slowly to a temperature of 180° F.

The jars used are provided with glass lids kept in position by metal clips or with a metal screw band. Rubber washers are placed between the lid and the bottle in order to ensure an airtight seal. As rubber perishes in the course of time, before using the rings should be overlooked carefully. The bottles should be washed thoroughly, first in warm, and then in cold water, and then allowed to drain. They should be packed as tightly as possible with the washed and prepared fruit, tapping the jar gently when filling with soft fruit and using the handle of a wooden spoon or a special packing stick for hard stone fruit, such as plums or greengages.

When packed the bottles should be

GOOD HOUSEKEEPING COOKERY FOLIOS

The small illustrated cookery folios listed below have been published by Good Housekeeping Institute. These give detailed instructions on various branches of cookery, and can be obtained from Good Housekeeping Institute, 49, Wellington Street, Strand, London, W.C.2, price 6d each, or 7½d including postage.

1. *The Making of Jams and Jellies, Pickles, Chutneys and Fruit Bottling. Detailed instructions and recipes.*

2. *Food in Relation to Health.* A reprint of the lectures and demonstrations given at the Institute on Food Values and Diet.

3. *Pies and Pastry Making.* The making of shortcrust, flaky, rough puff, puff and hot water crust pastries are given, with numerous recipes for pastry dishes.

4. *Lessons in Cake Making.* Directions and recipes for making cakes by different methods, (a) rubbing fat into flour, (b) creaming butter and sugar, (c) sponge mixtures, (d) girdle scones and cakes, and (e) meringue making.

filled with cold water or syrup to within ½ in. or so of the top. Fruit bottled in syrup has a better flavour and the sugar is also helpful in preserving it satisfactorily. For most fruits a syrup of suitable density is prepared by dissolving 1 lb. sugar in 2 pints water. Bring to the boil, remove any scum and cool. After covering the fruit either with water or syrup, covers and clips should be placed in position, or if screw top jars are used, the bands loosely screwed on.

Sterilising the bottles

For sterilising, the bottles require to be placed either in a special steriliser, such as that described in the article on page 42 or in a boiler or bath. If an ordinary boiler is used the bottom should be covered with wooden slats or several thicknesses of brown paper in order to obviate cracking of the glass. The heat should be gradual and from 1½ to 1¾ hours taken to raise the temperature to 180° F., the water being kept at this temperature for 15 minutes in order to ensure satisfactory sterilisation. The jars should then be removed from the boiler or steriliser and if screw top ones have been used, firmly screwed up. Next day the metal clips or bands should be removed and the bottles tested to see whether they are air-tight.

Preserving vegetables

As already mentioned, vegetables are more difficult to preserve satisfactorily on account of their lack of natural acidity and sugar. In addition, root vegetables are contaminated with soil and soil bacteria. The latter are often of the spore-producing variety, and these being specially resistent to heat are often extremely difficult to destroy. Young fresh vegetables should be selected, and after washing and suitable preparation varying with the kind of vegetable used, they should be loosely packed in bottles. The tight packing of vegetables is a mistake, as the liquid in which they are preserved is apt to become cloudy and tight packing makes it more difficult for heat to penetrate satisfactorily. The method of sterilisation varies to a certain extent, but in many cases the addition of lemon juice and salt to the water is advocated. The advantages of this are that the flavour is often improved, white vegetables do not become a bad colour, and the lack of natural acidity is compensated. This is an aid to successful preservation.

In one of the publications of the Ministry of Agriculture and Fisheries, the addition of 2½ oz. salt and 5 fluid oz. of brine to every gallon of water is advocated for the preservation of vegetables. These are added to the boiling water and when cool, the packed jars covered and placed in the steriliser in the same way as for fruit preservation. It is, however, necessary to heat them to a higher temperature and the water in the steriliser should be brought to boiling point and kept at this temperature for not less than 1½ hours. If the jars are not completely covered with liquid on removal from the vessel used for sterilising, they should be covered with more boiling, acidified brine solution and the sterilising continued for a further 20 minutes. Other methods of preserving vegetables include intermittent sterilising, when the bottles are kept at boiling temperature for one hour and the whole process repeated on three successive days, thus ensuring the destruction of all spores.

Vegetables are sterilised more rapidly by subjection to a higher temperature under pressure: but few housewives preserve in sufficient quantities to justify expenditure on the necessary equipment for this.

Any reader who is interested will find further details of the methods and also detailed instruction for different fruits and vegetables in the Ministry of Agriculture and Fisheries' publication referred to above.

Illustrations by Frank Rogers

The soup plate sat on the shelf among the noisy crowd who had taken his brothers' and sisters' places

The Story of a

THERE was once a soup plate named Simon, and he was the last one left of his set. All his brothers and sisters had been broken. But still he stood on the dresser shelf, as young and fresh-looking as on the day he was bought.

Of course a lot of new soup plates had come and taken the places of his brothers and sisters, but Simon found the newcomers a noisy, highly-coloured crowd.

" Too much pattern about them," he would say to himself, but he never said it aloud.

Simon himself was quiet and refined. He was a deep cream shade with a thin gold line round his edge and in the centre of him a gold crest. Sometimes, when there was extra company to dinner and not enough patterned soup plates to go round, Simon was taken down and placed with the others on the dining table. On these occasions he found he was never placed before the lady nor the master of the house, nor any of the guests, as in former days when his brothers and sisters were with him, but always before little Miss Gray, who was secretary to the master.

Simon liked little Miss Gray. She was quiet and refined, like himself. She

always drank her soup daintily, and touched him gently with her spoon, and did not tip him all on one side to get the last of the soup. Simon did not like people to tip him all on one side. It was so undignified. Besides it made him giddy.

The only part of a dinner party that Simon disliked was afterwards, when he was jumbled up with all the other noisy, chattering soup plates and given a bath in the sink. Not that he disliked baths. Simon liked them very much, but he would have preferred to take his in peace and quietness, with plenty of clean hot water. But once the bath was over, and he was dry and shining again and comfortably back in his place on the dresser shelf, he would settle down with a sigh and have a nice long think to himself. All around him the other soup plates would be giggling and chattering and whispering and telling each other what they had noticed at the dinner table that evening, and how Ruby, the clumsy kitchen-maid, had nearly dropped one of them again; while Simon would be thinking to himself in short sentences (he always thought in short sentences as he found it easier to think that way): " My bath water was too hot to-night. I hope I don't get a chill. Ruby nearly dropped me. She is careless. Her hands are

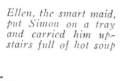

Ellen, the smart maid, put Simon on a tray and carried him upstairs full of hot soup

clumsy. I like Miss Gray. I am sorry for her. Her eyes looked tired. She looked sad. She only drank half her soup. . . ."

In the wall by the kitchen window there was a cupboard about which all the dresser folk were very curious. For the inside of this cupboard was a mystery. Nobody knew what was kept inside it. The position of the cupboard made it impossible for anyone on the dresser side of the room to see inside—and so, of course, all sorts of stories had grown up around it. Some said one thing and some said another.

The romantic little pepper-pot said she had heard there were fairies inside the cupboard! The squat, good-tempered salt-cellar said he

believed it was full of bags of macaroni! A large oval plate with a voice as big as himself said, " Rubbish! I believe it's full of precious silver and gold."

" Well, how is it we never see anything taken *out* of the cupboard?" asked all the teacups together.

The oval plate couldn't answer that. " Wait till spring-cleaning!" he used to say.

But when spring-cleaning time came nobody on the dresser saw anything be-

By Marion St.

Simon disliked his bath at the sink, with the risk that Ruby, the clumsy-fingered kitchen-maid, would drop him

Soup Plate

The romantic little pepper-pot believed that inside the mysterious kitchen cupboard lived fairies

John Webb

cause they were all taken down and carried into another room while the kitchen was washed and scrubbed, and when they were brought back the cupboard had been done and was fast closed as usual.

The oval plate's remark about silver and gold set Simon thinking. He had heard that he had some distinguished relatives somewhere, and he fell to wondering whether it might not be that his old Great-Grandfather the Silver

"My Lady wore the emerald ring last night," said Ellen. "She wouldn't have lost it for anything—and now it isn't there!"

Soup Tureen was kept away in the cupboard by the window. He could remember, years back, his brothers and sisters talking about this wonderful Great-Grandfather who was only seen on great occasions. Simon had never seen him; evidently there had been no occasion great enough in Simon's time to bring the Great-Grandfather out.

The kitchen table, who stood in the middle of the room and could see everything, used sometimes to give a titter and say, "I can see inside the cupboard! I can see through a crack! . . . It's all full of old broken china things waiting to be mended!" and she would chuckle away to herself.

But, as everybody knew, the kitchen table always exaggerated everything and was always making silly jokes. So nobody believed her. Besides, they didn't want to.

One evening, Ellen, the smart maid who waited at table, took Simon down from his shelf and put him on a tray; then she poured some hot soup into him and carried him upstairs to one of the bedrooms. Simon saw Miss Gray sitting by a gas fire. She wore a dressing-gown and looked very pale and ill.

When the maid had gone away she tried to eat a little of the hot soup that Simon held so temptingly in front of her. But she couldn't. Putting her spoon down she covered her face with her hands and began to cry.

Simon felt very sorry for her. He wished he could do something to comfort her. But what can a soup plate do? He waited patiently.

Presently he heard Miss Gray say between her sobs: "If *only* I had fifty pounds of my own!" Then she went on crying.

Simon waited patiently, and the

soup he was holding gradually grew colder and colder. . . .

Ellen came and carried the tray away, and after Simon had had a nice hot bath he was put back on his shelf again. He settled down to think.

"The water was just right to-night," he thought. "Not too hot. Not too cold. I'm glad Ruby didn't drop me. Her hands are very clumsy. I like Miss Gray. I wonder why she was crying. She didn't drink her soup at all. She looked ill. And very sad. I wonder why she wanted fifty pounds?"

Then he became aware that there was a great deal of noise and chatter and excitement going on around him. Not only on the dresser, but between Ruby and Ellen and Cook. They all seemed to be talking about a ring—an emerald ring.

"My Lady said she wouldn't have lost it for anything," said Ellen. "You know—it's that one she wears on her middle finger—the big green emerald."

"The one her mother gave her—I know," nodded Cook.

"My Lady wore it last night," went on Ellen, "and when she took it off she put it in her jewel case, and now to-night when *(Continued)*

"The ring!" cried Miss Gray, pointing at the broken soup-plate. "My Lady's ring!"

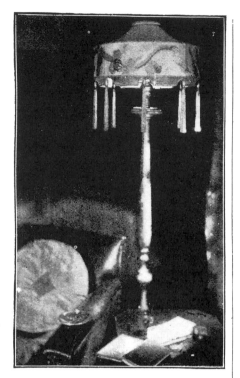

The Story of a Soup Plate

she goes to put it on again—it isn't there!"

They went on talking with growing indignation, and Simon gathered that this was because the maids had been told they were to go up to the Master's library as he wanted to ask them a few questions.

"He suspects that one of us may know something about how the ring got lost!" said Ellen.

"The idea!" exclaimed Cook angrily.

"Cheek!" said Ruby.

But by and by they all went out of the kitchen and in spite of the noise going on around him on the dresser, Simon settled down to think again. Of course the other soup plates and the cups and saucers and dishes were all talking about the lost emerald ring. But what did they know about it! Simon preferred his own thoughts.

The next morning the kitchen was buzzing with the news that the Master had offered fifty pounds reward to anyone who should find the ring and return it to My Lady.

Fifty pounds! The words seemed familiar to Simon. He thought a while. Ah, of course—it was just what Miss Gray wanted to make her stop crying!

He wished Miss Gray could find the ring and get the fifty pounds.

That evening there was a big dinner party and Simon was taken down and piled with the other soup plates.

As the hot soup was being poured into him Simon heard a slight *chink,* and felt something solid resting on his chest. What could it be?

While he was being carried from the sideboard to the table he tried hard to make out what it was. . . . And then he became aware that it was a ring—a small gold ring with a large emerald stone!

Before Simon could recover from his surprise he found himself once more on the table in front of Miss Gray. She had come down to dinner that evening, but she still looked very pale and ill.

When Simon realised that the missing emerald ring was actually resting there on his chest, hidden from Miss Gray's eyes by the thick soup, he began to feel very excited. Here was the ring, under Miss Gray's very nose! Here was her opportunity to win fifty pounds! And the chances were that she would only take one spoonful of soup and leave the rest to be taken away—and so she would never discover the ring at all. He waited anxiously. . . .

Simon was right about the spoonful of soup. Miss Gray took one spoonful, then placed the spoon back on the soup plate and allowed it to remain there. She had not seen the ring, but had turned her head and was talking to her next-door neighbour.

Simon grew desperate. What could he do? He wanted so badly to help poor Miss Gray.

He thought for a few moments.

And then he remembered a little trick that one of his brothers had shown him, but that he had never dared to try after seeing what had happened to his brother when he had tried it. Simon remembered that he knew the way to stretch himself so that he would *crack in half!* It was easier to do after very hot liquid had been poured over you, his brother had said. Simon thought of his brother. He thought of his own smooth cream surface. It seemed such a pity to spoil all that glossy creaminess and the beautiful gold crest on his chest with an ugly crack. Besides, what would become of him afterwards?

Simon hesitated. No, he felt he couldn't

make such a sacrifice. It was too much.

Then he looked up and saw Miss Gray's sad white face—and his kind heart urged him on.

Suddenly the guests around the dinner table were startled to hear a loud, sharp CRACK!

Right across Miss Gray's soup plate a huge crack had appeared.

And so thoroughly had Simon done his job that the soup was leaking rapidly through on to the table cloth.

Ellen, the maid, darted forward to the rescue, when all at once Miss Gray gave a little scream and pointed with a shaking finger to the soup plate.

"The ring!" she cried. "There's My Lady's ring!"

My Lady rose, pale and trembling. There was a stir round the table, and everybody stood up, and a buzz of talk began.

But Simon did not notice what was being said. The crack was hurting him too much. As Ellen picked him up he just caught My Lady's words: "Don't throw it away, Ellen. It's the last one left of that beautiful old set. We'll have it mended."

How long he had been lying in the cupboard he could not make out. He looked about him and saw various pieces of china, each piece chipped or cracked in some way or other. Some pieces had been mended, and some had not.

"Where am I?" said Simon aloud.

A deep rich voice from the back of the cupboard answered him. "In the cupboard by the kitchen window! The hospital *we* call it!"

In the cupboard by the kitchen window! Then the kitchen table had told the truth after all! It *was* a cupboard full of broken china.

"You had a nasty accident," said the deep rich voice.

Through the dimness Simon peered. And he saw that the speaker was a big Silver Soup Tureen with a mended handle.

"My Great-Grandfather!" gasped Simon.

"You are right, little Simon," said the deep rich voice. "I am your Great-Grandfather. I have heard about the way you behaved at the dinner table, and how My Lady's emerald ring was found!" He chuckled comfortably. "They said you cracked because your chest was weak! But I knew better. You learnt the trick that all our family know. And you wanted them to find the ring! . . . I am proud of you, little Simon."

Far into the night Simon talked with his Great-Grandfather and learnt many things. Among them that Miss Gray had received the fifty pounds, and was now going about with a happy face because she had been able to send the money to her mother who was ill. Also, Simon learnt that My Lady had said that he himself was to be put on a shelf in her own room, later on, when his crack had stopped aching.

Simon felt very proud and happy to hear this, and when his Great-Grandfather told him that probably his crack would hardly show at all Simon felt even happier still.

"But where had the emerald ring been all the time? How did it get into the soup? How was it lost? Did you hear that, too, Great-Grandfather?" inquired Simon.

"Cook left yesterday morning. She knew all about it," said the Great-Grandfather drowsily. "She took the ring and hid it, and it must have fallen accidentally into the soup."

"Ah!" said Simon, and settled down for a good think.

NOW…at last recaptured

the rare, smooth flavour of old-time cheeses

TIME was not a factor in cheese-making long ago! Months of cool ripening developed and brought the smooth flavour of old-time cheeses to perfection.

For, centuries ago, cheeses were first made in the sweet country dairies of England. Deep, thick walls and stone-flagged floors, wide windows letting the free moisture of the air reach every corner! There for six, nine, ten months, even a year — the cheeses were ripened slowly, carefully. No wonder that their flavour was so round and full and smooth!

But now, those sure leisurely methods which made old-time cheeses famous for delicious smoothness, are almost forgotten! Too often cheese is ripened hurriedly, under high temperatures.

At last, the Kraft Company have found a way to give you that very same rare flavour of the cheeses of long ago. For, owing to the wonderful resources at their command, they have been able to reproduce the long, cool ripening — to allow the full deliciousness of flavour to develop. Following the methods of the old-time dairies — they ripen Kraft Cheese almost three times as long as is the custom nowadays — in cool rooms with air **and** moisture perfectly adjusted.

MELLOWED 3 SEASONS TO GIVE IT THE OLD-TIME DELICIOUSNESS

By a secret method — the same mellow goodness in every single pound

By a wonderful combination of temperature, moisture and air currents, the Kraft Company reproduce the perfect conditions for ripening *always*. A special instrument has been devised — called a Kygrometer, which ensures that through the long months of maturing there is no variation at all from those conditions. This means that every single pound of Kraft has the same perfect texture, mellow smoothness you long for in cheese. Pasteurized and wrapped in tinfoil — Kraft keeps moist and fresh to the last creamy, golden slice!

Like old wine, Kraft Cheese is matured to perfection! It comes in 1-lb. and ½-lb. packets, 5-lb. blocks and Kraftet portions

KRAFT CHEESE
CHEDDAR

Made in England by Kraft Cheese Co., Ltd., Hayes Middlesex

HOUSEKEEPING
ON £1,000 A MINUTE

NIGHT AND DAY THROUGHOUT
THE YEAR WE ARE BUYING FOOD
FROM ABROAD AT THE RATE OF

£1,000	A MINUTE
£10,000,000	A WEEK
£520,000,000	A YEAR

How can you help to secure that this great order goes to
the Empire? By asking your grocer, butcher, and fruiterer
to fill your weekly order with Empire produce. That
will ensure your buying from your own best customers

ASK FIRST ● FOR HOME PRODUCE

ASK NEXT ● FOR THE PRODUCE OF
THE EMPIRE OVERSEAS

Write for a copy of the leaflet, 'Why should we buy from the Empire?', obtainable, post free, on application to the Empire Marketing Board, Westminster
—an official body, on which all the three political parties are represented.

ISSUED BY THE EMPIRE MARKETING BOARD

MAKING THE MOST OF THE KITCHEN GARDEN

III
Vegetables *for the* Gourmet

POTATOES are perhaps not exciting vegetables, but their romance lies in the fact that, as every schoolboy knows, they were introduced into England in the sixteenth century by Sir Walter Raleigh from Virginia, a country to which he never went, of which the potato is not a native, and where it was certainly not grown at the end of the sixteenth century. Potatoes were possibly first grown in Holland, and the best potato from a culinary point of view, the Dutch yellow potato, is still largely grown in that country. Potatoes are little grown in this country for salad, and for such purpose the fir-apple potato is distinctly worth trying. Curious in shape, it is difficult to peel, and a more convenient salad potato is the Hamburg egg-potato. Another interesting variety is Congo (Negress), which, when cooked, is a rich violet and looks very pretty in the salad. *Solanum Commersonnii,* the Uruguay potato, crops up from time to time. Vigorous and free from disease, it has considerable drawbacks in that the roots spread over about ten feet, the tubers are a foot apart, and when you have collected them you find that they have a pronouncedly bitter taste.

Scottish potato seed is indubitably the best and in most gardens it is better to give one's small potatoes to the pigs rather than to save them for seed. For high-class cookery the small potato *Quarantaine de la Halle* is indispensable (perhaps to the same degree as the apple *Calville Blanc* is indispensable to the French chef for apple sauce). Seed is generally scarce, the tubers are small and the yield per acre is low. The soup named after the immortal Parmentier who introduced the cultivation of the potato into France, whence it spread to England, is excellent and in some parts of France piquancy is

obtained by the addition of chopped water-cress.

There are many salad chicories, but the most interesting variety of *Cichorium Intybus* is *Witloof.* The cultivation of this vegetable was originally confined to Belgium, but it is now largely grown in France in the neighbourhood of Paris. The usual plan is to plant the trimmed crowns in trenches, and the crowns are forced as required by being covered with manure to a depth of some twenty inches. In a fortnight the manure can be moved to the next section and the exposed crowns, with their growths, covered with matting. *Witloof* is ready for cutting in about a month from starting the crowns. In Paris it is also grown in dark cellars at a temperature of about 58° F. In England it is grown as and along with seakale.

Of *Aralia cordata*, "Les Plantes Potagères" remarks: "It is one of the few Japanese vegetables that merit in-

Illustration

By

B. H. Follet

troduction into Europe." Called *Udo* in Japan, there are two principal varieties in cultivation—*Kan* (winter) and *Moyashi* (malt or late). *Kan* is cultivated like seakale and *Moyashi* like rhubarb. The stools are remarkably prolific, and *Kan,* forced and bleached, can be cut from ten weeks. It should be cooked *à la crème* and has a slight aromatic taste. Largely grown in Japan and China, it was introduced by Dr. Fairchild into America, where it has established itself; the Yokohama Nursery will supply stools which rapidly increase by division.

Fennel in this country usually suggests mackerel; this is the common fennel. In Southern Europe two plants are grown which appear to be merely varieties of *Foeniculum vulgare,* but have received the specific names of *officinale* (Allioni) and *dulce* (Miller). The first is sweet fennel, *Carosella,* and forms a large self-bleaching heart which is eaten raw as hors-d'œuvre; the latter is the well-known Florentine fennel, *Finoochio di Firenzi;* other varieties are grown near Bologna and in Sicily. Sown in rows it merely requires thinning out. When the "heart" is the size of an egg the row should be slightly earthed up, and the crowns will be ready for gathering in a fortnight. The crop is not always satisfactory in England, as there is often considerable loss through bolting. The best plan is to make sowings of seeds of some three or four varieties and at intervals of two to three weeks. It can be braised with veal, or served with melted butter or *au gratin.*

When the gardener sends in the broad-beans, the cook should invariably say she wants them half the size. Baby broad-beans are delicious *à la crème,* the large beans should be skinned before serving.

THE GOODE

Drawings by Elinor Lambert

UPON MY WYNE CUPBOARDE

As molten amber, here
Withyn this box
Are kept the April-tears of Apricocks ;
And here, more cool, more clere
Than Hippocrene,
Is stilled the Nectar of the Nectarine.

UNTO CÆSAR

My Colin hath a tal oake Chaire,
Made of a tal oake tree ;
And in its shaddowe standeth there
A lytell Stoole for me.

My Colin hath of Muggs for Beer,
In polished pewter, three ;
Wyth, tho' I drinke but water clere,
A lytell Mugg for me.

My Colin hath a goodly Presse
Wyth yron haspe and key ;
Yett gave, that I mighte have noe less,
A lytell Presse for me.

My Colin hath a great wide Bedd
Wyth postes carv'd cunninglie ;
And thus refews'd—since we are wed—
A lytell Bedd for me.

" AND ON THE SABBATH THOU SHALT DO NO MANNER OF WORK"

. . . Soe Monday shall be Washing Day ;
On Tuesday shall I bake ;
On Wednesday, brew ;
On Thursday, stewe ;
On Friday, butter-mayke.
I clene my house on Saturday,
But Sunday shall be free . . .
To Churche I goe,
Arraied for show,
And Colin walkes wyth me.

HOUSEWYFE

Poems in the Elizabethan Manner by C. W. D.

COLIN'S BREAKFASTE

Eache day I sett this oaken table here,
At eight o'clock, wyth Breakfaste for my dear ;
When, e'er to see how well my worke is done,
Through mullioned lattice peepes the morning sunne.
Whyle nod the new-waked roses, red and white,
He plays o'er panelled walls wyth golden lighte ;
And ere his greeting beames my Colin wake
These pleasures for his pleasing doe I take :

A linnen table-cloth of broidered mesh,
A patt of yellow butter, salte, and freshe ;
White, creamy milke the cow did yielde at dawne,
And fragrant coffee, newe from berries drawn ;
A ham for Colin's carving, pinke and leane,
With powdered crumbs engarnished, crispely clene ;
A browne egg in a Delften cuppe of blue,
A browne loaf on a wooden platter, too ;
And, that he may the more prefer his home,
A dishe of silverne honey in the combe—
When all at last is sett, and I made neate :
" My Colin, Breakfaste waits thee—come and eat."

UPON MY FEATHER BEDD

As Prewdence shooke
    My Bedd one day
She loos'd a piece
    Of feather grey.
" Have care . . . it tooke,
    Ere I was wedd,
A thousand geese
    To mayke this Bedd."

UPON MY FARMYARDE

I keepe my Farme for Colin's sake,
    Since he is kinde
        But poore.
My wheate for fine browne bread I bake,
    That he may find
        Goode store.
But since playne bread is dull, I trowe,
    And I but come
        To please,
I give him creame from my browne cow,
    And honey from
        My bees.

The Housekeeper's Dictionary *of* Facts

Buy Hygienically Wrapped Foods

—and protect your Family's health

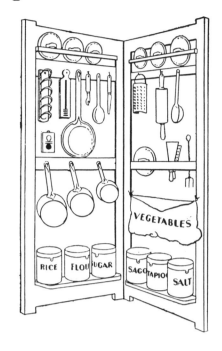

ONE often hears the remark, "Housewives of to-day are too fussy about foods." This alleged fastidiousness is to be encouraged, as one cannot be too particular concerning the condition and quality of foodstuffs. That the modern housewife is cultivating a discerning and almost scientific mind is all for the benefit of the home and the confusion of careless purveyors.

One of the signs of this scientific outlook is a demand for the more hygienic wrapping or protection of confectionery, preserved meat and cooked fish.

The introduction of transparent wrappers was welcomed by the public because it appeared that manufacturers of food products had at last overcome the problem of hygienic handling.

The best of these cellulose or gelatine wrappings are impervious to air, moisture, grease, dust and disease germs. They enable the prospective buyer to examine the food, even handle it, and yet be assured that when previously examined and touched, it was not contaminated. In these days of open shop windows, flies and dust from the streets settle upon foods which are not washed and in many cases are given to children for direct consumption. Every woman is keenly sensitive to this careless and dangerous handling and contamination of vital foods.

A word about these protective wrappers. The most popular variety at the moment is made of almost pure cellulose from spruce pulp or cotton pulp. The method of preparing

A Kitchen Corner in the Bed-Sitting-Room

It is comparatively easy to make a single room serve the united purposes of sitting-room and bedroom, but it is considerably more difficult to equip it satisfactorily to serve also as a kitchen. The construction of a screen such as the one illustrated solves the problem, for on it can be stored kitchen utensils, dry stores, etc., and it may conceal a small table on which cooking preparations can be made. Choose a wooden screen with two folds each measuring about 5 feet by 2 feet, enamel the inside white and fit several cross-bars, into which are screwed hooks for saucepans and other cooking utensils. A bar at the top holds saucepan lids in place and at the bottom are two small wooden shelves with rounded corners for holding canisters. Potatoes, carrots, turnips or other root vegetables can conveniently be kept in a long narrow bag suspended from two hooks.

The outside of the screen can be decorated to harmonise with the general colour scheme of the room, and in order to open it more easily castors should be attached to the outside corners

the cellulose is similar to that employed in the manufacture of viscose artificial silk. The thinness of the manufactured sheets is really amazing, about nine ten-thousandths of an inch being the usual substance. The wrappings may be printed or coloured according to desire. Nearly all the operations in the production of these delicate tissues are done by machine so as to avoid handling and possible contamination. They are admirably suitable for packing cakes, bread, nuts, sausages, bacon, cheese, cooked and cured fish, puddings, etc.

Another kind of wrapping consists of a gelatine which has been rendered insoluble so as to be unaffected by moisture and warm air. These gelatine tissues are indistinguishable from those made of cellulose, although at the moment the latter are more popular.

It is of interest to note that a recent patent provides for the covering of fruit with a special cellulose envelope. In this case the cellulose is not loose but is attached rather closely to the skin of the fruit. Unripened fruits may be suitably coated and allowed to ripen during transit, and in this way fresh apples and pears particularly full of flavour may be obtained. Apples, pears, plums, peaches, and even pineapples have been successfully treated in the above manner.

A doubt sometimes creeps into the minds of the more cautious people who see foods wrapped in these fresh, artistic tissues. They like the effect but fear the food may in some way be tainted with injurious chemicals. It is satisfactory to note that both cellulose and gelatine wrappers are guaranteed by the makers to be absolutely free from all traces of undesirable chemicals.

STURMERS

WORLD-FAMOUS FOR FLAVOUR

—*just as if you'd picked them yourself in* SUNNY TASMANIA

Apples from the other side of the world—yet crisp and fresh as if they'd been picked yesterday! Tasmanian apples and pears arrive just when we need them—before our own harvest is ready. Shipped in modern cold storage—not frozen—all their sun-fed goodness is retained and their flavour is perfect. Your fruiterer has them now and there will be fresh shipments every week for the next month or two.

BRITISH TO THE CORE

TASMANIAN APPLES

Issued by the Commonwealth of Australia

THE SUN ON THE HEARTH

So let it be a gas fire...

A BEDROOM isn't always comfortable in winter merely because it has a fire. That fire may produce smoke and dust; it may die down when it ought to burn up; it may make the room too warm or not warm enough; it may fail to provide good ventilation ....

A gas fire has none of these faults. It is as free from smoke as it is from dust. Completely under your control, it gives you instantly just the warmth you need .... It ventilates the room perfectly.

Moreover, when the budget is considered as a whole, gas is easily the most truly economical fuel.

So let it be a gas fire in each room this winter .... Order before the rush. Write, telephone or visit your gas showrooms and

Order your Gas Fires now

for summer warmth in winter weather

Which are your favourite English fruits

?

Blackberries?

Blackcurrants?

Cherries?

Gooseberries?

Loganberries?

Plums?

Raspberries?

Redcurrants?

Strawberries?

Thanks to a great new industry which has grown up in the past five years you can now enjoy them all the year round, canned within a few hours of picking and with all their natural freshness and flavour unimpaired.

To this new industry has been applied the new public service of the National Mark which, operated under Government supervision, makes it easy to identify the genuine home-grown product in the shops and also guarantees its quality.

Fresh picked peas, beans, carrots, celery, new potatoes, turnips, spinach, beetroots, and macedoine of vegetables are also canned under the National Mark.

Ask for

NATIONAL MARK

Canned English Fruits and Vegetables

Look for the Mark

on the Can

The finishing touch to an informal luncheon or dinner party is given by the serving in attractive glasses of one of the home-made liqueurs for which recipes are given in this article

Home-made *LIQUEURS*

By Anne Benshaw

WHO does not appreciate the added zest which a glass of liqueur gives to the after-dinner or after-luncheon coffee? Even those who have no palate for wines succumb to the syrupy tang of these strangely-flavoured drinks, and every informal party may be crowned with perfection by the serving of a bewildering range of them without extravagance too, if they are made at home.

Man, conservative ever, may scoff at home-made concoctions and stick to the austerity of chartreuse, benedictine or brandy, but woman, adventurous, likes to experiment in search of novelty and economy. Besides, the making of liqueurs provides an interesting change from jam-making and fruit-bottling. Almost all the fruits in season may be made into exciting liqueurs and a pound or two filched from the preserving-pan will not be regretted. Also, it is perhaps not generally realised in England what miracles of flavouring can be performed by the judicious use of liqueurs in cooking. A Frenchman once told me that his sister concocts a *compôte des fruits* in which she blends as many as ten different liqueurs—and her husband, on tasting the result, identifies them all.

Of course, the modern maker of liqueurs does not attempt the elaborate distillation process at which our grandmothers excelled, and for which the still-room existed. We buy our spirits from the wine-merchant, and, though naturally the finest brands give the finest results, it must be admitted that, to the ordinary palate, the fruit flavour will hide any lack of mellowness and bouquet.

Cherry Brandy

One pound of Morello cherries are stoned and picked over carefully, packed into a wide-mouthed jar with one pound of loaf sugar or 6 oz. of crushed sugar candy, and the crushed kernels from one-third of the cherries; cover this with brandy, keep well corked for three months and stir occasionally. The liqueur is then strained and bottled.

Damson Gin

This is made in similar fashion, using damsons and covering with gin. The damsons should be stoned and about sixteen damson kernels added to every pound of fruit and ¾ lb. crushed sugar candy.

Strawberry Whisky

This is a delightful liqueur, and is prepared by simmering together for 30 minutes a pound of strawberries and half a pound of lump sugar. Then strain, add a pint of whisky, 1 tablespoonful of lemon juice, 3 cloves, and leave for four or five months. Strain again and bottle.

Fruit Ratafias

All the soft fruits, red currants, black currants, raspberries, mulberries, may be used to make delicious fruit ratafias. To every 2 lb. of fruit allow ¼ lb. sugar. Prepare the fruit in the usual way, crush and sprinkle with the sugar and leave for 24 hours. Press out the juice, measure it and put into a stone bottle. To every pint of fruit juice add a quarter of a pound of sugar, a few cloves and a little cinnamon. After standing for a month, strain and bottle.

Apricot Brandy

Cut a dozen apricots in small pieces, crack the stones, peel and bruise the kernels, then put the latter with the fruit into a jar with a pint of brandy, half a pound of sugar, and two or three cloves. Cover the jar and infuse for a month, shaking frequently. After which strain and bottle.

That despised nursery fruit, the prune, may be treated in the same fashion to give a liqueur of distinctive flavour.

Sparkling "Pyrex" oven-tableware really is a most attractive Christmas gift. Most of us take such a pride in having lovely serving dishes. Washing-up halved too!

Glass cooking dishes are nice to have —

Food straight from oven to table in sparkling glass dishes like costly crystal

•

"PYREX" Pudding Dish (Round) No. 474. Lovely and useful — perfect for a Christmas Pudding. Price 3/6

"PYREX" Entrée Dish (Oval) No. 110. Very popular for entrées, vegetables and fish. Cover can be used as separate dish. Price 7/6

No Christmas present you can possibly give will please more than this lovely oven glassware—something just a little out of the ordinary.

You know yourself how nice it is to have lovely serving dishes. Especially when there are guests. Sparkling "Pyrex" glassware, piping-hot, straight from oven to table; the same beautiful ovenware as used in homes where cost is not counted.

Once a luxury, now with new low "Pyrex" prices you can offer this happiest of all presents at so little cost. And there's a practical side to it as well — washing-up halved, the same clean glass dish

for cooking and serving, no messy pots and pans!

Mothers who have families to cater for, young brides with modern views on housekeeping, bachelor girls — all will be delighted when they unwrap your lovely gift.

Here are some perfect "Pyrex" presents — the Blue Ribbon Gift Set, or even a single "Pyrex" Entrée Dish, or Casserole. Sold at all leading department stores, glass and china and hardware shops. Made in England by an all-British firm. With every piece sold there is a guarantee against breakage from oven heat for 12 months.

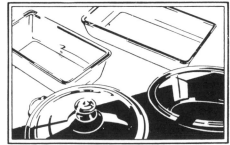

"PYREX" BLUE RIBBON GIFT SET makes a delightful present — lovely dishes for Christmas Day, and all the year. It costs only 16/6, or buy the pieces separately if you like. Four pieces: Round Casserole No. A268, 6/6; Utility Dish No. 231, 3/9; Bread or Cake Pan No. 212, 3/6; Oval Pie Dish No. 404, 2/9

"PYREX" *Ovenware*
(Regd. Trade Mark)

Made at Wear Glass Works, Sunderland, by

James A. Jobling & Co. Ltd.

118

When Baking Rich Cakes

TO prevent cakes which require long baking from becoming scorched and over-cooked, they should be protected by lining the tin with well-greased paper, and by tying several thicknesses of strong brown paper round the outside of the tin. When only small ovens are in use additional pre-caution is afforded by placing the cake on an asbestos board or tray of silver sand.

Preparing Currants and Sultanas

When possible the fruit for cakes and puddings should be washed several days before it is required in order that it may dry. In an emergency, however, it can be dry cleaned by sprink-ling generously with flour and rubbing over a sieve, when the stalks and any particles of dust fall through. Fruit—currants in particular—which are small and shrivelled, may be improved considerably by steaming. Place in a colander and put over a saucepan of boiling water. A few minutes are sufficient to cause the fruit to swell.

A Jelly Tip

Quite a novel Lemon Jelly can be made if ginger beer is used instead of water for dissolving the jelly. Exactly the same method should be followed, ex-cept that instead of water one pint of ginger beer should be boiled and added to the jelly.

Cream from Butter

The following is a new tested recipe for making cream from butter:

4 oz. salt-free	4 whites of eggs
butter	Little vanilla
3 oz. sieved icing	essence
sugar	Small pinch of salt

Melt the butter slowly and skim if necessary. Allow to get nearly cold, but not setting. Whisk the whites of eggs to a stiff froth so that they stand up in sharp points, and gently fold in the icing sugar, vanilla essence and a small pinch of salt. Then add the butter drop by drop, whisking hard all the time.

This cream may be used in all cases where real cream is used, but is not so liquid in consistency.

Baked Ham

Ham that is partly boiled and partly baked makes a change from one that is cooked entirely in boiling water. Weigh the ham, and allow 20 minutes to each pound and 20 minutes over. Soak it overnight and boil for half the required cooking time. Then take it out from

The Christmas Menu

Cream of Corn Soup
Roast Turkey.   Chestnut Stuffing.   Cranberry Sauce
Boiled Ham.
Stewed Celery   Roast Potatoes
Mince Pies   Christmas Pudding
Brandy Sauce
(See recipes for soup, stuffing and sauces on right)

Preparations to be made on Christmas Eve

Check the tradesmen's orders, all of which should have been given not later than the previous day.

Soak the ham in cold water; clean and stuff the turkey and leave ready for roasting.

Stew the giblets for gravy; make and bake the mince pies; make the cranberry sauce.

Preparations on Christmas Day

Cover the ham with cold water and simmer gently for the time required, allowing about 20 minutes to every pound and 20 minutes over.

Put the turkey into a slow oven of 400° F., lowering after 15 minutes to a temperature of about 340° F., which should be maintained throughout the whole of the cooking process. Baste the bird frequently.

For a turkey weighing from 10 to 13 lb. three hours should be allowed for cooking, or from 13 to 16 lb. three and a half hours, from 16 to 20 lb. four hours.

Prepare the vegetables, and put the pudding on to boil; make soup; make brandy sauce.

Put the water on for cooking vegetables; heat up cranberry sauce and cook the sausages. Warm plates and dishes, dish ham, skin it, sprinkle with bread-crumbs and decorate with a frill.

Dish turkey, remove string and place sausages round, then make the gravy, using stock from the giblets.

Dish up vegetables and sauces, heat up mince pies.

Turn out Christmas Pudding, and if liked pour over brandy and light it.

the water and allow it partly to cool. Make a paste with flour and water, and cover the ham entirely with this. It should be about half an inch thick, and should be kept in position by tying with string or by tying the whole ham in muslin. Then place in a moderate oven and bake for the remainder of the time. Remove the paste when the ham is cooked and return it to the oven for a few minutes to crisp it very slightly. Sprinkle with breadcrumbs and send to the table.

Unsweetened Evaporated Milk

The usefulness of sweetened con-densed milk is recognised by most housewives, but there are many that do not appreciate the possibilities of un-sweetened evaporated milk. This can be used to enrich innumerable dishes, both savoury and sweet, and is excellent for the making of soups and sauces, giving the dishes the flavour of fresh cream. It can be bought in tins from 3½d.

Cream of Corn Soup

1 large tin of corn
1½ pints water
1½ pints milk
2 oz. margarine
1 oz. flour
½ a small onion
1 teaspoonful salt
Pepper and chopped parsley

Cook the corn and onion in the milk and water, rub through a wire sieve, melt the margarine, cook the flour in it, but do not allow it to brown, and gradually add the sieved corn. Boil for about 10 minutes, season and serve in tureen with a little chopped parsley on top.

Chestnut Stuffing

1½ lb. chestnuts
¾ lb. sausage meat
3 oz. butter
4 oz. breadcrumbs
Seasoning and stock

Wash the chestnuts, cut a slice from the top of each, using the point of the knife. Place in a saucepan and cover with water, and boil for a few minutes. A few at a time should be taken from the water and the shell removed, using a pointed knife. Cover the shelled nuts either with stock or milk and simmer till they are cooked, and all the liquid has been absorbed. Rub through a sieve, add the rest of the ingredients to the purée and season to taste.

Cranberry Sauce

1 lb. cranberries
1–2 gills water
4 ounces sugar

Wash the cranberries and add the water. Stew until cooked, stirring and pressing the fruit from time to time. Sweeten with the sugar, to be added when the fruit is cooked.

Hard Brandy Sauce

2 oz. castor sugar	4 oz. fresh butter
2 dessertspoonfuls	1 tablespoonful
brandy	ground almonds

Cream the butter and sugar until light-coloured and frothy, then beat in the almonds. Keep cool until required and just before serving add the brandy.

The quantities given in the recipes would be suitable for eight or nine people.

NOTE TO READERS

The Institute is not only ready to answer readers' household or cookery questions, but their own solutions of domestic diffi-culties are gladly received. A small fee will be paid for any published.

FOOD *Glorious* FOOD

1932

Department of Cookery

Good Housekeeping Institute
49 Wellington Street, Strand, W.C.2.
Conducted by
D. D. Cottington Taylor
Certificate of King's College of Household and Social Science; First Class
Diplomas in Cookery, High Class Cookery, Laundrywork, Housewifery, A.R.S.I.

The First Meal of the Day

The value of cereals as a breakfast food

A LIGHT breakfast of cereals, fruit and coffee is becoming increasingly popular in this country, and manufacturers vie with one another in the variety of ways in which the different grains are treated and prepared for the table.

Barley, wheat, oats, corn, rice and rye are nearly all available not only in the uncooked condition, but also cooked and semi-cooked. Uncooked cereals, as a rule, require fairly prolonged cooking, but if partially cooked, a few minutes only are required to render them ready for the table. Being used largely as breakfast foods, this saving of time in preparation is an important asset, which is still further increased in the case of the completely cooked products which are ready for immediate consumption.

The different kinds of grain in themselves make a change of breakfast food an easy matter, but the possibilities of variety are increased considerably by the fact that most of the grains are available in several forms, including the whole grain, crushed, coarsely and finely milled, flaked and puffed, as well as in many cases malted or partially digested.

The main food constituent of cereals is starch, but most of them contain in addition a proportion of protein, fat, mineral salts, and particularly if manufactured from the whole grain including the bran, a fairly large amount of cellulose, which provides the body with the invaluable " roughage " required for correct intestinal action. Vitamin B is another valuable constituent of grains, as of seeds in general.

During the colder months of the year, especially in the North, oatmeal, which is one of the most nutritious of cereals, has always been appreciated in the form of porridge, and may be taken either as the precursor of the meal proper or as the main dish. Many people, however, find it difficult to give the long, slow cooking required by plain oatmeal, and for this reason usually prefer one of the prepared and partially-cooked products which are now on the market. These are subjected to pressure and steam heat, and in consequence of the pre-cooking during the course of manufacture the actual time required for the final preparation for the table is very much shortened, being in many cases no more than a few minutes.

There are some people who find oatmeal a little indigestible, this being no doubt largely due to the fact that after grinding it is practically impossible to separate the husk, which adheres very closely to the grain. For such people, however, there is a wide choice of preparations made from other grains. Either corn or wheat in the form of flakes, for instance, makes an excellent breakfast cereal served with milk or cream and fruit. One well-known brand of prepared corn flakes is slightly malted, thereby not only rendering digestion easier, but also imparting a pleasant flavour. The firm supplying this also markets an excellent prepared bran, also slightly malted, and usually eaten with milk and possibly a little sugar; if preferred, it may be used to make bran muffins, which are a much appreciated and healthful addition to the tea menu, or a little bran may be mixed with flour for many cooking purposes, such as when making suet pastry, scones, etc.

Barley is available in a number of forms; it contains a particularly large proportion of mineral matter, but only a very small proportion of gluten, and therefore unmixed with wheat flour, cannot be used for successful bread making. Pearl barley, patent barley, barley kernels and cream barley are well-known preparations of this grain. Its demulcent properties are high, and this is one of the valuable qualities of barley water. Incidentally, the easiest and most generally satisfactory way of making this often-ordered drink is from patent finely-powdered barley, which readily makes a very refreshing and not too thick beverage. Like most other cereals, the barley preparations can be used in a variety of unusual ways as well as in the more obvious ones with milk or cream for breakfast or prepared in the form of milk puddings. One or two out-of-the-ordinary suggestions for utilising the various prepared cereals for breakfast are given here.

A few words must finally be devoted to a consideration of wheat, which, in the form of bread, is a staple article of diet. In many cases, unfortunately, in the course of milling, the bran and germ, with their valuable constituents in the form of mineral salts, roughage and vitamins, are removed. However, in wholemeal flour or whole wheat in other forms, these valuable constituents are all conserved.

Shredded and puffed wheat are among the well-known preparations of this grain which will help to make variety on the breakfast table, or these again, with a little ingenuity on the part of the cook, can be used as a basis for an endless variety of nutritious dishes.

A New way with Scrambled Eggs

2 eggs	1 oz. butter
3 tablespoonfuls milk	Pepper and salt Cayenne pepper
1 oz. finely grated cheese	4 tablespoonfuls corn flakes

Beat the eggs, add the milk, finely grated cheese and seasoning. Melt the butter, stir in the beaten eggs, and scramble in the usual way. Meanwhile, warm the corn flakes in the oven and when crisp and hot place in a bed on a hot dish and pile the scrambled egg mixture on top.

For the sake of variety two tablespoonfuls of corn flakes to each egg can be added before scrambling, but those who prefer the crisp flakes should serve them as suggested in the recipe.

To make a more nourishing meal a gammon rasher should be grilled, cut in half and placed immediately on top of the flakes, and the egg piled on it.

By P. L. Garbutt

First Class Diploma King's College of Household and Social Science. Late Staff Battersea Polytechnic

Breakfast cereals as a nutritious and delicious food and as an ingredient in other recipes are becoming increasingly popular

hands and roll into shape. Then fry until golden brown and well cooked. When the sausages are done, stir the corn or wheat flakes into the batter.

Melt a nut of lard in a small frying-pan; when hot pour off the surplus fat and pour in sufficient batter to cover the bottom of the pan. Cook on both sides, turn on to a piece of kitchen paper, place one piece of sausage on each pancake and roll up. Continue until all the batter is used.

Fried Eggs with Corn Flakes

Bacon fat	6 tablespoonfuls corn
2 eggs	flakes

Fry the eggs in the fat remaining after cooking rashers, or use fresh bacon fat. Baste the eggs frequently with the fat to cook them evenly, and when cooked remove from the pan. Toss the cornflakes in the remaining fat; when hot through put on a plate and serve the fried eggs on top.

Savoury Pancakes

4 oz. flour	3 tablespoonfuls corn or
Good pinch of salt	wheat flakes
1 egg	4–5 sausages
½ pint milk	Nut of lard

Sieve the flour and salt into a basin, make a well in the centre, stir in the beaten egg and add the milk gradually to make a smooth batter. Then beat to introduce air, and allow to stand whilst the sausages are prepared. Remove the sausages from the skins, divide each into two, flour the

Bran and Oatmeal Bannocks

2 oz. wholemeal flour	¼ teaspoonful salt
2 oz. bran	1 heaped teaspoonful baking
2 oz. rolled oats	powder
1½ oz. butter	½ an egg
1 oz. sugar	Little milk to mix

Put the wholemeal, bran and rolled oats into a basin, and rub in the butter with the tips of the fingers. Add the baking powder, sugar, salt. Make a well in the centre, add the beaten egg and sufficient *(Continued)*

The First Meal of the Day

milk to bind. Turn on to a floured board, roll out and cut into rounds. Place on a hot girdle and cook on both sides. If preferred, the bannocks can be cooked in the oven.

Oatcakes

½ lb. medium oat-meal	½ teaspoonful salt
½ oz. butter, margarine or lard	Pinch of bicarbonate of soda
	A little boiling water

Put the oatmeal into a basin, rub in the butter, margarine or lard until it is finely divided, and add the salt and bicarbonate of soda. Mix to a stiff paste with boiling water. Roll out very thinly, cut into large rounds and then into triangular sections, put on a greased tin and bake in a moderate oven.

Barley Biscuits

6 oz. flour	4 oz. butter or margarine
½ teaspoonful salt	2 oz. barley kernels
1 teaspoonful baking powder	1 egg
	Little milk

Sieve the flour, salt and baking powder into a basin, rub in the butter or margarine with the tips of the fingers and stir in the barley kernels. Make a well in the centre, add the beaten egg and a little milk, and mix to a stiff paste. Roll out on a floured board, cut into round or oblong biscuits, put on a greased and floured baking sheet and bake in a quick oven until golden brown.

Bran Buns

2 oz. bran	1 teaspoonful baking powder
4 oz. flour	1 tablespoonful melted butter
¾ oz. sugar	¼ pint milk
Pinch of salt	
1 egg	

Sieve the flour, salt and baking powder into a basin, add the bran and sugar and mix well. Stir in the beaten egg, melted butter and milk and blend thoroughly. Put in spoonfuls on a hot girdle and when brown on the underside turn and brown the other side.

*Of course
they're tiresome
— they're tired out*

They use *twice*
the energy you do

JUST growing up is almost a day's work to children — everyday ! And then think of all they do as well : the tots at play — the others doing schoolwork, sports and endless tearing about.

It's bound to show : sometimes they are fretful, sometimes a bit backward — often one of them has a whole bad term at school.

And then someone says "they're growing too fast !" But ask a doctor and he will tell you, " actually it is undernourishment."

It isn't that the children aren't getting all they *want* to eat—but there's something they *need* and just *don't get enough of* in ordinary meals. That " something " is energy-food. So the doctor says " give them Horlick's — it's the best nourishment they can have — and, in addition, it makes them get more benefit from the rest of their food, and they like it."

Start today to give Horlick's Malted Milk to your children — they take to it because of its creamy

flavour. Chemists and grocers everywhere have Horlick's in sealed glass bottles in four sizes, from 2/-, and water is all you have to add. Horlick's Malted Milk Co. Ltd., Slough, Bucks.

★

HORLICK'S
Hot or Cold

Plain or Chocolate Flavoured
BRITISH THROUGHOUT

You should insist on TATE & LYLE'S *PACKET* SUGAR

because it is the best and purest sugar obtainable. Every packet of Tate and Lyle's sugar is guaranteed full net weight and to be of uniform high quality. Obtainable in Cube, Granulated, Caster and Preserving.

Also ask for

LYLE'S GOLDEN SYRUP

It is a food of very great nutriment and yields the full muscular energy of pure sugar. Give your children plenty of bread spread with Lyle's Golden Syrup.

SEND FOR THIS BOOK *NOW!*

free Write now for the interesting recipe book "SOME EVERYDAY DISHES." Post free on request from Dept. G.H.1. TATE & LYLE LTD., 21, Mincing Lane, London, E.C.3

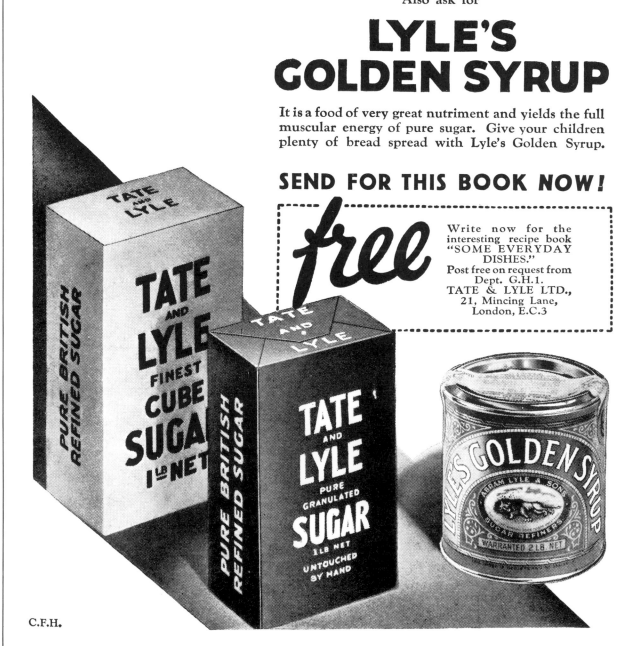

C.F.H.

SOME

COOKERY BOOKS

OF

YESTERDAY

ONE can hardly appreciate the intellectual value of cookery throughout the ages, the part it played not only in health and welfare, but in social life and in the development of nations, until one comes in contact with a great collection of cookery books or begins to collect them oneself.

The very prefaces to such books put one in a good humour. Who can resist being addressed as " Courteous Ladies and Gentlemen," or " Officers of the Mouth," and flattered or lectured with wit and charm? Who can resist the charming mention of old-fashioned flavourings which are like a stroll in the garden—the rose leaves, squash blossoms, parsnip seeds, basil, borage, marjoram, rosemary, saffron, musk angelica and elder flowers? Violets and cowslips made tanzies, roses formed the basis of fragrant conserves,and there were wiggs, pasties, frumenties, syllabubs and dozens of endearing delicacies to eat and drink.

The Greeks seem to have been the first to make an art of cookery. They travelled far and wide and brought back strange foodstuffs and methods of cooking or slaves who could tempt the palate. Their philosophers and poets did not disdain the pleasures of the table. Athenæus wrote enthusiastically of gastronomic ability and Plato, who said loftily that he preferred olives and fruit to any cooked food, was not above praising a certain confectioner who served him.

But it is from Ancient Rome that we have the first book of recipes, known as the *De Re Coquinaria* of *Apicius.* From this we learn the Roman method of serving meats, peas, beans, artichokes, cucumbers,cabbages,melons,olive oil and asparagus, a much-favoured vegetable. We think nowadays with something like horror of the rich and varied banquets of Roman days when people comforted their stomachs to the point of discomfort. " Going on a diet " was apparently unknown, and many, no doubt, died of a surfeit of food.

From Apicius one learns that the Romans loved pork and preserved it by covering it with a paste of salt, honey and vinegar and storing it in well-covered vessels. He gives a recipe for dressing a hog's paunch that is like veal stuffing of to-day, for boiling chickens with a rich sauce, for roasting white peacock with a gravy made of small birds, for carp's tongues and buttered eggs. Apicius gave much time and thought to vegetables. Sorrel must be stewed with mustard and seasoned with salt and vinegar, the tender part of broccoli boiled with pepper, chopped onion, coriander, a little sun-made wine and olive oil. It is from him that we get our first recipe for making cabbage tasty and comforting. He would have it cooked with herbs and gravy or with oil, cloves and raisins.

Alexandre Dumas, who it has been said was a better man than his son

BY

MARION

RYAN

because he knew more about food and who wrote a *Dictionary of Cookery,* dwells at length on the value and charm of cabbage and considered it at its best when boiled with ham.

In Italy cooking continued to be a fine art long after the conquest of Rome, catering to sight and smell as well as taste. The greatest chefs were those employed by dignitaries of the Church, such as that famous Scappi, who wrote a book for his pupils on kitchen etiquette as well as cookery, giving elaborate recipes and a hint which has come down to us that melon is a perfect beginning to a meal.

Though France has long been the acknowledged home of gastronomic perfection and produced the greatest cookery expert in the world, Brillat-Savarin, she was originally indebted to Italy, for Catherine de' Medici imported Italian cooks, who taught their art to the French masters of the kitchen at that time.

Louis XIV had two fine chefs, Béchemel, whose sauce pleases us to-day, and Vatel, who took his art so seriously that he killed himself when the fish did not arrive in time for a special royal banquet. One trembles to think what the King must have done to the recreant fishmonger !

There are several cookery books from the time of that other royal gourmet, Louis XV, and it may be noted that he made history for women cooks by admitting their possibilities and even bestowed the *cordon bleu* on the buxom wench who presided over the kitchen of Madame du Barry.

Any cookery book lover would thrill at the idea of a glimpse of that *Treaty on Utensils,* written in the twelfth century and probably the first book on kitchens and cookery in Great Britain, or *The Form of Cury,* said to have been compiled by the cook of King Richard II, who had a busy time satisfying the huge appetite of his royal master.

Tobias Venner, a Somerset doctor, wrote a manual of cookery (1620) which is probably the first book to stress the benefits and dangers of certain foods. He pronounces turbot, salmon, sturgeon and bull's beef hard of digestion and deplores the use of mushrooms, but adds that if one must eat them, it would be as well to wash the mouth out with vinegar and wipe the gums with a dry cloth after the experiment. He solemnly recommends ginger for the memory and a posset of roseleaves for a sleeping draught, suggests custards for the beginning or middle of a *(Continued)*

You can make this NEAPOLITAN MOULD *from Elizabeth Craig's Custard Book*

Elizabeth Craig, Britain's foremost cookery expert, is a great believer in custard. She thinks that British housewives could make very much more use of this wholesome, nutritious dish, and has compiled recipes for a hundred delightful ways of using it. For all these dishes she recommends you to use Foster Clark's Cream Custard, because it is made of the purest and finest ingredients and is so wonderfully economical.

Send a postcard (1d. stamp) to Foster Clark Ltd., Dept. P, Maidstone, Kent, for free sample and the Elizabeth Craig Custard Book containing 100 recipes. Please state whether you prefer Vanilla, Lemon, Almond, or Standard flavour.

HERE IS THE RECIPE

NEAPOLITAN MOULD

1 pint Foster Clark's Strawberry Jelly
*1 pint Foster Clark's Lemon Custard * ¼ oz. gelatine*

Make both custard and jelly according to instructions. Soak gelatine in 2 or 3 tablespoons cold water for ten minutes; drain and add to the hot custard. Stir till gelatine is dissolved. When jelly and custard are cool and ready to set, rinse out a jelly mould with cold water, and fill up with alternate layers of the jelly and custard, allowing each layer to set before adding the next. Dip mould in hot water for a second before turning on to a dish. Decorate round the base with a border of the chopped jelly remaining from what was used for the bottom lining. Enough for 6 or 8 persons.

" When I use a custard powder I always choose Foster Clark's Cream Custard, because I know how pure and wholesome it is. And I think it's delicious—don't you?"

Elizabeth Craig

6-pint packets **4½ᴰ** Large family tin 10½d

Foster Clark's
cream CUSTARD

C.8.

The Week-end House Party

Sandwich Fillings

Shrimp and Cheese

2 tablespoonfuls Parmesan cheese
2 tablespoonfuls thick creamy mayonnaise
½ pint shrimps (chopped)

Mix well together and pound.

Savoury Mixture

3 tablespoonfuls finely chopped nuts
2 hard-boiled eggs—sieved
2 tablespoonfuls cream
2 teaspoonfuls chopped capers

Mix thoroughly.

Lax filling

2 tablespoonfuls Lax
2 hard-boiled eggs
Salt and pepper
1 oz. butter
1 tablespoonful cream (thick)

Chop all ingredients up finely, pound with butter and seasoning.

Almond Sandwiches

2 oz. salted almonds well chopped

Cheese, Chutney and Cress

Season cream cheese. Spread rolls or bread and butter with cheese—put on this a layer of tomato or other chutney. Cover with a little cress.

Potted Meat

½ lb. ham and beef mixed (cooked)
3 ozs. cheese
Worcester sauce to taste

Put meat and cheese several times through mincer, mix with seasonings and sauce, and pot.

Veal Cutlets Parma

2½ lb. veal cutlets or fillets
3 oz. Parmesan cheese
Egg for coating
¾ lb. small mushrooms
Deep fat for frying
1 lb. tomatoes, cut into butterflies or left whole
Seasoning

Sauce Demi-Glacé (Half-Glaze)

1½ pint gravy from veal stock
½ pint espagnole sauce
Little sherry

Coat the cutlets in egg and cheese. Fry the mushrooms in butter. Bake the tomatoes lightly with butter and seasoning. Make the sauce by reducing the veal gravy to half and adding the espagnole sauce, seasoning and sherry. Fry the cutlets in deep fat. Arrange each cutlet on a dish with mushrooms and tomatoes and garnish tastefully.

Serve with demi-glacé sauce. This quantity will serve eight people.

Fruit Beehive

½ lb. ratafia biscuits
¼ lb. granulated sugar
1½ gills water
Teaspoonful glucose
1 pint rich egg custard
½ pint cream
½ pint strawberry pulp, or other fruit such as pineapple, apricot, etc.
1 oz. gelatine
½ gill wine
2 beaten whites of egg
Mixed glacé fruits

Boil the sugar, water and glucose until it begins to turn straw colour. Meanwhile draw a circle on a piece of grease-proof paper with a saucer. Oil well with salad oil. When the syrup is ready, dip the edges of ratafias in, and build up the beehive on the circle of paper, taking care to coat the biscuits with syrup, where they will touch. Build up about five or six rows and leave open at the top. Allow to get quite firm, then put on a silver dish. Make a second quantity of the syrup as before, and dip in a selection of fruits—orange quarters, grapes, cherries, strawberries, slices of banana, etc. Use a skewer or fork and lay the fruits on oiled paper for the glacé surface to set.

To prepare the filling dissolve the gelatine in the wine. Make the custard by boiling the milk and pouring it on to the eggs, reheat in a double pan until thick. Cool, and then add the fruit pulp. Whisk the cream, add the dissolved gelatine to the mixture, then the cream, and lastly the stiffly beaten whites. Just as it is setting pour this mixture into the beehive, decorate with glacé strawberries on the top, pipe with cream and serve glacé fruits round the dish.

Savoury Twists

¼ lb. puff or rough puff pastry
White of egg
Cooking salt
Chopped almonds

Cut the puff pastry into half-inch strips 3 to 4 in. long and an eighth of an in. thick. Twist two together, brush over with white of egg, sprinkle with chopped almonds and a little salt. Put into a hot oven and cook till golden brown and well risen.

Fillets of Sole Mayonnaise

3 soles—skinned and filleted (Reserve heads, bones etc., for stock)
Butter and flour for sauce
2–3 glasses Burgundy
1 onion
Bouquet Garni
Mushrooms

Make stock of the fish bones, add the wine and all the seasonings and cook gently till well flavoured. Add the filleted soles, rolled up, and cook slowly. When done strain the liquid off and make a sauce with flour and butter and prepared stock. Season well, then pour over the soles arranged in a silver dish and garnish with small mushrooms and lemon.

Braised Partridge (with Foie Gras)

2 brace partridges, trussed for boiling
Foie gras stuffing if liked

Braise

Fat bacon
2–3 shallots
½ bay leaves
Bouquet Garni
1 pt. good brown sauce
Blade of mace
Carrots
Good stock to moisten (about 2 pts.)
Truffles.

Lay the bacon at the bottom of the braise pan and slightly brown the partridges in the bacon fat. Add the flavourings, carrots and stock, season well, cover and cook gently for 1 hour. When cooked remove the partridges, strain off the liquor and add to the brown sauce and reduce. A little Madeira wine may be added. Dish up the birds with the sauce, which should be of creamy consistency, and serve very hot and well flavoured.

Fish Quenelles with Spinach

¾ lb. white fish
4 oz. butter
3 eggs
4 tablespoonfuls milk
4 tablespoonfuls breadcrumbs
Salt and pepper
Spinach

Put the milk and butter into a saucepan, melt, then add to the breadcrumbs. Leave at the side of the stove, stirring occasionally until thickening. Then allow to cool. Pound up the fish as finely as possible, and add it with the eggs, beating all together well, then pass through a wire sieve. Shape into quenelles and poach for 10 minutes in boiling stock or milk and stock. Strain well, coat with white sauce and serve on a border of spinach.

Glacé Pineapple

Prepare exactly as the glacé fruits in Fruit Beehive.

To Boil a Ham

Soak the ham for about 12 hours, changing the water from time to time. Scrape clean, weigh, put into a pan of cold water, and bring slowly to the boil. Allow 25 mins. per lb. Flavour with herbs and continue cooking 4–5 hours. Leave in the water until nearly cold, then remove the ham, and take off the skin.

To Coat the Ham

Make 2½ pints good white coating sauce and tammy. Add 1 pint liquid aspic. Stir the two together until thick enough to coat the back of a wooden spoon, then coat the ham evenly. Garnish with tomato skin, truffles, chervil, etc., and cover with one or two coats of liquid (cold) aspic. Finish with a ham frill and chopped aspic.

Neat pieces of chicken or other game may be dressed in this way, as shown in the illustration on page 76.

To Prepare a Tongue for Glazing

If the tongue has been dried, soak well for 12 hours, if fresh from the pickle 2–3 hours will be enough for soaking. Put into a saucepan of cold water and gradually bring to the boil, skim well and simmer for 2½–3 hours for a small tongue. When done remove the tongue, skin it, and trim the root. Secure on a wooden board with skewers through the tip of the tongue and the root, with a rolling pin underneath to preserve a good shape. When quite cold, glaze twice with meat glaze and garnish with piped butter, egg white and yolk.

Some Cookery Books of Yesterday

(Continued)

meal and says that two meals a day are enough for all but children or the infirm, who should not be bound by any rules.

During the latter part of the seventeenth and through the eighteenth century cookery books appeared in astonishing numbers. Indeed it seemed a pleasant way of distinguishing oneself, especially during the eighteenth century, and zealous collectors can get interesting little volumes of that time.

Hannah Woolley, who was an early intruder into a field which had appeared to belong to men, in 1670 wrote *The Queen-like Closet or Rich Cabinet*. She was as wildly extravagant as all her male predecessors and she added beauty culture to cookery and probably started the first registry office, for she got servants for many of her friends and acquaintances and was not above taking a fee for her services.

Mrs. Mary Tillinghast followed Mrs. Woolley's example in 1678 and wrote *Excellent Recipes Experienced and Taught and Now Printed for the Use of Her Scholars Only*. She was apparently a cook of some note, but one would hardly consider her practical to-day. In fact, her nonchalant extravagance as to eggs and butter would turn a twentieth-century housewife grey if she had to follow such directions.

Here's the *new* Beefex bottle –
why does it take a teaspoon?

"*Better than ever*"

So that . .

you can reach every part of the bottle. Consequently none of the Beefex is wasted — surely a great improvement? Beefex of course, is the BEST of BEEF, a sustaining and refreshing drink for all times, and ideal for wintry nights. Many housewives use it to enrich gravies and soups as well. From all grocers, chemists and stores. 1-oz. 7d., 2-oz. 1/1, 4-oz. 1/11, 8-oz. 3/6, 16-oz. 5/6.

Also cubes 1d., dissolve instantly.

TRY BEEFEX RISSOLES

4 ozs. cold mutton. Pepper and salt to taste.
1 teaspoonful Beefex.   1 small onion.
2 ozs. mashed potatoes. 1 egg. Breadcrumbs.

Mince meat and onion very finely; add Beefex, potatoes, pepper and salt, mix well together, then add sufficient egg to make the mixture into a fairly stiff paste. Form into rissoles, dip first into beaten egg then into breadcrumbs, and fry a golden brown.

Drink Beefex — and cook with it, too.

Advert. of Beefex Ltd., West Smithfield, E.C.1   royds 3a

None of these female cooks, however, won the fame which came to Hannah Glasse and Elizabeth Raffald. Hannah Glasse's *The Art of Cookery* was her most successful book. She was the wife of an attorney and had a large acquaintance through which she was able to gather much material, especially directions for the cure of various ailments. In fact, so great were her pretensions to being a wise woman that Dr. Johnson scorned her and said that no woman could write a good cookery book, but that he could. An idle boast, however, for he never even tried, while Hannah's many editions of cookery and cures pleased women of her time and are a boon to collectors of to-day, who often find copies in unexpected places and at reasonable prices, though one of the 1745 editions is said to have fetched £30 at a sale not so long ago.

If you can face the difficult script of an early *Art of Cookery* you will be charmed with Hannah's variety. She appears to know everything from how to cook and to clean a white frock with gold threads to treating an hysterical patient, the bite of a mad dog, an attack of the plague or mere heartburn. One of her draughts calls for twenty different roots, sixteen flowers, nineteen varieties of seeds and a bit of mistletoe. Her cure for hysteria requires equal diligence in wood and garden at all times of year, but probably owes any efficiency it has to the two quarts of brandy she threw in for good measure!

Cheesecakes were very popular in her day and she incorporated a favourite recipe in her book.

To make Almond Cheesecakes

" Take half a pound of Jordan almonds and lay them in cold water all night the next morning blanch them in cold water then take them out and lay them in a clean cloth beat them very fine in a little orange flower water then take six eggs leave out four whites beat them and strain them then take half a pound of white sugar with a little beaten mace beat them well together with a marble mortar take ten ounces of good fresh butter melt it a little grated lemon peel and put them in the mortar with other ingredients mix all well together and fill your patty pans."

To make Little Fine Cakes

" One pound of butter beaten to a cream a pound and a quarter of flour a pound of white sugar beat fine a pound of currants cleaned washed and picked six eggs two whites left out beat them fine mix the flour sugar and eggs by degrees with the butter beat it all well with both hands either make it into little cakes or one cake."

Elizabeth Raffald was a remarkably energetic woman. She wrote her cookery book after she left domestic service and dedicated it to a former mistress. It is called *The Experienced English Housewife*, and its eight hundred recipes were " for the use and ease of ladies, housekeepers and cooks etc." One could buy it at her confectionery shop, which could not have been altogether successful since she gave it up and, with her husband, ran three inns at different times.

Like most of the cookery-book writers of her day, she gives great space to sweets and pastries and is lavish with butter and eggs. Of her Transparent Pudding she says, " It is a pretty pudding for a corner for dinner and a middle for supper."

Transparent Pudding

" Beat eight eggs very well and put them in a pan with half a pound of butter and the same weight of loaf sugar beat fine a little grated nutmeg set it on the fire and keep stirring till it thickens like buttered eggs then put it in a bason to cool roll a rich puff paste very thin lay it round the edge of the dish then pour in the pudding and bake in a moderate oven half an hour it will cut light and clear."

To make King William Cream

" Beat the whites of three eggs very well then squeeze the juice of two large lemons or three small ones take two ounces more than the juice of double refined sugar and mix together with two or three drops of orange flower water and five or six spoonfuls of fair spring water when all the sugar is melted put in the whites of eggs into the pan and the juice set it over a slow fire and keep stirring till you find it thickens then strain it through a coarse cloth quick into a dish."

In the early nineteenth century cookery books began to change in style. They became more practical as to recipes, less pompous in directions, less flowery in phrases. They no longer commended, lectured and flattered. In 1808 Mrs. Helene Russell wrote *A New System of Domestic Cookery Founded Upon the Principles of Economy and Adapted to the Use of Private Families*, adding, in a foreword, that it was for the use of her married daughters and that she wished she had had some such guide when she began housekeeping.

It became so popular that many others followed her example and the collector can browse among nineteenth-century cookery books to her heart's content. They do not all quite follow the promises of their titles as to economy according to our present ideas and very few of them have any commercial value. Eliza Axton's *Modern Cookery* in 1845 and all the books of Alexis Soyer, the famous cook of the Reform Club, which came a little later, were very much used. But it was reserved for Isabella Mary Beeton to become the real household idol of Victorian days.

Use Our Shopping Service

if you live out of reach of London's shops and yet would have the advantage of buying direct from them. Our staff will gladly purchase for you any of the articles shown on the Shopping Service pages or in the advertisement columns. Send order or cheque, stating clearly what you require, to Shopping Service, 153 Queen Victoria Street, London, E.C.4

Cooking without an oven provides a pleasant change from office work for the girl who is interested in the art

The business world of to-day is crowded with bachelor girls who would rather cook a simple meal at home than eat out expensively every evening of the week

BUSINESS girls living alone represent a large part of the life of every city, and this article has been especially compiled for them. "What shall I have for supper?" is an ever-recurring, knotty problem, and in the experience of more than one business girl, our very old and valued friend, the egg, serves as an answer; but eggs in time become monotonous. It is hoped, therefore, that the suggestions herewith may be of interest. The menus are simple and easily cooked, as time and trouble is a factor to consider at the end of a day's work. Quite apart from the actual value of the food prepared, the restful effect on the nerves and mind of a dainty meal varied from day to day is not to be belittled, so that a short time at the beginning of the week is well spent in planning and ordering in advance.

The bachelor girl usually has friends who are pleased to entertain one or two evenings a week, and the return of hospitality is part of the fun of living in this way. Cooking in the evening provides a pleasant change from office work for the girl who is interested in the art, while those who have never cooked before can accomplish a good deal by the aid of one of the many excellent simple cookery books to be bought at a trifling cost, more satisfactory to the uninitiated than the rather terrifying Mrs. Beeton.

The cooking apparatus in bed-sitting-rooms or small flatlets seldom exceeds a gas-ring and griller; the accompanying menus are based on this assumption. Those who are lucky enough to have small ovens or even gas cookers will be able to vary the dishes and have foods which can be prepared in the oven. The list of cooking utensils need not be large but must be adequate. Economy can be effected by buying a small steamer in which two or three foods can be cooked at once, and a fireproof casserole will prove a valuable friend. A frying-pan, kettle, saucepans, and if possible a small girdle for cooking scones will complete the utensils.

A word or two about stoves will not be out of place here, and may be of help to those who live or are contemplating living alone. Tiny cookers with one small oven, a griller and one boiling ring may be had from £2 15s. upwards according to finish. Without the oven the price is very much less; a griller and boiling ring costs from 25s. They are convenient in size and are easily concealable when not in use. The measurements vary from about 20 in. by 16 in. to 11 in. by 8 in.

Setting aside a special time in the week for planning the menu is the first step towards making the work of catering an easy one. Friday evening is a useful time for all kinds of odd jobs, so the half-hour for planning can be added to the list, along with the sewing on of buttons and mending of stockings ready for the week-end. Breakfasts are usually simple affairs when there are early buses and trains to catch, so that only the evening meal needs consideration. It is as well to remember that even when only small quantities of foods are ordered, scraps have a habit of lingering, so that little ways must be devised for using them up. Next take stock of the store-cupboard and order the staple foods such as sugar, butter, seasonings, tea, vegetables, etc. The weekly order can be left at the respective shops on Saturday morning so that the goods can be delivered during the day. Perishable foods should be bought or ordered the day they are required, and as early as possible, so that a good choice is obtained. "Left-overs" are apt to be the lot of the late shopper.

An inexperienced housekeeper will be ignorant of how much should be spent on food for one person. Taking into account visitors and evenings out when no food is needed, an average week will cost about 12s. to 15s. exclusive of gas or heating. This figure is a fluctuating one however, as appetites and tastes vary.

The girl who is interested in getting the best value for money would be well

Meals for the Business Girl

By
Phyllis Peck

*Combined Domestic Science
Diploma, and First Class
Needlework and Dressmaking
Diploma*

Department of Cookery
Good Housekeeping Institute
49 Wellington Street, Strand, W.C.2
Conducted by
Mrs. D. D. Cottington Taylor
Certificate of King's College of Household and Social Science : First Class
Diplomas in Cookery, High Class Cookery, Laundrywork, Housewifery, A.R.S.I.

advised to look out for shops supplying small quantities of cooked and ready prepared foods, only requiring to be heated. One well-known catering firm supplies most delicious foods ready packed in waxed cartons, at extremely reasonable prices, which makes it hardly worth while preparing and cooking such small quantities at home.

The following meals can all be prepared without the use of an oven, but where one is available, a little more variety will be possible.

MENUS FOR ONE WEEK

Sunday
Breakfast
Prepared cereal
Small Finnan haddock
Toast, butter, marmalade
Tea or coffee

Mid-day Meal
Hot veal cake
Mashed potatoes
Sprouts or marrow
Raspberry cream. Stewed fruit
Cheese and biscuits

Tea
Hot potato scones—frying-pan or girdle
Bread and butter
Honey
Cakes

Supper
Scrambled egg with tomato and cheese
Fresh fruit. Finish raspberry cream
Biscuits and butter
Celery

Monday
Evening Meal
Cold veal cake
Potato and tomato salad
Stewed apples. Custard
Cheese and biscuits

Tuesday
Evening Meal
Tomato soup (tinned)
Scotch eggs (bought ready for frying)
Mashed potatoes. French beans
Chocolate mould
Bananas
Cheese and biscuits

Wednesday
Evening Meal (with one guest)
Gammon rasher and spinach (tinned)
Tinned peas
Boiled potatoes
Orange and banana salad and cream
Cheese and biscuits

Thursday
Evening Meal
Liver and bacon with gravy
Mashed potatoes
Jam tarts
Cheese and biscuits
Celery

Friday
Evening Meal (with one guest)
Grapefruit (tinned or fresh)
Fried scallops
Casserole of beef (make Thursday evening, using up tinned peas and celery)
Boiled potatoes
Coffee creams

Saturday
Breakfast
Prepared cereal or porridge
Fried egg and bacon
Toast, marmalade, butter
Tea or coffee

Tea (visitor)
Scones
Watercress and jam
Cake

Supper (visitor)
Sausages and mashed potatoes
Sprouts
Bananas or apples
Nuts
Cheese and biscuits

These dinners at home need not be a worry. Half an hour spent in planning simple menus and marketing lists once a week, makes them a very easy matter

HOW OTHERS LIVE

—

MAID'S TIME TABLE (Monday to Saturday)

7	a.m.	Light Boiler.
		Sweep and dust rooms on ground floor.
		Cook breakfast.
8.15 a.m.		Breakfast.
8.45 a.m.		Wash-up.
		Tidy kitchen.
9.30 a.m.		Make beds.
		Sweep and dust upstairs rooms.
		Stairs and landings.
11—1		Special duty.
1 p.m.		Lunch.

SPECIAL DUTIES

MONDAY	Washing	THURSDAY	Dining-room
TUESDAY	Bedrooms	FRIDAY	Landings and hall
WEDNESDAY	Lounge	SATURDAY	Kitchen

Tuesday afternoon clean silver ($1\frac{1}{2}$—2 hours)
Wednesday evening ironing (about $1\frac{1}{2}$ hours)

TYPICAL MENUS FOR ONE WEEK

SUNDAY

Lunch   Roast leg of lamb.
Potatoes. Cabbage.
Queen pudding.

Supper   Buck rarebit.
Jam tartlets.
Cheese. Fruit.

TUESDAY

Lunch   Irish stew.
Apple pudding.

Dinner   Durham cutlets (made
with remains of
lamb).
Cabbage. Potatoes.
Pancakes.

THURSDAY

Lunch   Casserole of rabbit.
Potatoes.
Baked jam roll.

Supper   Smoked haddock.
Bread and butter.
Cheese. Fruit.

MONDAY

Lunch   Soup.
Cold lamb.
Potatoes. Pickles.
Syrup pudding.

Dinner   Dinner out.

WEDNESDAY

Lunch   Roast cutlets.
Potatoes. Turnips.
Milk pudding. Baked
apples.

Dinner   Dinner out.

FRIDAY

Lunch   Beans and bacon (a
Good Housekeeping
recipe).
Potatoes.
Sponge pudding.

Dinner   Grilled steak.
Potatoes, onions, tomatoes.
Chocolate pudding.

SATURDAY

Lunch   Steak and kidney pudding.
Potatoes. Parsnips.
Steamed custard.

Dinner   Dinner out.

WHEN asked by the Director of Good Housekeeping Institute to give an account of my household management and expenditure, the thought came to my mind, "How much of all this will be of any real interest to others?" But having searched my brain—and our household receipts file—for the information required, I came to the conclusion that such a form of exercise is definitely enlightening to oneself, and my regret in the matter is that I cannot compare notes, as it were, with others more or less similarly placed. By so doing I should, I am convinced, learn much to guide me, but I hope the facts I give will interest others to the extent at least of making them take stock of their own endeavours, and profit as I have done by the experience.

We are a family of four: my husband, myself, our little boy of between two and three years of age, and a maid. Our house contains two living-rooms, a rather large entrance hall, four bedrooms, a dressing-room, kitchen and usual offices. It is a modern house, having been built only six years, and is sensibly planned with a kitchen of good size and no wasted space on landings or staircase. The water is heated by means of an independent boiler, beside which stands the gas cooker. Gas is also used for heating purposes in the living and bedrooms, so that fire lighting and its attendant labours is ruled out. There is, however, plenty of work to accomplish thoroughly, but it is so planned that with the exception of one afternoon a week in which the silver is cleaned, and one evening devoted to ironing, it is confined to the mornings. We have what perhaps some people would consider a rather large amount of polishing to do, for all our furniture is of the modern type which relies on plain outlines and the natural grain of

AVERAGE WEEKLY EXPENDITURE

	£	s.	d.
Maid's Wages . .		16	0
Milk		6	0
Bread		1	3
Butcher . . .		12	6
Fishmonger . .		3	0
Grocer . . .		15	6
Greengrocer . .		5	0
Laundry . . .		1	6
Cakes . . .		2	6
Papers . . .		1	0
	£3	4	3

OVERHEAD AND MISCELLANEOUS EXPENSES

Average per Quarter	£	s.	d.
Gas	2	13	2
Electricity . . .	1	6	7
Coke	1	15	0
General Rate . .	9	3	0
Land Tax . . .	4	15	0
Commons Conservators Rate . . .		2	7
Water Rate . . .	1	5	4
Income Tax . .	15	0	0
Life Insurance . .	15	4	2
House and Contents Assurance . .	2	0	0
Doctor and Dentist .	3	0	0
Gardener . . .	1	10	0
Piano Tuner . .		6	0
Charity . . .	1	10	0
	£59	10	10

An account of the management, menus, and tables of expenditure of a family of four, including maid

Described by
A Reader of the Magazine

frequent and regular wax polishing, using the minimum of wax (and that thinned with turpentine), is in the long run the best and easiest method of obtaining really good results. I must also mention that we have lately purchased an electric floor polisher. In addition, we maintain the light clean look of the wood floors by washing them over twice annually with turpentine and so removing all accumulated wax and the dirt that gets inevitably trodden in with it. The floor is scrubbed over with a brush dipped in turpentine, and then plenty of old rags, which I save for the purpose and which are afterwards burnt, are used to clean off the loosened wax and dirt.

Needless to say, I do not expect one maid to do all the housework and the cooking. My husband comes home to lunch daily, and as he possesses the rather annoying habit of disliking cold food, this meal, with the exception of the meat course each Monday, is invariably a hot one. The menus appended to this article are typical, and give meals actually consumed by us during the past week—a cold one with a biting east wind. Breakfast is not included, as this without exception consists of eggs and bacon (or bacon and tomatoes on a few occasions) followed by toast, marmalade, honey and tea. The first course of the lunches mentioned (and this is the same throughout the year) is, Sunday excepted, a dish that requires little preparation, one which may be prepared the evening before.

the polished wood for its beauty, and the hall, lounge, dining-room, landing and half-landing have parquet floors.

The kitchen and one bedroom are covered with linoleum, the latter supplemented by rugs, and the remaining bedrooms have surrounds of linoleum. All these—furniture and floors—are wax polished weekly, and if, as already mentioned, the labour involved is somewhat more than some people may consider necessary, we have the reward of that brightness which only well cared for wood, whether old or new, can give to a house. If this point appears to have been laboured it is only on account of my conviction born of experience that

By FLORENCE WHITE

(Author of "Good Things in England," and founder of the English Folk Cookery Association)

A man's thoughts are influenced by the things he eats—so these revelations of the tastes of some of our notabilities are interesting as well as amusing

Lord Hailsham likes apple pie; Lord Snowden's standing order is for jam tarts

IF it be true "not soul helps flesh more than flesh helps soul" and that a man's thoughts are influenced by the food he eats and the drink he drinks, the education of the palate and a study of the psychology of food assume as much importance as that of the eye, hand, ear and nose. In fact they cannot be dissociated without the whole personality suffering. Pains in one's tummy or a diseased appendix may have disastrous æsthetic and even international consequences, whilst a sense of well-being may contribute to the world's peace.

Nor need this attention to food be dull. A lively interest in one's dinner adds to the gaiety of life and a mere cursory and haphazard observation of the favourite food of men and women of distinction may be most amusing. There is even something to be said for a scientific collection of data from the time when Esau sold his birthright for a mess of pottage. How did that affect the destinies of Israel? And what effect did Mr. Gladstone's favourite dish of lobster followed by rice pudding have on his soul and therefore on his policy?

William the Conqueror is said to have invaded Britain for the sake of an oyster bed, and Talleyrand to have governed by means of truffles. When setting out on an important embassy he would simply ask to be supplied with the best chefs France could produce. Given them, he confidently asserted he could answer for the success of his diplomacy. There are more ways than one of achieving the conquest of a nation.

To-day, Monsieur Herbodeau, President of the Association Culinaire in London and Controller of the kitchens of the Carlton Hotel and Restaurant, is frequently asked by English diplomats to create menus for dinners for which matters of national policy have been the *raison d'être,* and no one is better qualified to do this without bias. In addition to being the best French cook in the world since the retirement of Maître Escoffier who trained him, Monsieur Herbodeau has probably more knowledge of gastronomy than any other man living. He has just published a study of the *Deipnosophists.* He has the supreme advantage of being in his early prime. It is a great intellectual treat to explore with him the volumes of the unique library he has

Favourite Foods of Famous Men

Among the dishes preferred by the notable figures on the left are: Pachmann, boiled rice; the Master of Sempill, haggis; Lord Balfour, dressed crab; Sir Arthur Quiller-Couch, ham and sweet-pickled damsons

Photos: Peter North, Claude Harris, Elliott & Fry, Lenare, Vandyk, Topical

This is the grill at Simpsons in the Strand, a restaurant famous the world over for its perfect English cooking

Among the few remaining dishes of mediæval sumptuousness is roast swan. Each year the King presents a swan to certain high officials

Monsieur Herbodeau, of the Carlton Hotel, who is President of the London Association Culinaire

already collected, as well as a gastronomic treat to eat a dinner he has arranged.

The mistake so many English people make is to undervalue the artistic and psychological side of the pleasures of the table and to narrow down the study of food to the practical work of the kitchen. There is much more "to it" than that, and it is in this direction, not in the actual preparation of food, that France scores.

Reverting for a moment to Mr. Gladstone, a quotation from Monsieur André Maurois' *Disraeli,* a picture of the Victorian Age translated by Hamish Miles, seems to fit into the picture.

"At a dinner at Lyndhurst's when both Disraeli and young Gladstone, then an Under-Secretary of State, were present, they were served with a swan, very white, very tender and well stuffed with truffles, and that itself was good company."

The King, of course, has his own Swanncries at Norwich and every year he sends presents of swans to certain high officials.

When Mr. Arthur Balfour left the House of Commons at 1 a.m. in days gone by, he liked nothing better than a dressed crab.

Mr. Lloyd George's particular fancy is for grilled steaks and peaches; not together, of course.

In the days before Members were paid, when the House of Commons was justly considered the best club in Europe, a favourite dish cooked for special dinners and luncheons in the small dining-rooms on the Terrace was quail stuffed with truffles and *foie gras,* enveloped in a thin wrapping of puff paste, "light as love," *(Continued)*

135

1934

FAVOURITE FOODS OF FAMOUS MEN

and equally melting, and then baked. This probably is the most perfect way of cooking quail and similar small birds, the effect is even superior to *en papillotte,* because whilst the flavour is equally well preserved we have in addition the delicate and delicious enveloping crust, through which, by the way, the quail's legs protrude. This is not an article on cookery, otherwise now would be the time to discuss the merits of ham baked, and leg o' mutton boiled, in a plain crust.

To return to the favourite food of our legislators; Mr. Reginald Vaughan, one of the Directors of the Carlton, who during forty years of hotel management has catered for Kings, Queens, Princes, Premiers and other famous people, was from 1920 to 1932 controller of the Refreshment Department of the House of Lords and naturally knows more about the tastes of the members of the Upper House than anyone.

"It is," he observes, "a curious fact that our peers eat almost no meat; they may have an occasional cutlet but mainly it is fish, omelettes, apple pies and the like. Teas they want served in the old-fashioned way with plenty of cherry cake and buns on the table, but no cream buns or sticky chocolate confections. They do like simplicity at all costs—bread and butter, watercress, scones and jam but no pastries."

The higher a man's position the simpler his taste, is Mr. Vaughan's experience. Personally I think this is because these people alone know how really good the best simple English cookery can be. In their own homes they have become accustomed from childhood to the best home-grown produce, served in its prime, vegetables and fruit freshly cut and gathered at the right moment and cooked and served simply at once; meat and game well-hung. Whereas the men and women who rave about elaborate foreign cookery have been brought up on imported produce that has travelled from producer to market, from market to shop, from shop to kitchen, where it has been prepared for table in the English fashion by an indifferent cook.

When Lord Birkenhead was Chancellor, he asked Mr. Vaughan to make arrangements for a dinner for H.M. the King in the Royal Gallery. Malmaisons, his Majesty's favourite flower, were on the table, and his favourite dish, roast saddle of mutton, on the menu.

Lord Sankey, the present Lord Chancellor and one of the most unassuming of men, is among the few remaining epicures. He prefers chops to steaks.

Lord Snowden has a standing order for jam tarts.

Lord Lansdowne prefers a cut from the joint, and Lord Evesham's weakness is for a plain grilled sole.

Perfect grills are a feature of both Refreshment Rooms of the Houses of Parliament, and when Don Alfonso lunches at the House of Lords he generally chooses "one of your famous English grilled steaks."

Grilled mutton cutlets and tomatoes, and sausages and mashed potatoes are general favourites.

The usual drink in the House of Lords is water, or barley-water, the latter being the particular fancy of some well-known judges and other legal dignitaries.

Lord Hailsham and Lord Cecil love apple pie, real apple pie made in a deep dish. The kitchens of the Houses of Parliament are famous for making them per-

fectly in the correct manner. I have seen them being made there, by a woman cook who knows her job and does it well.

The Lord Dudley who was Foreign Secretary in the nineteenth century hated a dinner without apple pie. The story goes that even when at an important official dinner at Prince Esterhazy's he was terribly put out on finding that his favourite delicacy was wanting, and kept on murmuring pretty audibly: "God bless my soul! No apple pie!" He also insisted on its being called apple-pie, the word "tart," he affirmed, being correctly applied only to pastry filled with fruit and left uncovered. This is an old dispute and those interested in such matters may be glad to know there is a good essay on the subject in the *Cambridge Review* for 11th November, 1897.

The Master of Sempill, who is a whole-hearted supporter of the English Folk Cookery Association, thinks "There is no better dish than haggis, but one would not appreciate it to the same extent if one were to have it continuously." He thinks "one should eat what is customary in the various countries that one visits. If one does this, then one gets a nice change in diet and appreciates one's own national dishes all the better on returning from a sojourn abroad." He says many of the Japanese dishes are particularly good, both satisfying to the eye as well as to the palate.

Sir George Duckworth, another of the few remaining *gourmets,* who frankly owns to being a *gourmand* also, is omnivorous and likes everything good, but two of his particular favourites are firstly, a small Dover sole fried in butter with a dressing over it of finely chopped chervil in lemon juice; and secondly, fried fillets of sole with a thick mushroom sauce to accompany them.

The last, he tells me, was a cunning device of Major G. H. Cartwright, himself a noted Eton cricketer and Secretary to the famous Eton Ramblers Cricket Club, of which Sir George is a member. Major Cartwright invented this dish for a dinner (at Claridge's) which the Ramblers offered to a still more famous Eton cricketer, the Rt. Hon. J. E. K. Studd, then Lord Mayor of London.

Lady Clark of Tilliepromie, whose collection of recipes were, at Sir John's request, after her death made by Miss Catherine Frere into the famous cookery book that bears her name, was a cousin of Sir George Duckworth, and they still serve at Dalingridge, his Sussex home, a special dish of neck of mutton made from one of her recipes. It goes by the amusing name of "Lady Clark's Neck."

With Sir George we will leave royal, political and diplomatic circles and pass on to art, music and literature. He is a fitting link, as his mother, Mrs. Herbert Duckworth, married Sir Leslie Stephen, and he knows literary and artistic circles in Paris as well as London as well as he does those of legislation and diplomacy.

In the novels of Balzac we can see how the food habits of his characters are used to make us visualise their personality. He makes them dine before us. A chapter will describe a recipe which in the space of a second will reveal the mentality of the housewife. Jane Austen, Mrs. Gaskell, Charles Dickens and George Eliot also use this method, and it has been adopted increasingly during recent years by modern English writers, notably by the late John Galsworthy.

Writers and musicians, how do they re-

act to this gastronomic test? Augustus John says the Old Mill Restaurant at West Harnham, half a mile from Salisbury has "the best cook and the best food in Wessex," and I know for a fact when he goes there he asks for a mixed grill and likes it highly seasoned.

Sir Arthur Quiller-Couch thinks there is nothing to beat home-cured ham and sweet pickled damsons. This, with his own claret or cider-cup, he considers makes a perfect light supper.

Mr. Aubrey Bateman, of Bath, who, when he was Mayor created such a storm in a teacup by saying no Englishwoman can cook, always has a French chef, but owned rather shamefacedly that for luncheon there is nothing better than a slice of good home-made English brawn, adding with amusement, "And the fellow can't make it!" Apparently traditional food habits die hard. Brawn with mustard was always served at dinner in England from November to March in the days of Elizabeth.

Herman Finck makes up parties and goes down from the Savage Club to Simpson's-in-the-Strand to eat chicken pudding, and although I don't know Mr. Finck I am very proud of this, because the recipe from which the pudding is made has been in my mother's family for generations and I gave it to Simpson's only last year. It promises to be as famous as the beefsteak pudding at the Cheshire Cheese.

Chaliapin, the great bass, is most fastidious about his food, and is very proud of the fact that he can cook. He insisted once on showing a famous chef how to cook a steak *à la Russe.*

Madame Patti every day before performance used to ask Mr. Vaughan to send oysters and champagne to her room. She looked on them as a tonic for her wonderful voice.

Pachmann was the despair of chefs; he would look at several menus and then order boiled rice.

Sarah Bernhardt loved omelettes; Duse was so fond of fruit she could live on it. Caruso was as fond of ices as a schoolboy.

Monsieur André L. Simon found a luncheon at the Savoy at which were featured salmon trout with the wonderful Bacchus sauce, and baby lamb with mushrooms—"the best chosen and best cooked luncheon he had enjoyed this year or last" (1932–1933). The lamb, he says in *Tables of Content,* where the full menu is given, "would have brought tears of joy to the eyes of Rabelais himself."

The gastronomic trend at the moment lies in the direction of preserving the best food tradition of every nation on the assumption that it probably represents the survival of the fittest; that which best suits each country's climate, soil, character and habits. This is, however, only a safe guide if the particular nation is perfectly satisfied with its state of health, mental and physical. There is tremendous scope for interesting study in this direction, not merely from the scientific dietetic point of view, but from the æsthetic and psychological. The Japanese are even said to be considering whether by altering their diet slightly they cannot add to their stature.

As a rule the menus arranged by vitamin and other experts are so deadly dull and same. They need not be if only the cook would study science and food resources that are never tapped; and the scientist learn to cook; and both at the same time exercise their imaginations.

Why is **HARTLEY'S** marmalade made in January?

Because January is the month in which the Seville oranges arrive in this country. No other oranges can give the true marmalade flavour, and therefore Hartleys use *only* the genuine Seville. Nothing else goes into the jar except pure sugar.

If you would like to make a convincing test of the superiority of a real Seville orange marmalade, don't wait until your present jar is finished. Get a jar of Hartley's now and taste them side by side.

Seville oranges alone give the true marmalade flavour

Every year HARTLEY'S *import the pick of the Seville orange crop*

Only Seville oranges and pure sugar go into HARTLEY'S *Marmalade*

The standard "old-fashioned" kind hitherto known as Hartley's Marmalade has been renamed Hartley's *Aintree* Marmalade to distinguish it more clearly from Hartley's Jelly Marmalade and Hartley's Bitter-Sweet Marmalade.

HARTLEY'S
A I N T R E E   M A R M A L A D E

M I

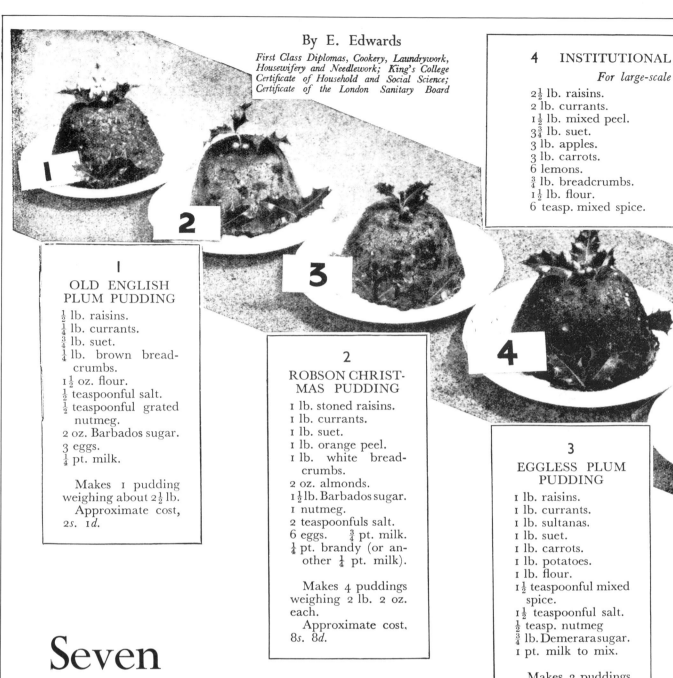

By E. Edwards

First Class Diplomas, Cookery, Laundrywork, Housewifery and Needlework; King's College Certificate of Household and Social Science; Certificate of the London Sanitary Board

1 OLD ENGLISH PLUM PUDDING

½ lb. raisins.
¼ lb. currants.
¾ lb. suet.
¼ lb. brown bread-crumbs.
1½ oz. flour.
½ teaspoonful salt.
½ teaspoonful grated nutmeg.
2 oz. Barbados sugar.
3 eggs.
¼ pt. milk.

Makes 1 pudding weighing about 2½ lb.
Approximate cost, 2s. 1d.

2 ROBSON CHRISTMAS PUDDING

1 lb. stoned raisins.
1 lb. currants.
1 lb. suet.
1 lb. orange peel.
1 lb. white bread-crumbs.
2 oz. almonds.
1½ lb. Barbados sugar.
1 nutmeg.
2 teaspoonfuls salt.
6 eggs.   ¾ pt. milk.
¼ pt. brandy (or another ¼ pt. milk).

Makes 4 puddings weighing 2 lb. 2 oz. each.
Approximate cost, 8s. 8d.

3 EGGLESS PLUM PUDDING

1 lb. raisins.
1 lb. currants.
1 lb. sultanas.
1 lb. suet.
1 lb. carrots.
1 lb. potatoes.
1 lb. flour.
1½ teaspoonful mixed spice.
1½ teaspoonful salt.
½ teasp. nutmeg.
¾ lb. Demerara sugar.
1 pt. milk to mix.

Makes 3 puddings weighing 2½ lb. each.
1 pudding weighing 1½ lb.
Approximate cost, 4s. 5d.

4 INSTITUTIONAL

For large-scale

2½ lb. raisins.
2 lb. currants.
1½ lb. mixed peel.
3¾ lb. suet.
3 lb. apples.
3 lb. carrots.
6 lemons.
¾ lb. breadcrumbs.
1½ lb. flour.
6 teasp. mixed spice.

Seven Christmas Puddings

with costs and quantities for making them

THERE is something so special about family Christmas puddings that most people prefer to make them at home, usually calculating a quantity that will include presents for friends and relatives abroad or away from home at the festive season.

When old recipes are available, there is little difficulty in choosing one which pleases the young as well as the older members of the family and which is invariably declared incomparable. However, many of our readers, to judge by the inquiries we receive, are pleased to have help with their puddings. Some

need an inexpensive mixture suitable for a school or institution, others want vegetarian puddings and others puddings which have no carrot or apple in them. With a view to meeting this need, seven recipes are given here. Each has been made, tested and eaten in Good Housekeeping Institute and all have been declared excellent in their respective classes. One particularly interesting point noted was that the pudding which contained no eggs could not be distinguished in appearance or taste from those which contained a generous quantity.

A difficulty which frequently con-

fronts young housewives is knowing exactly how many basins a particular recipe will fill. As a guide, the exact size of the basin and the number used are given.

In order to save repetition the method has been tabulated and can always be followed unless otherwise stated.

Method for Making Christmas Pudding

Size of basin—approximately 6¼ in. across, 3¾ in. deep.
Number of servings of average size—eight to ten.

CHRISTMAS PUDDING

catering

6 teaspoonfuls bicar-
   bonate of soda.
6 teaspoonfuls salt.
3 lb. Barbados sugar.
1½ pts. milk.

Makes 9 puddings
weighing 2½ lb. each.
Approximate cost,
12s. 4½d.

5
VEGETARIAN PLUM PUDDING

½ lb. raisins.
½ lb. currants.
¼ lb. peel.
½ lb. brown bread-
   crumbs.
½ lb. carrots.
½ lb. flour.
½ lb. Barbados sugar.
½ lb. butter.
½ teaspoonful salt.
½ teaspoonful ground
   ginger.
1½ teaspoonfuls spice.
4 tablespoonfuls black
   treacle.
2 eggs.   ½ pt. milk.

Cream the butter
and sugar together,
add the eggs singly,
beating well be-
tween each addition.
Stir in the flour and
breadcrumbs. Lastly
add spices, salt, fruit,
carrot, treacle and
milk.

Mix thoroughly.

Makes 2 puddings
weighing 2¼ lb. each.
Approximate cost,
2s. 7d.

6
AN EXCELLENT PLUM PUDDING

½ lb. raisins.
½ lb. currants.
2 oz. mixed candied
   peel.
1 lb. suet.
1 lb. breadcrumbs.
1 lb. Demerara sugar.
1 teaspoonful salt.
6 eggs.
¼ pt. brandy (or
   milk).

Makes 2 puddings
weighing 2 lb. 6 oz.
each.
Approximate cost,
6s. 9½d.

7
GOOD HOUSE-KEEPING CHRISTMAS PUDDING

2½ lb. raisins.
1½ lb. sultanas.
1½ lb. currants.
¾ lb. peel.
2 oz. sweet almonds.
2 oz. bitter almonds.
1 lb. suet.
½ lb. breadcrumbs
   (white).
1 lb. flour.
½ teaspoonful grated
   nutmeg.
½ teasp. cinnamon.
2 teaspoonfuls salt.
1 lb. Barbados sugar.
6 eggs.   1 pt. milk.

Makes 5 puddings weighing
2 lb. 5 oz. each.
Approximate cost, 8s. 8d.

FOOD Glorious FOOD

1934

Illustrations
by
Harry
Morley

The children stared, then shrieked with delight at the sight of the goose. "Oh, Charlie," said Margaret, "Wherever did you get it?"

MARGARET FRANCIS came down from putting the last of the children to bed, and quietly resumed her mending. Her husband, Charles Francis, stirred the fire, for outside the cottage window the wind was whining from the north-east, with a sound of yet more snow. A man of infinite moods, he responded to the sudden glow; for whereas all that evening he had been irritable as a man will be when the weather checks him in his work, he could now speak more philosophically of the desperate winter that had set in, and the thaw that seemed as far off as ever.

"I reckon we shall get a change o' weather one o' these days, me old beauty?"

"I hope so, Charlie." She was a wisp of a woman, set in a finer mould than her handsome, specious husband, and as she said the words there came a nervous hesitation. She knew his quick, impatient rages, but duty with her was an insistent thing, and she had to speak.

"Don't think I'm keeping on at you, Charlie, but what about Christmas dinner? It's only three days now."

He flared up at once. "Now ain't that a master funny thing? Didn't I say I'd as good as got somethin'? What d'you want to keep mobbin' about it for, then?"

Her voice held the same quiet level. "I'm not mobbing, as you call it. But you know how you forget things." She hesitated again. "If you hadn't really spoken for anything, I was wondering if someone might let us have a fowl. Just a cheap one."

"A fowl!" He sneered. "We ain't got no jolly money for fowls, nor nothin' else, neither—and well you know it. But you've allust had a Christmas dinner, hain't ye? Well, then!"

He was settling to his accustomed

It was Farewell to Pheasants

when Charlie Francis, the poacher, at last brought home the family Christmas Dinner

By MICHAEL HOME

(Author of "God and the Rabbit," and "In this Valley")

nap, but his wife's voice came in again. "Look here, Charlie, I must speak. If you're planning to get something you shouldn't, then you can save your time, for me and the children would sooner have a crust of bread. Once before you brought home those pheasants and made out you'd bought them, and all the time you'd got them off the squire's land; and Field knew it, and Mrs. Field told me herself that if it hadn't been for me and the children, you know what'd have happened."

"Field!" He gave a little sneering laugh. "Who care a button about him —nor his jolly keepers, either? And what about the squire's pheasants eatin' my corn? Did Mrs. Field tell you about that? I lay a farden cake she didn't." The irony was soothing him and the anger partly went. "And never you mind about Christmas dinner, Mrs. Francis. I told you I'd got my eye on somethin', didn't I? Well, then!"

She nodded. "Very well, Charlie. Only, if you bring home here what you shouldn't, then I'll not cook it, and that's flat. My conscience tells me what's right, if yours doesn't."

"Conscience!" He glared again. "I can cook it myself, can't I?" He settled again to the chair and the brief storm subsided with his final rumblings. "And am I to have any peace and quiet in this house or am I not? A master funny thing a man go workin' all day long and can't have no rest when he do get home?"

But no man in Breckland had more irons in the fire than Charles Francis, and all the next day his hands and thoughts were busy, and at idle, inconsequential, unremunerative things which he liked doing. Village work was slack and there was a crowd of men in his workshop-barn to watch him work and laugh with him and gossip. But as he walked home in the dusk and Farmer Cordy gave him the seal of the night, with the remark that it looked like being a rare sharp Christmas, he remembered the meal and it was on the tip of his tongue to speak to the farmer about an old hen. Then he was glad he had said nothing. He had no half-crowns for old hens when pheasants lay handy for a man with brains. He would show Field and his keepers who was the cleverer man. He would make Squire Green pay for the corn his birds had eaten. And if Margaret started that mobbing again, or was obstinate about the cooking, he would show her once and for all who was master in the house.

But Margaret said no word that night, and the next day Francis was busier than ever. Chaff had to be cut to save work over the holiday; mangolds cleaned; wood brought home and kindling chopped, and the sow's stye cleaned out, for she was soon due to litter. It was late afternoon, then, when he remembered again the Christmas meal, and when the thought came to him so that he knew himself at grips with a problem that could be no longer shelved, his mind stirred among hopeless schemes and old hypotheses, till he knew himself pathetically for a baulked man. If it were moonlight, and if he could borrow an air-gun, he could yet knock over two roosting pheasants that night. If he had not been so jolly busy he might have gone to Ouseland and got some birdlime from a man he knew. If the frost were not so hard, late as it was he could have laid down some traps.

But something had to be done and already the dusk was coming on, so that it was useless to venture down to his holding at Parson's Patch with the hope of a lucky shot. Then an idea came as a last poor hope, and he filled his pockets with corn from the cob's bin and, making his way through the dung-yard at the back of the barn, came in the dusk out at the Illborough Lane. There the wind cut to the bone, and the bare trees so overhung the narrow track that it would have been dark but for the crisp whiteness of the frozen snow.

Ten minutes, and he was in the shelter of his tiny haystack, peering across the white valley to the ride between the woods where that early summer the squire's pheasants had been reared. Then he moved cautiously to his far boundary and reconnoitred from the hedge. Against the white of clean snow he thought to discern a pheasant making its way to the larches where already a cock was squawking. In a moment he was through a gap and in the ride. As he shuffled his feet so that no clear track should stay, he threw the corn with wide scatterings. Then he was gone again —a mere darkness in the gloom of the narrow lane.

That night his tongue held, ready the words that should silence his wife's questionings, but Margaret had made her protest and, for all his sneering, was not one to nag. The children were excited too and kept her busy, till at last she brought down from upstairs the tinsel toys for the tree and the tiny holders for the candles. Then the girls went to bed, and the two boys, and it was Jim who broached the subject when he had kissed his father good-night.

" What are we havin' for Christmas dinner, father? "

The hasty words leaped to Francis's tongue—then he laughed.

" Christmas dinner? Never thinkin' about anything but your jolly bellies. And never you mind what we're havin'. You allust have had somethin', ain't ye? Well, then ! "

He settled ostentatiously to his nap, breathing heavily with a pretence of sleep. Then sleep came, and bedtime, and still Margaret had said no word.

Christmas morning had the same icy frost. The children would be stirring early to hunt through their stockings, but long before dawn Francis was up and away. By the light of the lantern he mucked out the cob and gave it an early feed. He broke the ice in the tub, mixed the sow a pail of meal, and left her stye door open, with a beet or two thrown in the yard where she could come at them. Then he got out his gun and cartridges from their hiding-place beneath the bench, and by the yard way slipped out to the lane.

To him night was the same as daylight, and ten minutes later he lay in the seclusion of a holly clump in his far hedge, and with the barrel of the gun alone protruding, awaited the first dawn.

There was no irksomeness in the wait. In his poachings he was a man of tireless patience, and time was nothing provided that at last the one great moment came. Slowly the sky lightened towards Larford Heath. Then his blood, as it always did, stirred at the squawk of a pheasant, and his right hand closed round the stock of the gun as he peered into the whitening grey.

Now his legs were cramped and the cold was numbing him. Five minutes, and he could make out the trees that bordered the ride. Five minutes more and a slow, impotent rage began to mount as he knew his planning had been in vain. Broad daylight was hard at

hand. The grey landscape held no sign of a moving thing, and soon it would whiten and betray, so that it would be madness to try a shot. Then suddenly, as he half-rose to go, he caught his breath at the miracle that was happening. A pair of pheasants—cock-birds both—were picking a dainty way across the frozen snow. A scant fifty yards away, they were—and coming nearer. Then one caught sight of the corn and ran forward. The other followed and in a minute the two were pecking together.

Then the barrel of the gun straightened imperceptibly out. There was the roar of a shot—and like a man bursting from hell itself, Charles Francis broke from his shelter and was across the snow. The kicking birds were whisked

Slowly the sky lightened towards Larford Heath. Charlie's blood, as it always did, stirred at the squawk of a pheasant, and his right hand closed round the stock of his gun as he peered into the whitening grey

into his pockets, snow was scattered to cover feathers and blood, and he was back in the hedge again. Two at a shot. A family feed for a penny cartridge. And, Margaret's scruples or no scruples, a Christmas dinner!

Now he was chuckling to himself and filled with a superb confidence as he looked round. There was no movement on the visible landscape, and as he moved off it was scarcely yet full light. But he hid his gun in the haystack at the height of land, and gave yet another look across the valley. And one look was enough to send a quick terror through him, for down the far slope a man was coming headlong, and that man was Field, the head-keeper!

In that first panic Francis took to his heels. Then he slowed to a walk. Field was no runner, and he sneered to himself as he remembered that, and how in the village there was no man that he himself could not outrun. And though the shot had come from Charles Francis's land, Field could never prove who fired it, for of the one thing he was certain—that he had caught no glimpse that could identify himself. Yet a panic was still on him so that he broke into a trot, slowing only when he neared the barn. It was as he slipped through the back way, glancing towards the park, that there came a new, tremendous terror, which for a moment blanched his face. Field had taken the private way across the hall meadows, and was almost on him!

With a quick movement he thrust the two pheasants beneath the bracken of the stack he had stored in the yard corner against winter bedding. As he slipped through the barn door, and kicked the sow on the snout to keep her back, he was already summoning a courage, so that when Field drew in from the yard he was singing a carol and mixing a skep of chaff and beet When the keeper's feet sounded on the stone floor of the barn he could look round with a start of enormous surprise.

"Whuh, Mas' Field, if you didn't fair scare me!" He gave a smile of relief. "Wondered for a moment whoever it was. And what d'you reckon you're a-doin' of this time o' day?"

"Mornin', Charlie," said Field. He was a bearded, stocky man, whose soberness *(Continued)*

FAREWELL TO PHEASANTS

fools had often taken for stolidity. His manner and voice were quiet, as became one who had much to do with gentry. Many a time he had threatened Francis, but his own wife's pleadings and her friendship with Margaret Francis and the thought of the children had stayed his hand. Even now he came to the matter circuitously, for in the presence of so plausible a rogue, it was hard to bear malice or wish the man ill.

"I suppose you didn't hap to hear a shot just now, Charlie?"

"A shot?" He laughed. "I been too busy to hear any shots." The laugh became more friendly. "What do you want to go worryin' about shots for, a mornin' like this? Christmas don't come every day, ye know."

"No," said Field deliberately. He chewed upon the thought, then moved a step or two nearer the yard door, and Francis, moistening his lips, watched him where he stood. But slowly, and in that chill air, Field made up his mind. He liked Charles Francis, rogue though he was. His wife was a nice little body, and there were the children—but duty was duty, and the time had come for Francis to be brought to a full stop. But as he steeled his heart to say the ominous words, a something caught his eye, so that he

stared amazed. Then he gave a grunt and a dry laugh.

"I suppose you didn't hap to fire that shot, Charlie?"

"What, me?" said Francis indignantly. "Whatever make you think a thing like that. What should I want to go firin' shots for?" Then he laughed. "This ain't Guy Fawkes' Night, ye know."

"You might have been after a Christmas dinner," said Field quietly, his eyes still on the yard. Then he glanced back quickly over his shoulder. "Come ye here a minute and have a look."

Francis came to look. There was no need to ask for what, for the tragedy

(Continued)

THE COOKING OF GAME

Partridge and Pheasant

Draw and truss, cover breast with bacon, cook in a moderate oven, allow about 30 minutes for partridge and 45 to 50 for pheasant. Baste frequently with butter. Dish on toast, garnish with watercress. About 1 lb. beefsteak is sometimes placed inside a pheasant to keep it moist and to improve its flavour, while cooking.

Accompaniments

Gravy	Bread sauce
Brown crumbs	Chipped potatoes

Teal, Ptarmigan, Blackcock

These birds are served on rounds of buttered toast. They should be basted frequently with butter while cooking. Roast in a moderate oven for about 30 minutes. Garnish with watercress and quarters of lemon.

Accompaniments

Gravy	Bread sauce or
Brown crumbs	Orange sauce

Snipe, Plover, Quail, Woodcock

After trussing, cover breast with a slice of bacon. Place on toast in order to catch the drippings from the trail. Cook for about 15 minutes, basting frequently. Serve on toast and garnish with watercress.

Accompaniments

Gravy	Browned crumbs
	Chipped potatoes

Roast Venison

After being hung for the required length of time—from six to nine days is

generally sufficient—brush the joint with fat and cover with a stiff paste made of flour and water, and wrap in an outer layer of greased paper. Roast in a moderate oven, allowing 25 minutes per lb. Half an hour before serving remove the paper, baste well and dredge with flour. Serve with thick brown gravy and red-currant jelly.

Salmi of Game

2 small game birds (any kind)	1 oz. butter
	1 oz. flour
1 onion	1 tomato
1 carrot	A few mushrooms for
¾ pt. game stock	garnish
	Glass of red wine

Roast the birds, removing them from the oven when barely cooked. Remove the skin and the ends of the legs and cut the flesh into neat pieces. Pound up the carcases and fry them with the chopped onion and carrot in the butter. Add the flour and allow to brown. Next add the tomato cut into quarters, the red wine and stock. Bring to the boil and simmer for an hour. Strain the sauce over the joints of game and heat. Serve garnished with small mushrooms which have been cooked in butter.

Jugged Hare

1 hare	1 glass port wine
1½ pints stock	Tablespoonful lemon juice
¼ lb. bacon	3 ozs. flour
2 onions stuck with cloves	Forcemeat
Bunch of herbs	Red-currant jelly
	Seasoning

Cut the hare into ten or twelve neat joints and flour them well. Fry them in the bacon cut into dice. Turn them into a casserole or jar with the onions, herbs,

and lemon and cover with the stock, cover and cook in a very moderate oven for three hours or until tender. In the meantime form the forcemeat (made according to the following recipe) into small balls, egg, crumb and fry them. Dish the hare. Mix the flour to a smooth cream with cold water. Stir into the gravy and bring to the boil. Add the wine and seasoning of the hare and the blood of the hare if liked. Do not reboil, but heat meat and forcemeat balls in gravy. Dish and serve with red-currant jelly.

Forcemeat for Jugged Hare

The liver of the hare	Little grated lemon rind
4 oz. breadcrumbs	1 oz. suet
1 tablespoonful chopped parsley	1 teaspoonful dried herbs
	Egg or milk to mix
	Seasoning

Part boil the liver and chop it finely. Mix all the dry ingredients together and moisten with the egg or milk. Form into small balls, coat with egg and crumbs and fry.

Partridge en Casserole

Partridge	Lemon juice (dessertspoonful)
2 oz. butter	½ pt. stock
Onion	1 gill cream
	Seasoning

Heat the butter in the casserole and when smoking hot brown the partridge and the onion cut into quarters. Then remove the onion and add the lemon juice, seasoning, and stock. Place casserole in the oven and baste the bird frequently. When barely cooked pour the cream over the bird. Finish cooking and serve in the casserole.

"You must try these...

Cadburys

CHOCOLATE BISCUITS • Not just chocolate biscuits — but chocolate biscuits made by *Cadbury*. There's a difference ... smoother, more delicious chocolate. Hand them round in the fashionable Drum. This attractive-looking tin is practical, too. It keeps the biscuits fresh and unbroken. Here is shown a ½ lb. Drum of the Digestive variety. It costs only 1/-. Other varieties are at your grocer's.

TABLE FINGERS
½ *lb. Drum* 1/2

DIGESTIVE BISCUITS
½ *lb. Drum* 1/-

RASPBERRY WAFER
½ *lb. Drum* 1/3

*BOURNVILLE
BISCUITS*
½ *lb. Drum* 1/2

STIRLING BISCUITS
(*Milk Chocolate*)
½ *lb. Drum* 1/3

PICKWICK
(*Shortcake Finger*)
½ *lb. Drum* 1/-

MADE AT BOURNVILLE
THE FACTORY IN A GARDEN

CADBURY'S CHOCOLATE DIGESTIVE BISCUITS

½ lb. DRUM 1/-

146

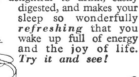

FAREWELL TO PHEASANTS

lay beneath his eye—and was still in progress. The old sow had rooted beneath the bracken and found the two pheasants. One—but for the head—she had already eaten, and the other she was now finishing with greedy slaverings and little pleasureable grunts as her jaws smacked. The old Adam flared out in Francis beyond his prudence, and his voice came in a mad bellow.

"You old davul, you!"

Field's arm shot out to hold him back. "You're not soon enough, Charlie bor. Your Christmas dinner's gone."

It was too late for lies or plausibilities. Francis knew himself a lost man, and it was not his way to cringe. Yet in a quick, pathetic moment he saw Margaret and the children.

"All right, Mas' Field." He spoke gently, like a man who accepts fate. "Only, don't have the summons sent round, or breathe a deen to a soul till Christmas is over. We don't want no upset."

"No," said Field reflectively. "As you say, Charlie, we don't want no upset—not at Christmas."

Then his eye fell again on the foraging sow, and the incongruous feathers that hung by her slavering jaws, and all at once he began to chuckle. Then he gurgled and his body began a quivering, which was the nearest he ever came to a laugh. Then at last he shook his head, and with his knuckles wiped the corners of his tear-blurred eyes.

"Blest if ever I seed the like! A fair masterpiece."

Once more he shook his head, and with a glint of hope Francis watched him. Then the face straightened and he turned challengingly.

"If I say nothin', you can keep your own mouth shut about this?"

"That I sartinly can," Francis assured him solemnly.

Field's eyes narrowed. "You'd better— or I'll have you yet for that job you did a fortnight ago down the Drove, what you thowt I knew nothin' about." He looked away for a moment, stirring with his stick the snowy dung of the yard. Then with another challenge: "Was them two birds your Christmas dinner?"

Francis mumbled a something, and for once looked sheepish.

"Well, if you come along o' me," went on the head-keeper, "I got somethin' you might have—though my missus needn't know nothin' about it. The squire sent me his usual turkey, and then blowed if someone else didn't go and give me a goose—so you can have the goose."

Francis stared. Then he saw that Field was in earnest, and a new miracle happened. Charles Francis, the Radical, to whom all keepers—as such—were the scum of the earth and its veriest dolts, flicked his fingers humbly to his forelock.

"Thankee, Master Field; thankee, very kindly."

He was half an hour late for breakfast. The family had finished, though they were still at table, and Margaret began scolding as soon as she heard his step in the kitchen. There had been sausages that morning as a Christmas treat, and the children had had a half-one each.

"Come on, Charlie, do! There's your breakfast all getting cold."

To him the dramatic was ever the salt of life and all at once he was at the partition door and holding up the goose by its legs. The children stared, then shrieked with delight. Margaret was startled, too.

"Oh, Charlie!" And then, suspiciously: "Wherever did you get it?"

"From a man what I know." He laughed, and beneath his black moustache his teeth showed pearly white. "And it didn't cost nothin', neither. Now what about your Christmas dinner? Didn't I tell you I'd have one?"

For a moment she felt like crying. "I believe you knew about it all the time!"

"Knew about it!" The sneer gave time to fit the lie deftly into place. "And what if I did? I ain't forced to tell you everything, am I? Well, then!"

He ran his fingers caressingly along the feathers from head to tail, then with a last chuckle laid the goose on the rag rug by his chair and drew up to the table. Margaret put before him the plate with its two sausages and gravy, and he reached over for the pepper-pot.

"The squire give all the farmers a brace o' pheasants," said Jim. "I know, because Arthur Cordy told me—and I see 'em."

"Goose is better than pheasants, isn't it, father," said little Eva loyally.

"Pheasants!" He sneered. The pepper-pot in hand, he looked round the circle of young, admiring eyes, and his other hand was raised in a scornful gesture. "Pheasants! Who want pheasants? Let 'em have their jolly pheasants. I wouldn't have 'em—no! not if they was to give 'em me."

The Books to Choose

When you are selecting presents for a woman who loves homes and home-making, give her one of these. The prices are very moderate, and we will send them direct, if you prefer:

Sweets and Candies - - 1s., or 1s. 2d. post free
Pies, Puddings and Pastry 6d., or 7½d. „ „
A.B.C. of Cookery - 2s. 6d., or 2s. 9d. „ „
Cakemaking - - - 1s., or 1s. 2d. „ „
Menu and Recipe Book 2s. 6d., or 2s. 9d. „ „
Cooking by Electricity - 6d., or 7½d. „ „

Send your orders to Good Housekeeping, 153 Queen Victoria Street, London, E.C.4

The
Fascination of Old English
County Cookery

❧

I RECENTLY came across what I considered to be a very appropriate wall decoration for a country house dining-room—a gastronomic map of France, attractively framed in red. After studying it carefully for a short time, I realised that it gave an immense amount of fascinating information on gastronomic matters which could not have been portrayed so successfully by any other means. I was not surprised to find that the map had proved a much appreciated and welcomed wedding gift.

Although England is small, and has never claimed the same distinction as France as far as the art of gastronomy is concerned, it seemed to me a matter for regret that no similar map of England had ever been published, particularly as at the present time there is a great revival of interest in good English cookery. To compensate for this deficiency, we have had this map of England and Wales drawn specially for GOOD HOUSEKEEPING readers in the hope that it will serve to arouse interest in a subject which might be forgotten, but which appeals to almost every housewife.

I do not claim that the dishes given are comprehensive; in fact, in some counties, where it would appear that cooking is thought far more of than in others, almost half the dishes have had to be omitted from the map for want of space. Some of these are given in the panel on this page.

It is interesting to note that Warwickshire, Herefordshire and Hertfordshire are devoid of names. This does not imply that these particular counties cannot boast some special dishes, but that so far I have not been successful in tracing them.

It is surprising how easy it is in the rush of modern life to lose touch with old English customs, pursuits and foods, and in an effort to collate in a convenient form some of the best of our old county dishes, I am hoping to publish during 1936 a series of articles dealing with this subject.

In my brief preliminary search, I have received much help from the County Federations of Women's Institutes, of which I am very appreciative. Some Federations have published their own cookery books, most of which con-

SOME ADDITIONAL COUNTY DISHES

CORNWALL
Black Cake, Apple and Mutton Pie, Fairings, Sly Cakes, Kettle Broth, Hog's Pudding.

DORSET
Apple Cake, Blackmore Vale Cakes, Crock Cake, Jugged Steak, Dorset Delight.

WILTSHIRE
Syllabubs, Girdle Cakes.

SURREY
Guildford Manchits, Surrey Tea Cakes.

KENT
Oast Cakes, Kentish Cheese Pasties, Well Pudding, Rabbit Pudding, Browsels Scrap Cake, Scran Cakes, Pork Cake, Haslet.

BUCKINGHAMSHIRE
Aylesbury Game Pie, Bacon Badger, Bucks Mutton Pie, Chiltern Hills Pudding.

WORCESTERSHIRE
Spiced Beef.

NOTTINGHAMSHIRE
Nottingham Pork Pie, Mansfield Pudding.

YORKSHIRE
Yorkshire Yule Cake, Bread and Oat Cake, Savoury Pudding, Spiced Bread, Yorkshire Christmas Pie, North Country Sweet Pie.

LANCASHIRE
Goosenargh Cakes.

tain at least three or four recipes peculiar to their county, but others could not assist me for they had no collection of recipes or any information on the subject which they could pass on.

From a glance at the map it would appear that counties farthest removed from London have a greater wealth of special dishes, for there seems to be no shortage of recipes from Cornwall, Devonshire, Yorkshire, Cumberland and Lancashire, although Kent provides a good number. Whether this is so or not remains to be proved.

From the letters I receive and from my personal contact with GOOD HOUSEKEEPING readers, I know there are many who possess a mine of information on matters appertaining to the home, including county customs, food and cookery. I take this opportunity, therefore, of inviting any reader who has genuine old recipes, preferably those which can be attributed to a county or district, to send them to me. Payment will be made for those published.

The work I have already done in connection with old English recipes has proved fascinating and full of interest. Among other things, I have discovered that most counties have their special dishes for utilising "flead," and although to-day, comparatively speaking, few people kill their own pigs, it would be a pity to lose sight entirely of the old ways and means our grandparents had of utilising the materials that were available in their day.

"Frummity" is another dish which appears in different counties, although the spelling varies slightly. For instance, it is "Frummity" in Durham, "Frumetty" in Lincolnshire, and "Firmety" in Yorkshire.

From Kent I received a very comprehensive list of recipes, of which Oast Cakes, Flead Cakes, A Pound of Butter Roasted, and Huffkins, all sound so exciting that one immediately wants to rush off and make them. In addition to these, and other less well-known dishes, such popular ones as Eccles Cakes, Lancashire Hot Pot, Bath Buns, Maids of Honour, Cornish Pasties, Melton Mowbray Pies, will also be tried and tested in the Institute kitchens before appearing in print.

D. D. COTTINGTON TAYLOR

The Director invites all readers to co-operate in a survey of the traditional foods of our countryside

Gastronomic map of ENGLAND

STEPS TO
HEALTH
AND
APPETITE

NEW ZEALAND

NEW ZEALAND BUTTER

NEW ZEALAND BUTTER

Sunshine is health. In the fresh, green pasturelands of sunny New Zealand wonderfully rich cream is produced to make the butter which brings to you all the natural sunshine vitamins in the most delightful form. No other butter gives so much enjoyment and so much nourishment at so relatively small cost. New Zealand cheese is just as good.

If you want the best, you must get—

The importance of plenty of New Zealand Butter for growing boys and girls cannot be over-estimated.

Read the following extract from the officially published report of Dr. H. C. Corry Mann, O.B.E., of an Investigation conducted under the auspices of the Medical Research Council :—

"A group of 26 boys who were taking the butter ration remained under observation during 12 months and during that time gained an average 6·30 lb. per boy and grew an average 2·22 in. per boy. 11 of these 26 boys completed a two years' test, and the average gain in weight remained steady at 12·32 lb. for the two years' period."

The Butter used was New Zealand Butter

New Zealand Butter and Cheese

Chichester Cross, 15th Century

This Christmas again
Shippam's
delicious pastes of
MEATS, FISH & FOWL
will be present at all
the jolliest parties

HALF A MILLION WISHBONES — each one from a plump Sussex chicken which has joined a mellow ham to make Shippam's Chicken and Ham paste. This is one of the sights of Shippam's factory, over which

YOU ARE INVITED to see — any time — any day — without appointment. Just call in — we like to show people the perfect ingredients of our pastes and the ideal conditions under which they are made. If you cannot call yourself, please write for our illustrated brochure, free on request. C. Shippam Ltd, Dept 13K, Chichester, Sussex

" To my mind a picnic should be
somewhat unsophisticated and pastoral,
imbued with the spirit of Rousseau "

THE PLEASURES OF PICNICS

Illustrations by Rex Whistler

PICNICS, necessarily diversions for a safe countryside, do not suit Asia and Africa, where Nature, "red in tooth and claw," reigns at her reddest; there they become a dangerous indulgence. However much you may love them, your devotion is scarcely an altruistic one: you cannot yourself wish to provide the picnicking for other creatures, lion or tiger. In America even, though the animals be fewer and less fierce, the continent seems too large for the sense of outdoor intimacy essential to a picnic. You can hardly feel secure, at your ease, in it. Therefore Europe is the continent where this art has been most fully developed, and in England, especially, we have been obliged to develop our own rainproof technique. For, although eating in the open air has always had its devotees, on the Continent you can eat under these circumstances meals that would have appealed to Lucullus himself, while here in England is but a little opportunity to sit under a striped umbrella, by the side of a lake, feeding deliciously. We are, generally speaking, a nation of indoor-eaters, and if you go out you must take your food with you.

As for the lure of the picnic, it is a kind of illusion, fascinating because of the Petit-Trianon element of make-believe simplicity which it brings with it to you and your friends. For it takes two—or more—to make a picnic, as much as a quarrel. Eating alone out-of-doors does not constitute a picnic. You are savages once more, or mariners wrecked upon a desert island, or members of the eternal Swiss Family Robinson, waiting, with the same not unjustified confidence as theirs, for Providence most properly to provide.

Two things alone are supreme, all-important; the situation you choose, and the food. The picnics that you may observe in progress throughout England on any fine Sunday during the spring or summer are pointless, are not picnics at all; when hundreds of cars are parked on the remaining commons—many of them beautiful in themselves—while crouching and lolling on plaid rugs beside them, their owners unwrap unappetising parcels with the noisy crackle and rattle of old gentlemen reading *The Times* in the bow-windows of London clubs. That does not constitute a picnic: it is just eating out of doors, *déjeuner sur l'herbe*.

A picnic should be dedicated to an occasion or pitched in some transient paradise, such as a wood of bluebells; where you may sit on the silver trunks of fallen birches, with a prone oak tree as your awkward table, while round and under you floats a mist of blossom, the perfumed, blue-smoke-cloud that every year imparts to the English spring an unparalleled beauty. Or again, the meal can be offered to the autumn; because, in a sense, we become, as we eat in these surroundings, the representatives of the old gods to whom our ancestors made sacrifice, and every mouthful, as we contemplate the rowan berries that flicker like fire upon the branches of their trees, is a hymn of praise to the English autumn. . . . Nearby, too, you should light a bonfire, so that the acrid smell of it, the very seal and token of the season, should accompany each course. And you should most carefully select beforehand, at whatever time of year your banquet takes place, the particular kinds of food due to the season.

The bane of ordinary picnics is bread—thick Stonehenge slices of buttered English bread, between which lies a thin film of pink paste. . . . Avoid then, if possible, bread, which was re-

Osbert Sitwell

an epicure in eating out-of-doors, tells of alfresco meals that have delighted him and that may perhaps please you

sponsible in times past for the inevitable post-picnic indigestion. Bring wheat or rye biscuits, the crispness of which matches the tang of the fresh air, and other biscuits (for they, and rightly, are one of the glories of England). Bring cold trout, which swam in the stream beneath where you are sitting, and plenty of fresh butter, cold chicken, all the fruits of the season, and cheese with the goaty taste of mountains clinging to it. If possible, let the food be wrapped in leaves—vine leaves and the like rather than in everyday, greaseproof paper. In the autumn you should prepare cold partridges, which a few short days ago flew and nested among the golden branches round you (you should, too, throw aside gentility for the moment and eat the legs, after the manner of a true Crusoe, with your fingers!) and provide bilberries and apples and raw celery. For to my mind a picnic should be somewhat unsophisticated and pastoral, imbued with the spirit of Jean Jacques Rousseau.

Yet other kinds of picnics are not without their own appropriate joys, and I look back with pleasure to those early spring days in Portugal, when I was staying with a German friend, a connoisseur of life and of many countries. There, with a few other companions, we used to set out at an early hour, motoring to distant parts of the country, and often obliged to wait for twenty minutes or so on the ferry that plies across the lime-green waters of the Tagus; a pleasant break, comparable to the oasis of the English Channel in that long, dreary ride from London to Paris. After a considerable drive, my friend would give a signal; and the chauffeur and footmen would jump down and produce enormous patent boxes. Thereafter they would unfold Bokhara rugs, stagger forward with collapsible chairs and table, and then proceed to bear in dish after dish, hot dishes and cold dishes, French and Austrian and Spanish, bottles of white wine and bottles of red, Rhine wines and the wines of Bordeaux, while the friendly Portuguese sun of February and March traced for us increasingly complicated patterns among the leaves of cork tree and palm.

Nevertheless, in meals such as these, the trees seemed the one essential factor: because trees *are* necessary as a

"Throw aside gentility for the moment and eat after the manner of a true Crusoe, with your fingers"

rule to a picnic, so that they may offer you their kindly shade. But not always, for the temples of Pestum in Italy, of Girgenti and Suggesti in Sicily and of Cape Sunion in Greece, provide you with the age-old artificial shade of their immense columns . . . I have said before, that in my opinion picnics should, many of them, be dedicated to an occasion; and the antique world should furnish you with one such, at least.

"Other kinds of picnics are not without their appropriate joys . . ."

Does your Child know these signs of the Happy Healthy OVALTINEYS?

***Boys and Girls!
Join the League of
Ovaltineys to-day!***

Send a postcard to-day to THE CHIEF OVALTINEY, The 'Ovaltine' Factory (Dept. 67), King's Langley, Herts, asking for the Official Rule Book and full details of the League.

P214A

MANY thousands of boys and girls are enthusiastic members of the League of Ovaltineys. They get endless fun and amusement from the secret high-signs signals and code. And more important still, they are told how to be always fit and vigorous.

The League of Ovaltineys was founded by the proprietors of 'Ovaltine' in the interests of children everywhere. Parents welcome the League because they appreciate its objects and the great benefit which 'Ovaltine' confers on the health of their children.

Delicious 'Ovaltine' is the perfect food beverage for children. It provides every nutritive element required to build up a strong, sturdy body, sound nerves and abundant vitality. For this reason make 'Ovaltine' your child's regular daily beverage. And be sure, too, that he or she joins the League of Happy Ovaltineys.

'OVALTINE'
Builds up Brain, Nerve and Body.
Prices in Gt. Britain and N. Ireland, 1/1, 1/10 and 3/3.

The Housekeeper's Dictionary *of* Facts

FOOD
Glorious
FOOD

1936

Green Tomatoes

I SHOULD be very glad if you would tell me whether green tomatoes are really wholesome articles of food, as we have a good many growing outside which will never ripen, and the only recipe for the use of them I have ever seen is green tomato chutney.
(M. N., Nottingham.)

Since green tomatoes are immature, they lack flavour, and it is therefore advisable to use them for chutneys in which a very definite flavour is obtained from the addition of spices.

You may be interested to hear the personal experience of a member of the Institute Staff, who for many years grew a large number of tomatoes, and naturally had a good many green ones left over each autumn. After picking, these were placed in a box in a hot cupboard, and a large proportion of them gradually developed and ripened. Although they were not as deep a red as those which ripened in the sun, they were quite palatable, and could be used satisfactorily for soups, sauces and salads.

Thank you very much for your reply to my question about green tomatoes. The ripening process has been quite a success and we can now use the tomatoes in the ordinary way as well as for chutney. We have no hot cupboard, so I keep them in a covered box and basket on the rack over the fire. The first lot I did not disturb, but took them out when I thought they were all beautifully ripe, only to find that those underneath were quite green. Now I am turning them occasionally, with good results.

It is splendid to be able to write to the Institute when in any difficulty with regard to food. I only wish I could come up to London and take some of your courses.
(M. N., Nottingham.)

Mistress and Maid

I feel I would like to send you a word of sincere thanks for all your kindness and the trouble that you and your staff have taken with my cook, who was having lessons with you last week. I think she has profited very greatly by what she has learnt, and I notice a distinct difference in many of her dishes, and I know you do not take household cooks as a rule, and I appreciate very much your consideration in making this exception.
(C. T., Tockington.)

One Reader to Another

Having lived in India, I can sympathise with one of your correspondents, Mrs. D., Rotherhithe, who writes of the difficulty of keeping food even moderately fresh during the hot weather in an outpost in the northern part of Argentina, very far from civilisation. During my time in India we had no electricity or refrigerators, and ice could be obtained only from a distance. One there-

---

A NEW YEAR RESOLUTION

"I WILL BE A BETTER COOK"

For anyone interested in the subject, this is a resolution very easy to carry out. At Good Housekeeping Institute instruction is given in all branches of cookery by a fully-trained staff, and one of the advantages of our work is that it is not arranged in terms or sessions and therefore the lessons may be taken at any time at which we have a vacancy.

Household cookery, high-class cookery, cake-making and the icing of cakes, with many other branches, may all be studied; and of particular importance at this season, when early Seville oranges will soon be available, are the lessons on the making of marmalade.

Full particulars of our courses, which range in length from a single half-day to a year, may be obtained from :

Good Housekeeping Institute,
49, Wellington Street,
Strand, W.C.2

---

fore had to devise ways and means of keeping things cool and fresh. Our water-pot of drinking water had to be kept wrapped round with a cloth continuously kept wet, where the wind would play upon it. In an open basket hanging from a branch of a shady tree, lined with straw or grass, we would place our milk, butter and eggs, where they would swing in the wind and be beautifully cool and fresh. We also put cooked meat in the air like this, but it had to be used within twenty-four hours.
(Mrs. A. M. R., Somerset.)

Paraffin Cookers and Lamps

I am proposing to complete some useful hints on the general use and care of paraffin cookers and lamps, for the assistance of those who use them in schools, and who have little knowledge of the scientific handling of paraffin. I have seen your seal on some of the stoves, and it occurs to me that you may have literature dealing with them from your research department.

I am sure that there are many points regarding paraffin and the kinds and care of suitable stoves, that should be known by people in rural areas who use oil for lighting and cooking.

We have carried out a considerable number of tests on paraffin cookers and

---

lamps of different types and have found that, as a rule, very detailed instructions for use are supplied by the manufacturers. I am enclosing a list of our Approved Appliances, from which you will see the names of firms who have submitted oil-operated cooking, heating and lighting equipment for our tests. You may care to communicate with some of these. We have published articles from time to time on oil equipment, although I am afraid these have not been very recent.

I am enclosing a booklet dealing with oil cookers, which I think you may find helpful.

Thank you very much indeed for your reply to my letter regarding oil cookers. I have been able to obtain much information on the subject, and shall find your enclosures most useful for reference. I am much obliged for your help.

A Water Softener for a Small House

I have been interested recently in water softeners, and noticing that these articles are dealt with from time to time in the pages of your most interesting journal, I hope it may be in order to ask for some advice.

We would like to install a water softener in our small house—three in household—but have been rather worried by the fact that prices vary so much. We inquired at the Ideal Homes Exhibition and were told of a model costing £12 12s. A recent call from a representative of another firm estimated the price of a suitable model at somewhere near £30. I would be most grateful for some advice as to how much one should expect to pay for a satisfactory plant for this size of house (to work off the main), and as to whether the model at £12 12s. is likely to be satisfactory.
(R. M., London, N.2.)

You will find that prices vary for water softeners of very similar capacity, largely on account of the fact that some of them are filled with natural softening medium and others with an artificially prepared one. The former is the more expensive of the two and is not so readily affected adversely by water conditions. On the other hand, the artificial medium has considerably greater exchange value than the natural medium and consequently a very much smaller and less expensive plant will often suffice. In the ordinary way the softeners filled with artificial medium are perfectly satisfactory.

We have tested both of the softeners you have in mind, and can thoroughly recommend them.

Thank you very much for your most helpful letter about water softeners. I very much appreciate the trouble you have taken in this matter and the satisfactory way in which you have answered my questions.
(R. M., London, N.2.)

155

FOOD *Glorious* **fOOD**

1936

Right: the principal cuts of beef (the numbers referring to tables included in the article and the bones shown in the sections in which they will be found). The most expensive joints are in Section III

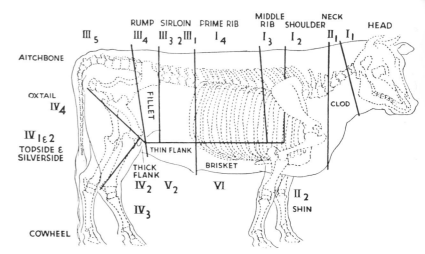

Below: the principal cuts of pork. These are different from the other three cases in several ways. The shoulder is unheard of, joints called the spare rib and the hand replacing it, and there are fewer sections

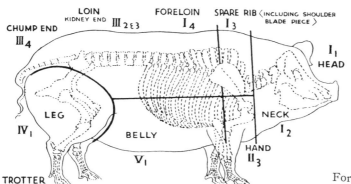

WHAT DO YOU KNOW

by RACHEL AND

Help for the young
to learn how to choose

NOTHING is more difficult to buy than meat, and the young house-wife is generally rather afraid of her butcher. Uneasily, and, as a rule, quite unjustly suspicious that she is being laughed at and imposed upon, she is not sufficiently familiar with the structure of the animals used for meat to be sure of grounds for complaint. Her best way of acquiring this information is by making a friend of her butcher and besetting him with questions, but as this is not always easy, perhaps we can clear the matter up a little on paper.

All the animals used for meat have certain features in common—notably, four legs and a backbone running from head to tail. Although butchers vary their cuts a little with the demands of their customers, they must be guided in cutting up a carcass by the bony structure of the animal, and they therefore tackle an ox, a pig, a sheep and a calf in much the same way. Every animal is first divided into sides by splitting the backbone in two from head to tail. The two sides are identical and each side falls roughly into five sections. The ox, being much larger than the others, is subdivided into a larger number of joints. Bacon is cut up quite differently and must be dealt with separately.

In studying the diagrams on these pages and the details which follow, it should be remembered that conditions vary considerably in town and country.

For example, a butcher in a sparsely-populated area, who kills his own animals, has quite a different trade from one in a large city, who is a purveyor only and never kills, but always buys carcasses from a central market.

The following practical facts will serve as a good shopping guide, telling you what you can and cannot ask your butcher.

You Can Ask Your Butcher

1. For *half* a leg or shoulder of mutton or lamb. (If you are taking the top or fillet half, ask him to bone it for you or you will find it nearly impossible to carve.)

2. To bone (i.e. remove the bones from) mutton (leg, shoulder, breast, loin), beef (sirloin, rib, brisket, aitchbone), veal (leg, bladebone, breast, loin), pork (leg, spare rib, loin, hand).

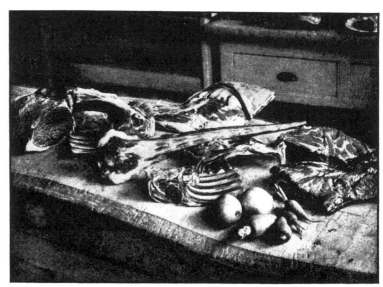

This is a group of the less expensive cuts of meat, suitable for stewing and casserole cookery. It includes silverside of beef, oxtail and neck of mutton and veal

HEAD I1

SCRAG END
NECK I2
MIDDLE NECK I3
14
BEST END NECK
III 2
LOIN
LOIN CHUMP END
III 5

LEG IV1

SHOULDER
II 3

BREAST
V1

Left: the principal cuts of mutton and lamb. As with beef, the best and most expensive joints come from Section III, and may be roasted. Sections II and IV are one whole joint, but can be halved

Below: the principal cuts of veal The leg and shoulder are divided into smaller joints, the former being suitable for roasting and the latter, termed blade-bone, oyster and knuckle, for stewing

ABOUT MEAT?

MARGARET RYAN

housewife who has yet

joints at the butcher's

HEAD I1

SCRAG END
OF NECK
I2
MIDDLE NECK I3
BEST END NECK
I4
LOIN
III 2
CHUMP END
II 5

BLADEBONE
& OYSTER
II 3

FOREKNUCKLE
II 2

BREAST
V1

FILLET
IV1

KNUCKLE
IV 3

3. To cut the approximate weight you require of steak, topside, silverside, flank or any other meat without bone. He cannot do this with the large bony joints; for instance, he cannot chop half a pound off a leg of mutton to reduce the joint to the exact weight you want without spoiling both the joint and the piece cut off. But a well-stocked butcher's shop ought to provide you with a joint within half a pound of the weight you require.

4. To cut up liver, stewing steak, fillet of veal, etc., into slices of the thickness you require.

5. To trim cutlets (i.e. take away the superfluous fat and skin and leave the lower part of the rib bone bare).

6. To salt and cook an ox tongue for you.

7. To salt silverside for you. Some butchers do this regularly, others only salt silverside to order and therefore require about two days' notice.

8. For a few pennyworth of bones for soup and stock, or pieces for your dog, but only if you buy all your other meat from him.

Do not be afraid that your butcher will look down on you for buying either small quantities or the cheaper cuts of meat. In the former case the price covers him; in the second place he is only too glad to get rid of the cheaper parts of the animal. He can always sell the best parts. The only thing to remember is that your butcher cannot perform impossibilities.

You Cannot Ask Your Butcher

1. To divide a rib of beef or a loin bone in mutton, pork or veal and sell you part. Some butchers will divide a sirloin bone in beef to oblige a customer who wants a very small quantity, but you must not be surprised if he says he cannot do this. He will, of course, *separate* the bones one from the other in the joint after you have bought it (in loin of mutton, for example).

2. For a leg of beef. This would be a huge joint, and is divided into shin, round (topside and silverside), thick flank or veiny piece, and the aitchbone joint.

3. For a shoulder of beef. This is sold partly as stewing steak, partly as shin and partly as clod—all pieces for stewing.

Although a butcher cannot always give exact weight in large, bony joints, he should cut within half a pound of your order if he carries a reasonable stock

CORONATION
Catering

by E. J. M. CRESWELL

of Good Housekeeping Institute staff, in collaboration with
Mrs. MONTAGUE of Good Housekeeping Restaurant

Whether you are helping
taining a party on the
or spending the day in
gestions will help you

A S far as our history books go back, the celebration of joyful events has been associated with "groaning tables," so it is inevitable and quite natural that the Coronation festivities should bring English cooking and entertaining into the limelight. We are more scientific, though perhaps not so lavish as, say, our Tudor ancestors, but this event is calculated to be of unprecedented immensity, and during Coronation week catering, in London particularly, may become a rather difficult problem.

One of the most important points to be borne in mind, with whatever type of catering is being undertaken, is that all arrangements should be made very well in advance, with nothing left to chance, or disappointments will result.

This especially applies to the hiring of china, chairs, tables, urns, and the booking of halls, etc., as there will be a more than usually big demand for them, but wise organisers will already have all such arrangements well in hand, and this article is intended to help mainly with the choice and cost of the food.

On such occasions as these the children are not forgotten. The presentation of mugs or some such memento is usually accompanied by a tea or similar function, and many school teachers will find that to their lot falls the task of organising the Coronation tea for their pupils. The money that is to be spent on these teas varies considerably according to the size and type of school, so we have planned two such teas, one for 500 children at 6d. per head, and one for 200 children at 1s. per head.

In some districts it has been suggested that the allowance should be only 4d. per head—a lamentably low figure, and it is to be hoped that such a tea, which could be only a meagre affair, would be supplemented by gifts from private individuals to make it more worthy of the occasion. There are generous people everywhere, and many who are interested in children would be only too pleased to give presents of home-made jam or cakes, biscuits, sausage rolls, etc., if they were approached.

It is assumed that for as large a number as 500 the cakes and buns will be bought from a caterer, but for smaller numbers the Domestic Science departments of the schools concerned will in many cases be responsible for producing them. Well-made scones, rock cakes, queen cakes and biscuits should not be beyond the older children, and are preferable to cheap bought cakes, as well as being more economical, but this calls for hard work and careful organisation, and as early as January of this year the Institute began to receive letters from Domestic Science teachers asking for advice on various catering difficulties they had foreseen.

In one instance the school had only recently been opened, the girls were all young and of course not very experienced in the art of cooking, and the teachers felt a little diffident in undertaking so much with them. In such a case the best thing is to keep to very simple cooking, put in as much practice beforehand as the syllabus will allow, and if possible arrange to have picked classes to carry out the actual work. Jelly, which is always popular with children, could be substituted for some of the cakes in this case, as it is very simple to make and easy to serve if it is set in little individual waxed cups with cardboard spoons.

It will be noticed that in each of these menus tea has been allowed for

with a school tea, enter=
route of the procession
the country, these sug=
plan successful menus

the drink. If, however, lemonade is
more popular, or if the meal is going
to be taken picnic-fashion, say on the
school sports ground, the money allowed
for tea, milk and sugar can be used for
providing the lemonade, thus doing
away with the difficulty of urns, hot
water, etc., and as lemonade is less expensive than tea, there will probably be
some balance in hand, which can be
spent in augmenting another item of
the meal. It will also be noticed that
in calculating the quantities of tea, milk
and sugar there has been a rather
generous allowance of milk, to enable
the smaller children to have either very
weak tea or perhaps milk alone.

Where time and talent permit, enterprising caterers or Domestic Science
teachers could add to the feast with a
well-decorated red, white and blue
Coronation Cake, such as the one illustrated in this article. The cake, which
need not be a very expensive mixture,
should be large enough for every child
to have a piece, and will cause much
more excitement and interest than the
slab cake, which can then be dispensed
with. The design chosen, especially if
the children themselves are going to
execute it, should be simple, and a geo-
metrical design such as that used on
our Coronation Cake is very effective
in deep red and blue on a white ground.

A SHILLING CORONATION TEA FOR SCHOOLCHILDREN

Quantities are calculated for 200 children
Food allowance at 1/- per head : £10 0s. 0d.

MENU

	£	s.	d.
Sandwiches *(3 per head)*			
10 quartern loaves, sliced, at 9d.		7	6
7 lb. butter (approx. ¾ lb. per loaf) at 1s.		7	0
16 lb. tomatoes at 6d.		8	0
10 tins sardines at 6½d.		5	5
7 lb. jam		3	3
Bread and Butter *(1 white and 1 brown piece per head)*			
2 white quartern loaves, sliced, at 9d.		1	6
2 brown quartern loaves, sliced, at 10d.		1	8
4 lb. butter at 1s.		4	0
Scones *(2 halves per head)*			
17 doz. at 6d. per doz.		8	6
4 lb. butter at 1s.		4	0
Cakes			
34 doz. assorted cakes at 1s. 6d. per doz.	2	11	0
Fruit Salad			
50 tins fruit salad at 1s. 4d. (or, if preferred, 25–30 tins of various fruits, with the addition of fresh bananas, oranges, etc.)	3	6	8
12 pts. half-price cream at 1s.		12	0
Tea			
3 lb. tea at 2s.		6	0
6 galls. milk at 2s.		12	0
6 lb. sugar at 3d.		1	6
	£10	**0**	**0**

A SIXPENNY CORONATION TEA FOR SCHOOLCHILDREN

Quantities are calculated for 500 children
Food allowance at 6d. per head: £12 10s. 0d.

MENU

	£	s.	d.
Bread and Butter *(2 pieces per head)*			
8 quartern loaves, sliced, at 9d.		6	0
6 lb. butter (¾ lb. per loaf), at 1s.		6	0
Jam Sandwiches *(2 per head approx.)*			
15 loaves		11	3
7½ lb. butter (½ lb. per loaf)		7	6
14 lb. jam (home-made if possible)		4	0
Cakes *(2 fancy cakes, 1 bun, 1 piece slab cake per head)*			
Small currant buns	1	0	0
85 doz. cakes at 1s. 3d. per doz.	5	3	9
60 lb. slab cake at 1s. per lb.	3	0	0
Tea			
5 lb. tea at 1s. 9d.		8	9
10 gall. milk at 2s.	1	0	0
Sugar		2	9
	£12	**10**	**0**

Which way do you dress salads?

1: LIKE THIS: take one young hostess all of a dither because her in-laws are coming to supper. Add an awful mess in her kitchen, dismal failure to get the complicated ingredients of salad dressing to do anything but curdle, season with exasperation and an over-flushed face — and serve with embarrassment.

2: OR LIKE THIS: take one charming young daughter-in-law, full of self confidence, because she is perfectly aware that with Heinz Salad Cream she can produce a perfect salad. Add the delightful knowledge that Heinz chefs use nothing but new laid eggs, pure olive oil and rich cream to make this wonderful dressing. Mix with fruits and crisp young vegetables—and serve with applause.

AND DON'T FORGET that because Heinz Salad Cream is made from nothing but new laid eggs, the purest olive oil, and plenty of rich cream, it adds that extra nutriment to a salad which makes it a perfectly balanced meal! And that is a big consideration when planning light meals

6ᵈ and **10ᵈ** **1/1½**

"SALADS AND WHEN TO HAVE THEM"—not just a jumble of recipes but a really intelligent little book on salad-making out of everyday ingredients. Full of bright ideas ' Monday Salads,' ' Health & Beauty Salads,' etc. Send a card for your free copy to H. J. Heinz Co. Ltd., Harlesden London, N.W.10.

HEINZ *Salad Cream*

MADE IN OUR LONDON KITCHENS—ONE OF THE 57 VARIETIES

A NEW COLD SWEET

A new pudding which does not entail cooking and which makes a cool and healthful summer sweet is named " Jellicrest." Everything is ready for use in a packet, with the exception only of half a pint of milk, and the finished pudding is interesting, as it is in two sections, the top a semi-transparent jelly and the lower half creamy and opaque. This sweet is one that should appeal to mothers who find their children have a natural dislike of milk.

DAMSON WINE

4 lb. damsons	9 pints water
3 lb. sugar	1 oz. yeast

Wash and pick the damsons and boil until tender in the gallon of water plus 1 pint (to allow for evaporation). Strain on to the sugar and cool until lukewarm. Add the yeast, spread on toast and leave for 24 hours. Remove the yeast, put into a cask or bottle and leave open to work. Fill up with wine. When the fermentation has finished cork tightly or bung. Rack off and bottle after 6 months.

PICNIC MEAT PASTE

Cold beef, mutton, ham or tongue may be substituted for the white meat in the recipe for Eggs for Gastronomes, and table sauce or chutney may be added instead of the wine. Follow the directions for preparing the mixture and use in sandwiches or bridge rolls.

A convenient way of using the paste on a picnic is to put it into a pot and spread it on buttered wheaten biscuits, thus obviating the tedious business of making sandwiches beforehand.

JELLIED HAM AND CHICKEN

1 boiling fowl	1 teaspoonful chopped
1 lb. raw ham	parsley
1 onion	½ oz. gelatine
Small blade of mace	Salt and pepper
2 hard-boiled eggs	Watercress

Wash and wipe the fowl thoroughly and put into a pan of boiling water. Bring to the boil, skim, add the mace, onion and seasonings, and simmer for 1½ hours or until tender. Add the ham half an hour before the chicken is cooked, and at the end of this time lift the fowl and ham out of the liquor. Remove the skin from the flesh, divide the chicken into joints and carve all the flesh from the bones and carcase. Return the bones and skin to the liquor and boil it rapidly, without the lid, until it is reduced to one-third of the original amount.

Meanwhile, cut the chicken and ham into neat dice. Strain the liquor on to the gelatine and allow to dissolve. Then add the meat and parsley and re-heat all together. Decorate a wetted mould with slices of hard-boiled egg, adding the trimmings of the meat. Pour mixture into the mould and allow to set for several hours until cold and firm. When the mould is cold, dip it in a basin of warm water, turn out and garnish with watercress.

GALANTINE

1½ lb. stewing steak	2 oz. fat bacon
3 oz. breadcrumbs	4 oz. sausage-meat
1 thin slice of onion	1 teaspoonful grated
1 teaspoonful chopped	lemon rind
parsley	1 egg
Salt and pepper	

Pass the meat, bacon and onion through a mincer; add the sausage-meat, lemon rind, parsley, crumbs, seasoning and beaten egg. Mix very thoroughly with the hand until the mixture binds, adding a little stock if necessary. Shape into a roll on a floured board and then put into a greased and floured cloth. Tie securely and put into a saucepan of boiling water. Boil for 2 hours. Remove the cloth and roll the galantine in breadcrumbs. Serve cold with a salad, or use for sandwiches.

BLOATER PASTE FOR PICNIC SANDWICHES

Butter	2 bloaters
	Salt and pepper

Cook the bloaters either by baking in a moderate oven or by poaching in water. Remove the skin and bones whilst the fish is still hot and rub the flesh through a sieve. Weigh the sieved fish and add to it an equal weight of butter. Pound both well together or, if a pestle and mortar are not available, cream the butter and work in the fish gradually but thoroughly. Season to taste and press tightly into small glass jars. Cover with melted butter and keep in a cold place.

This home-made paste should not be kept for more than a few days.

EGGS FOR GASTRONOMES

6 hard-boiled eggs	4 oz. cold chicken, duck
2 oz. stale bread	or veal
1 oz. butter	½ raw egg
Salt and pepper	1 teaspoonful finely-
Lettuce leaves	chopped parsley
A little wine, if liked (Sherry or Madeira)	

Soak the bread in cold water for half an hour, then squeeze out the moisture. Mince the meat, then put it into a mortar, together with the rest of the ingredients, except the cooked eggs. Pound very thoroughly. If the wine is omitted, add a little more beaten egg. Pass the mixture through a sieve. Cut the hard-boiled eggs in half and remove the yolks. Cut a little off the bottom of the whites, so that they stand level, and fill with the prepared mixture. Arrange on a bed of lettuce and sprinkle with the finely-chopped or sieved yolks.

PINEAPPLE AND BANANA MAYONNAISE

4 slices of fresh or tinned pineapple	
1 lettuce	2 bananas
Mayonnaise	1 oz. hazel nuts
	2 small tomatoes

Arrange the heart leaves of the lettuce on a flat dish. If tinned pineapple is used, drain the slices and dry on a clean tea towel. Cut the pineapple into small pieces and mix with a little mayonnaise and half of the chopped nuts. Put this mixture on to the bed of lettuce. Cut the bananas in half and cut each half into two slices. Arrange the slices star-wise with the blunt ends to the centre. Coat each slice with mayonnaise and sprinkle with the remainder of the chopped nuts. Garnish with thinly cut quarters of tomato.

SUGGESTIONS FOR SANDWICH FILLINGS

Meat

Minced cold mutton and mint sauce

Minced cold beef and horseradish sauce

Cold fried bacon and chopped pickled onions

Minced cooked liver and bacon with mustard

Minced chicken and ham

Tongue and chopped olives

Fish

Cold salmon, mashed potato and cucumber

Cooked smoked haddock and parsley sauce

Flaked crab and capers

Kipper and mustard

Any cooked white fish and chopped pickled walnuts

Finely chopped shrimps, mayonnaise, and lettuce

Miscellaneous

Seeded raisins and cream cheese

Mashed bananas and raspberry jam

Lemon curd and ground almonds

Marmalade and chopped walnuts

Sliced strawberries and cream cheese

Chopped currants, finely chopped mint, castor sugar

CHIVERS JELLIES

MADE IN SIXTEEN DELICIOUS FLAVOURS

Your Old Favourites

ARE NOW SUPPLIED IN BRIGHT NEW PACKETS

There's nothing more festive than Chivers Jellies; gay, sparkling colours and real fruit juice flavours make them ideal for special occasions—and for ordinary warm weather meals as well. Now, in Coronation year, the packets have been made festive too—each has its own fruit illustration to enable you to choose your favourite flavour more easily. The best jellies are now in the best packets—order some for to-morrow's menu.

Try this nourishing economical recipe

RICE CUPS

1 pint Chivers Raspberry Jelly	¼ lb. sponge fingers
1 oz. rice	½ pint milk	Sugar to taste

Dissolve jelly as directed, pour a little into individual glasses and allow to set. Dip sponge fingers in jelly, remove and put aside to set, after which arrange them in the glasses. Cook rice in milk, adding sugar to taste. Whip half the jelly when on the point of setting and mix with the rice, then fill up the glasses with this mixture. Decorate with chopped jelly.

CHIVERS & SONS LTD., THE ORCHARD FACTORY, HISTON, CAMBRIDGE

DO YOU KNOW...

*Here, in question and answer form, is much
useful information on cooking problems*

... Why Bacon is pink in colour?

MOST readers are probably aware that the red colour of meat is due to the presence of hæmoglobin, and some may have been curious enough to wonder why the flesh of bacon and ham is of a pinkish rather than a red colour. Research on these colour changes occurring in meat is in progress at the present time, for it is obviously of some importance from the commercial point of view to know how and why such alterations occur. In the case of bacon, the change in colour occurs during the pickling process, and is caused by the action of the saltpetre, the hæmoglobin present in the meat undergoing a chemical change, with formation of the pinkish-coloured nitroso-hæmoglobin.

•

... What is meant by Accredited Milk?

PARTICULARLY in households where there are young children or invalids, it is useful to know something of the different grades of milk which are now available. The following are the official Ministry of Health designations for Accredited, Tuberculin Tested and Pasteurised Milk.

Accredited Milk comes from cows that have passed a veterinary inspection, but not a test for tuberculosis.

Tuberculin Tested Milk comes from cows that have passed the tuberculin test for freedom from tuberculosis.

Tuberculin Tested Milk (Pasteurised) is Tuberculin Tested Milk which is also pasteurised.

Tuberculin Tested Milk (Certified) is Tuberculin Tested Milk which is bottled on the farm.

Pasteurised Milk has been heated at 145° Fahr. for 30 minutes to destroy any disease germs.

Wherever the expense can be considered it is probably wise to purchase Tuberculin Tested (Certified) Milk, which takes the place of the older designation of Grade A (which is no longer recognised) for infants and young children, but for adults in ordinary health Pasteurised Milk is considerably less expensive and, provided it is purchased from a reputable dairy, is entirely satisfactory. The temperature to which it has been subjected can be counted on to have destroyed harmful bacteria.

So much publicity has been given to the subject of milk lately that few people can fail to realise the exceptional value of this food, particularly for children. Those sufficiently interested to pursue the subject further may like to know of the pamphlet entitled *The Nutritive Value of Milk,* recently issued by the Ministry of Health, price 3d. This points out its extreme value in providing in an easily assimilable form not only the main body-building and energising constituents of the diet, but also vitamins and the highly important calcium and other salts which without milk are often difficult to include in adequate proportions. For children, from one to two pints daily should be the rule, and wherever possible adults should make a habit of consuming at least a pint per day in one form or another, including, of course, that taken with tea, coffee and in sauces, puddings, etc.

... How to prevent Chestnuts breaking when preparing Marrons Glacés?

AFTER removing outer and inner shells by blanching for a few minutes in boiling water, tie them in special parchment cooking paper, and steam until tender.

•

... Why Fruit sinks to the bottom of a cake?

THE cause may be one or more of the following:
(1) Adding too much liquid to the cake mixture, so that when put into the tin the mixture is not stiff enough to support the fruit.

(2) Putting the cake into too cool an oven. This causes the butter or other fat to melt before it is absorbed by the flour, again resulting in a semi-liquid mixture.

(3) Using fruit which is too heavy to be suspended; for example, whole cherries which retain their moisture are frequently too heavy to be supported in a light mixture. This can be remedied by cutting the cherries into halves or thirds.

(4) Using the wrong proportion of ingredients; too much sugar or butter to the quantity of flour, or adding baking powder to self-raising flour.

.. Old-world charm .. in this ...

Skippers Sandwich dish *in Spode*

WITH STERLING SILVER - PLATED HANDLE AND SERVING FORK.

FREE
FROM YOUR GROCER

It would cost you 6/- to buy this lovely Dish — yet it's FREE! Specially made for Skippers, in two old English designs, by the manufacturers of Spode ware. To get it you need only 20 Skippers top labels. Begin with the free starting coupon, worth 5 labels, from your grocer's counter. Then save 15 labels from Skippers tins. Take coupon and labels to your grocer and exchange them for the Dish in either of the two designs. Then start collecting for the other design, to make a pair! But you must hurry, because supplies of the Dish are strictly limited. If your grocer cannot supply the Dish, send coupon and labels, with 9d in stamps for packing and postage, to Angus Watson & Co. Limited, Southall, Middlesex. We'll send you the Dish by return. (*This offer does not apply to the Irish Free State.*)

There's DOUBLE nourishment in Skippers!

Cold weather makes heavy demands on children's reserves of strength. *Extra* nourishment is needed to renew these reserves and build up greater power of resistance. Give them Skippers, Mother! There's double nourishment in every tin! The pure olive-oil they're packed in doubles their value — makes Skippers far richer in food value than ordinary fish! Give your youngsters, and grown-ups, a chance to get safely through the winter. Insist on Skippers, and serve them often!

Skippers *The tasty fish with the DOUBLE nourishment*

SKP 252-5

ANGUS WATSON & CO. LIMITED, SOUTHALL, MIDDLESEX, AND NEWCASTLE-UPON-TYNE, ENGLAND

164

SELECTED RECIPES FOR THE MONTH

FOOD *Glorious* FOOD

1937

It is by no means too early to start making Christmas puddings, mincemeat and other traditional fare

OLD ENGLISH PLUM PUDDING

½ lb. raisins	2 oz. Barbadoes sugar
¼ lb. currants	½ teaspoonful salt
½ lb. suet	½ teaspoonful grated nutmeg
¼ lb. brown breadcrumbs	3 eggs
1½ oz. flour	¼ pint milk

(Makes 1 pudding weighing about 2½ lb.)

INSTITUTIONAL CHRISTMAS PUDDING

2½ lb. raisins	1½ lb. flour
2 lb. currants	6 teaspoonfuls mixed spice
1½ lb. mixed peel	6 teaspoonfuls bicarbonate of soda
1¼ lb. suet	6 teaspoonfuls salt
3 lb. apples	3 lb. Barbadoes sugar
3 lb. carrots	1½ pints milk
6 lemons	
¾ lb. breadcrumbs	

(Makes 9 puddings weighing 2½ lb. each.)

EGGLESS PLUM PUDDING

1 lb. raisins	1 lb. flour
1 lb. currants	1½ teaspoonfuls mixed spice
1 lb. sultanas	1½ teaspoonfuls salt
¾ lb. suet	½ teaspoonful nutmeg
1 lb. carrots	¾ lb. Demerara sugar
1 lb. potatoes	

1 pint milk

(Makes 3 puddings weighing 2½ lb. each.)

VEGETARIAN PLUM PUDDING

½ lb. raisins	½ teaspoonful salt
½ lb. currants	½ teaspoonful ground ginger
¼ lb. peel	1½ teaspoonfuls mixed spice
½ lb. brown breadcrumbs	4 tablespoonfuls black treacle
½ lb. carrots	2 eggs
½ lb. flour	½ pint milk
½ lb. Barbadoes sugar	
½ lb. butter	

(Makes 2 puddings weighing 2¼ lb. each.)

METHOD OF MAKING A CHRISTMAS PUDDING

1. Stone the raisins, unless seeded ones are used. 2. Wash, dry, and pick sultanas, currants and raisins. 3. Remove sugar from peel and shred it finely. 4. Blanch and chop the almonds. 5. Grate the suet and chop any large pieces finely. 6. Make the breadcrumbs. 7. Grate apple, carrot and lemon rind (when included in recipe). 8. Put pan or steamer on to boil. 9. Sieve flour, salt and spices into a basin large enough to hold all the ingredients. 10. Put all the prepared ingredients and sugar into the basin. Mix thoroughly by hand. 11. Beat up the eggs (if used). Squeeze lemon, measure milk. Add these to the dry ingredients and mix to a soft dropping consistency. If time permits, leave for several hours and mix again. 12. Grease basin, covering paper and pudding cloths. 13. Fill basin to the top, cover with paper, tie on pudding cloth securely, pinning or tying up the corners. 14. Boil for 5 hours, replenishing the water as required, or steam for 7½ hours. 15. Remove, allow to cool. Take off the pudding cloth, wipe the basin, cover with a clean, ungreased cloth. 16. Hang in the larder or put in a cool place.

TO SERVE THE PUDDING

Tie on a greased cloth and boil for 4 hours or steam for 6 hours. Turn out on to a hot dish.

MINCEMEAT

1 lb. apples	2 oz. almonds
1 lb. currants	Grated rind and juice of 1 lemon
½ lb. peel (mixed)	1 teaspoonful mixed spice
1 lb. sultanas	¼ pint brandy
1 lb. raisins	
1 lb. suet	

1 lb. Barbadoes sugar

Prepare the fruit. Chop or mince the fruit, apples and suet. Add the spice, sugar, lemon rind, lemon juice and brandy. Mix very thoroughly. Pack closely in clean, dry jam-jars. Cover as for jam and store in a cool, dry place.

N.B.—If difficulty has been experienced with the keeping qualities of this mincemeat, the quantity of apples can be reduced to ½ lb.

CHRISTMAS CAKE No. 1.

6 oz. butter	3 oz. peel
9 oz. flour	2 oz. almonds
¾ lb. currants	½ lb. dark brown sugar
½ lb. sultanas	Grated rind and juice of 1 lemon
4 eggs	

2 oz. cherries

Beat the butter and sugar to a cream, add the eggs one at a time, and beat each thoroughly in. If the mixture shows signs of curdling, add a little flour. Add the lemon juice and rind, lightly stir in the flour, and, last of all, the prepared fruit. Mix thoroughly, pour into lined caketins, and bake in a cool oven of approximately 300° F. for 6–8 hours, reducing the temperature when the cake begins to brown.

CHRISTMAS CAKE No. 2.

10 oz. butter	¾ lb. sultanas
11 oz. sugar	¼ lb. almonds
12 oz. flour	¼ lb. cherries
1 lb. currants	¼ lb. peel
1 teaspoonful spice	6–8 eggs
1 wineglassful brandy	Milk

Method as in above recipe.

YULE BREAD

1¾ lb. flour	2 oz. mixed peel
5 oz. margarine	¾ pint milk and water (approx.)
1 oz. yeast	½ teaspoonful mixed spice
½ lb. sugar	1 teaspoonful salt
½ lb. currants	
½ lb. raisins	

Sieve the flour and salt together. Mix the yeast with a little warm water. Rub the fat into the flour, make a well in the centre, pour in the yeast and allow to sponge for 20 minutes. Add the rest of the ingredients, beat very thoroughly until a soft but not sticky dough is obtained. Grease and warm eight loaf tins and half fill with the dough. Put to rise in a warm place until the dough comes to the top of the tins (about 1¾ hours), then bake at a temperature of 360° F. for ¾ hour. Turn out and cool. Eat either plain or with butter.

HOT-WATER CRUST RAISED PORK PIE

1½ lb. lean pork	1 lb. flour
Salt and pepper	4 oz. lard
Onion	1½ gills milk and water

Egg for coating

Cut up the pork into dice and sprinkle with the seasonings. Put the bones and onion in a pan, cover with water and simmer for 3 hours, replenishing the water occasionally. Sieve the flour and a pinch of salt into a warmed basin. Bring the lard, milk, and water just to the boil, pour into the middle of the flour, and stir with a knife until the pastry is cool enough to handle. Knead until smooth, adding more hot water if required. Cover and stand in a warm place for half an hour. Keep warm throughout, but do not over-heat. Cut off one quarter of the pastry and keep warm. Mould the remainder with the hands or line a pie-mould with it. Put the pork in the middle of the pastry, add two tablespoonfuls of the prepared stock, cover with a lid of pastry and decorate with leaves of pastry. Brush with egg and bake in a hot oven for 1½ hours. Pour in stock to fill while the pie is still hot. Do not remove the paper or pie-mould until the pie is cold.

HOME AND SCHOOL CATERING

In the course of Lecture-demonstrations this Autumn, the Institute is laying great stress on the importance of a well-balanced diet in connection with the health, not only of the individual, but ultimately of the nation. In *Good Housekeeping with Modern Methods*, clear and concise information is given on the question of Food Values, which should make it easy to work out satisfying meals that contain the proper degree of nourishment for children and adults. Suitable menus for Schools, Colleges, etc., are also worked out, with costs and quantities.

The catering section in this book has been written as a direct result of the many letters that the Institute has received, which show that there is a great deal of interest and need for information on catering subjects. For example, one reader writes, "I should be very glad to know of a book which gives menus for meals for a household of 30 children and 6 adults at an allowance of 10*s.* per head per week." Another writes: "Where can I get a weekly menu with approximate costs suitable for a household of ten adults, where the cooking is done single-handed by a cook-housekeeper?"

The answer to your own catering problems may also be in this book, which can be obtained from Good Housekeeping Institute, 49, Wellington Street, Strand, W.C.2, price 7*s.* 6*d.*, plus 6*d.* postage.

Tray meals simplify cooking for one. The article opposite makes some suggestions for easily-prepared and appetising tray meals

LIGHT LUNCHEON PARTY TRAY

Fish Soufflé
with Mushroom Sauce
Cucumber and Radish Salad : Peas
Nut and Date Bread
Cherry Tartlets
Iced Tea

MEALS on a TRAY

by C. F. PALMER

ANY woman who lives alone knows the advantages of tray meals which can be eaten comfortably by the fire or at an open window without the effort of moving furniture or setting tables. And it is with almost a holiday sense that the busy mother of a family settles down to eat a meal from a tray when all the members of her family are out. There is something of the spirit of a picnic about eating in this way and the food seems to have that subtle added flavour of sausages fried over a twig fire in the open air or tea made from spring water.

Although most men would not appreciate it, this charm of informality can be introduced into the entertaining of your feminine guests. Any woman friend would enjoy an intimate tray luncheon by the fire or on a sunny verandah, and if you have a morning bridge party or a committee meeting your guests would be intrigued to find individual luncheon trays ready for them to carry to any convenient place in the house or garden.

With a little careful planning, delicious hot tray meals can be served as attractively as cold ones. The food looks best if cooked and served in small individual dishes and this involves very little extra time in the preparation, even for a number of people.

A supply of cocotte dishes, small soufflé dishes, dariole moulds and marmites are useful for hot foods, and for cold sweets and salads the glass department of any large store displays suitable small dishes of every colour, shape and price.

There are inexpensive light-weight trays of such pleasing designs that no tray-cloth is necessary, and useful trolleys with detachable trays are obtainable in delightful colours. A trolley is rather useful for fireside meals in the winter for more than one person, as it provides extra space for plates and dishes. In the picture opposite the sweet is served in a basket tray, which is particularly suitable for meals out of doors, and fresh leaves may be used to line a tray of this type.

LUNCHEON PARTY TRAY

Globe Artichoke
with Melted Butter

Cold Pigeon or Grouse: Salad

Stewed Damsons with Cream

WARM WEATHER LUNCHEON TRAY

Shrimp Salad

Brown Bread and Butter

Fresh Pears or Peaches

Cream Cheese and Crackers

Lemonade

QUICKLY PREPARED HOT TRAY LUNCHEON

Mushroom Omelette

Baked Apple with Cream

Coffee

VEGETARIAN LUNCHEON TRAY

Tomato Soup

Egg and Spinach Cocotte

Russian Salad   Wholemeal Toast

Blackberry Trifle

Coffee

COLD WEATHER LUNCHEON TRAY

Leeks au Gratin

Mashed Potatoes

Steamed Castle Pudding

Coffee

We give below recipes for the dishes in the menus appearing on pages 62–3.

Fish Soufflé

½ lb. fish	2 eggs
2 oz. flour	1½ oz. butter
½ gill cream	1½ gills fish stock

Seasoning

Bone the fish and put the bones on to boil with ¾ pint of water to make the stock. Grease or butter four small moulds and tie a band of greased kitchen paper round the outside of the moulds. Melt the butter, stir in the flour, add the strained stock and stir until it thickens, then beat thoroughly. Continue to cook for about three minutes. Put this paste and the flaked or chopped fish into a basin and mix thoroughly. Add the yolks of egg separately, and the seasoning and mix well. Rub the mixture through a sieve and add the cream. Whip the whites of egg very stiffly and stir lightly into the fish mixture. Pour into the prepared moulds, cover with greased paper and steam for about one hour.

Mushroom Sauce

To ½ pint of Béchamel sauce add ¼ lb. of button mushrooms which have been peeled, washed and lightly fried in butter.

Simmer the sauce for ten minutes after adding the mushrooms. (Sufficient for four people.)

Nut and Date Bread

¾ lb. wholemeal flour	½ pint milk
3 teaspoonfuls baking powder	1 egg
1 teaspoonful salt	2 oz. stoned dates
2 oz. sugar	2 oz. chopped nuts
	2 oz. butter

Mix together the wholemeal flour, baking powder, salt and sugar. Make a well in the centre, and add the milk and the well-beaten egg. Mix in the dry ingredients gradually, and then beat all together. Finally add the melted butter, and the dates chopped and mixed with a little flour, and the chopped nuts. Put the mixture into one or two well-greased bread-tins and bake in a moderate oven about forty-five minutes or until done. This makes a good-sized loaf.

Cherry Tartlets

Pastry

6 oz. flour	1 yolk of egg
3½ oz. butter	1 dessertspoonful cold water
1 dessertspoonful sugar	1 pinch salt

A small tin bright red or morello cherries

Syrup

1 gill fruit syrup and water	The juice of ¼ lemon
1½ oz. loaf sugar	1 teaspoonful red currant jelly
1 teaspoonful powdered arrowroot	A few drops carmine

To prepare the pastry rub the fat into the flour and add the sugar. Mix the egg yolk with the cold water and add the pinch of salt. Bind to a stiff paste. Roll it out thinly to ⅛ in. thickness. With a plain or fluted cutter, slightly larger than the top of the tartlet tin, stamp out rounds of pastry. Fit a round into each tartlet tin, pressing well where the side of the tin joins the bottom. Prick each at bottom. Put a small piece of greaseproof paper in the bottom of each and fill up with uncooked rice. Bake until the pastry is set and brown in a hot oven. Remove the papers and the rice (the latter should be stored for future use). When cool, fill the cases with stoned cherries and cover with the syrup.

To make the syrup add the liquid to the sugar in a small saucepan. Dissolve and boil for five minutes. Add the lemon juice and jelly and the arrowroot mixed smoothly with a little cold water. Stir with a wooden spoon and boil thoroughly until the syrup is quite clear. Add the colouring. Strain it over the fruit. Allow to set and serve cold.

Note.—This quantity makes about one dozen Cherry Tartlets.

Egg and Spinach Cocotte

1 egg	1 tablespoonful cooked and sieved spinach
1 tablespoonful white sauce	

Pepper and salt

Butter a cocotte dish and put the spinach into it. Break a whole egg on to the spinach and cover with the white sauce. Season and bake in a moderate oven for about ten minutes or until the egg is set and the sauce lightly brown. (To serve one person.)

Blackberry Trifle

1 small sponge cake	Cream
Stewed blackberries	1 Macaroon
Jam	Angelica

Split the sponge cake and spread with jam. Arrange it in a small dish and soak with blackberry juice for ½ hour. Sprinkle with the crushed macaroon and cover with blackberries. Whip the cream, sweeten and flavour it, and spread it over the blackberries. Decorate with blackberries and angelica. (To serve one person.)

Globe Artichokes

Wash carefully, cut off the stem, tops and any outer leaves. Put them into boiling salt water and cook for forty minutes. When tender the leaves pull out easily. Drain upside down. Serve with melted butter.

Shrimp Salad

½ pint shrimps	Sliced cucumber
1 tablespoonful mayonnaise	Shredded lettuce
	Tomato

Stir the shrimps into the mayonnaise, pile the mixture into a salad bowl, garnish with lettuce, cucumber and sliced tomato. (Sufficient for two persons.)

Russian Salad

Cooked mixed vegetables, such as carrots, peas, beans, potatoes, asparagus, turnips, etc.	2 anchovies
	A little cold fish
	A few gherkins, capers and olives

Mayonnaise sauce

Cut the vegetables into small dice or rounds, chop the gherkins and capers, fillet and shred the anchovies and flake the cooked fish. Mix all the ingredients with some mayonnaise sauce and serve in small individual dishes. If aspic jelly is available, cut into fancy shapes, or chop and use for garnishing.

Leeks au Gratin

4 leeks	2 oz. cheese
½ pint white sauce	½ oz. butter

Pepper and salt

Wash the leeks well, cut off the tops and bottoms and cook for thirty-five minutes in boiling salted water. Drain and put them into two buttered fireproof dishes. Add the cheese to the white sauce, season well, and pour over the leeks. Sprinkle the top with a little grated cheese and few small pieces of butter. Bake until brown. (Sufficient for two people.)

Castle Puddings

1 egg	2 oz. flour
2 oz. butter	⅛ teaspoonful baking powder
2 oz. sugar	

1 tablespoonful milk

Sieve the baking powder and flour and beat the butter and sugar until soft and white. Beat the egg into the butter and sugar. Stir in the flour and the milk. Half-fill four greased dariole moulds with the mixture and bake in a fairly hot oven for twenty-five minutes. Turn out on to a hot dish and serve with jam sauce. (Sufficient for four people.)

The service of meals on a tray is simplified if the food is cooked in individual fireproof dishes, of which there is now a varied range

Seasoning is

SAYS THE

One of the signs of the makes full use of herbs

CONSIDERABLE publicity was recently given to a criticism addressed to five hundred wives of British Rotarians by an American-born woman novelist that British women are not good cooks. I think most readers will agree that general and sweeping criticisms of this kind are often inaccurate, and whilst I would not deny that some English maids show little aptitude or interest in the preparation of meals, I count myself fortunate that my work brings me in contact with thousands of women who have an extremely high standard of cooking and excel at the art.

If the novelist had claimed that English women are not adept at the art of seasoning I might have been more ready to agree, for the majority are reluctant to experiment and to make full use of herbs, condiments and spices, and it is with the object of offering suggestions along these lines that this article has been written.

Not only is far too little use made of herbs and spices, but when they are used it is frequently with too heavy a hand. Skill is essential not only to know how and when to use each herb, spice or condiment, but to know how little, rather than how much, to use.

I should not be surprised if my suggestion to include a little powdered or whole ginger in a mutton stew were received with trepidation and some misgiving, but the result will be surprisingly good. One only needs to take a little trouble to discover how best these valuable aids to cookery can be utilised. A little allspice, or whole or coarsely ground pepper, used with a pinch of ginger, create an entirely new and unusual flavour in a stew, which I have never found to be unappreciated. The secret lies in using them sparingly and with greater discrimination than most cooks would think necessary.

By way of setting a good example, and putting into practice what I preach, I have devoted to herbs a space of generous size in my new garden, and it is my intention to care for them myself, and to add the more unusual varieties

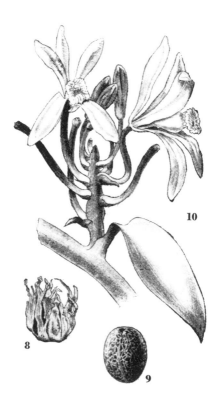

1. *Common Mint, essential to the English for their mint sauce.* 2. *Another variety of mint, sometimes referred to as eau-de-Cologne mint.* 3. *Rue.* 4. *Bergamot.* 5. *Savory.* 6. *Rosemary; the last four are little used to-day, but are well worth cultivating.* 7. *Common sage is the popular adjunct to roast pork and duck.* *Mace (8) and Nutmeg (9) should be used more extensively for flavouring savoury dishes.* 10. *Vanilla Pod proves more economical in use than the essence*

a Subtle Art

DIRECTOR

good cook is that she
and spices as flavouring

from time to time. Not only shall I grow them, but I shall not lose an opportunity to utilise them to create new flavours, and I have little doubt that, as time passes, more space still will be devoted to cultivating these valuable adjuncts to good cooking.

Mint, sage, thyme, marjoram and parsley are the herbs most likely to be found in country gardens, but I am going to make a plea to Good House-keeping readers that they also find room for some lesser known ones, so that they may always have at hand a means of subtle seasoning.

The lack of interest and the ignorance which exist nowadays about herbs and spices among young housewives are probably the result of their being unaccustomed to seeing them used in the kitchen in their childhood days, for beyond the occasional use of dried herbs from a packet, or ground ginger in ginger-breads, and of mixed spice in Christmas puddings and cakes, spices, condiments and herbs do not play a very important part in cooking as practised to-day.

This state of affairs must be remedied, and I hope that each reader will set aside a small corner of her store cupboard for a collection of as many aids to subtle seasoning as possible, including herbs, spices and such well-known sauces as Yorkshire Relish, Worcester Sauce and Tomato Sauce. In the summer fresh herbs should always be used in preference to dried ones, but in the winter months reliance must be placed on those that have been sun-dried, with the exception of parsley.

Parsley. Almost every kitchen garden boasts its border of parsley, but I doubt whether as much use is made of it as might be. It is, however, not only as a decorative medium—its bright green colour cannot be obtained by any other means—but recent researches have proved that it is a very good source of Vitamin C. We all know that Vitamin C is destroyed by heat, and that to cook parsley is to spoil its beauty, and these two simple facts should teach us to use it uncooked

(Continued)

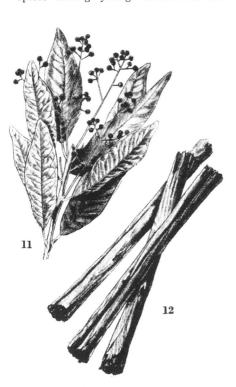

11. *Pimento is commonly known as allspice.* 12. *Cinnamon is obtainable in stick and powdered form.* 13. *Tarragon should be cultivated for its delicate and unusual flavour. Alecost (14) and Balm (15) have few devotees to-day, but can be added to stuffings.* 16. *Bay Leaf improves a " bouquet garni," and gives a pleasant flavour to milk dishes and blancmange. Marjoram (17), Silver Thyme (18), Lemon Scented Thyme (19), and Common Thyme (20) are probably the most commonly used of all our British herbs*

WHY THE VICAR OFTEN CAME TO TEA

A lesson for every housewife ..

No one would suggest for a minute that the vicar was influenced by anything other than his duties — but it was strange that he called so often at the house where they had Shippam's Pastes for tea. The vicar had to eat a good many *ordinary* teas, which made him appreciate Shippam's all the more — because Shippam's are *real food* pastes, made with real chicken or lobster or salmon as the case may be. No wonder they're so tasty and nourishing. Have Chicken and Ham, Turkey and Tongue or what you will. But have Shippam's every time for picnics, parties or everyday tea.

Seasoning is a Subtle Art

and in generous quantities whenever possible.

In Maitre d'Hôtel butter and salads both its vitamin value and beauty are retained at their fullest, while in the making of parsley sauce it should be added after cooking is completed. In fact, I advocate cooling the sauce slightly by stirring it for half a minute before adding the finely chopped parsley. For mutton or any other meat or vegetable broth it should be sprinkled, chopped finely, in the bottom of the soup tureen and the hot broth poured on to it; or if preferred, it can be sprinkled on top of the broth after it is in the tureen. In this way the full flavour, beauty, and anti-scorbutic value are unimpaired.

Bouquet Garni. These words appear so frequently in the list of ingredients for soups, stews and other savoury dishes that it comes almost as a shock to those who have a sound knowledge of cooking to find that there are some people who are at a loss to know what the term implies. A *bouquet garni* consists of a small bunch of herbs, with some spices, and it is added to many dishes during cooking for the purpose of extracting the various flavourings. It should always be discarded, however, before the food is dished. A sprig of thyme, parsley or marjoram, a bay leaf, a few peppercorns, a blade of mace and sometimes celery seed are included. For ease in removal the herbs are tied together with white cotton, and the celery seeds, mace, allspice, whole pepper or ginger root— when used—should be put into a small muslin bag. When the food is sufficiently flavoured the *bouquet garni* and bag of spices can easily be removed, even if the main ingredients are not completely cooked.

Mint is so well known in this country that it needs no introduction, and nothing can enhance the flavour of English roast lamb better than sauce made with freshly gathered mint. There are, however, several varieties of mint, including eau-de-Cologne mint, Bergamot and Peppermint, but it is the common mint that one should cultivate for mint sauce. This herb unfortunately has an annoying habit of suddenly changing its character, due to hybridisation, or possibly to the character of the soil. I speak from experience. In my old garden the most perfect mint possible was produced for many years, but after it was transferred to my new garden in the heart of the country the flavour deteriorated almost beyond recognition.

I have already mentioned the value of mint sauce, and I would like to suggest that, for a change, cyder vinegar be used for making it, with sufficient sugar to sweeten it slightly. Whilst many recipes for mint sauce suggest adding one third, or sometimes an equal part, of water to vinegar, I consider that mint sauce made thus is a poor apology for the real thing, and those who find the addition of water a necessity should try the vinegar made from English apples.

In the past cyder vinegar was generally imported from France and was regarded as a luxury, but to-day that made from West of England apples can be bought at only a few pence more per pint than malt vinegar.

There is one criticism that an epicure might make against using mint sauce with hot meat—namely, that it chills the gravy. Even this criticism can be eliminated if the flavour of the mint be stored in jelly form. Apple jelly is the basis, and the mint flavour is imparted by cooking a handful of fresh young mint with the apples. When the jelly is ready for potting I recommend the addition of a fairly generous quantity of finely chopped mint. This, of course, produces a thick, instead of a clear, jelly, but the improvement in the flavour justifies it.

Although mint sauce and jelly are usually associated with hot and cold roast lamb and mutton, it is a flavour that can, with advantage, be introduced into other dishes and beverages. Crushed mint added to cooling drinks, fruit cups, cyder cup, etc., is an asset, and a spray of mint should always be cooked with peas and introduced into soups, whether made from fresh or dried peas. It also improves the flavour of mutton stews, if used judiciously. I leave it to the imagination of my readers to experiment, remembering that whether one is trying out herbs, spices or condiments, it is advisable always to start with a very little, and to increase the quantity, rather than to season too generously in the first instance.

Thyme and Marjoram. Although they are often confused, the sketch shows that marjoram leaves are slightly larger, although the arrangement on the stem is similar. Marjoram is frequently included in mixed herbs, but, again, it is only necessary to try it alone with simple savoury dishes to find that, used skilfully, it adds interest to what might otherwise be a dull dish.

Silver Thyme, Lemon Thyme and Common Thyme are all valuable herbs, and one variety is the principal ingredient of stuffing or forcemeat. A little added to beef, rabbit and hare stews is a distinct improvement, but, again, thyme, like all other herbs, should be used with discretion, particularly in a dish such as veal and ham pie, where the flavour has less risk of being lost by evaporation.

Tarragon and Chervil. I have never discovered the reason why tarragon is used so sparingly by most home cooks, for, along with chervil, it was always to be found, day in and day out throughout the year, with other more common herbs, in my training kitchens. Chervil is used chiefly for garnishing savoury dishes, and for the decorating of moulds, but tarragon is invaluable on account of its delicate flavour.

For a change try cooking a small handful of fresh tarragon, with a nut of butter, inside a roast fowl. The flavour of the bird is completely changed thereby, and as monotony should always be avoided in cooking this is a tip worth remembering. Tarragon leaves should also be included in some salads, and pounded with butter for savoury fillings, and chopped tarragon added to veal stuffing is a change worth trying.

Rue, Alecost or Costmary, Balm, Rosemary and Fennel should all be cultivated when even a small garden is available, for if used with discrimination, either alone or combined with some of the more common herbs, they are of immense help to the cook.

No less important for subtle seasoning are the spices and condiments which, unlike herbs, cannot be grown in our country, and which are imported from tropical and sub-tropical lands. It was therefore to the Port of London Authority I went for reliable and up-to-date information regarding this subject. I learnt that most spices come from East India, Malaya and the West Indies. The best cloves are grown in Penang, but the largest quantity reaches us from Zanzibar and Madagascar. Ceylon provides cinnamon. Pimento comes from Jamaica and ginger from China. From the West Indies we have nutmegs, although many also come from the East Indies and

Penang. From the Straits Settlements and Java come the bulk of pepper. I only wish it were possible for my readers to visit the Port of London Warehouses, where they could see for themselves the spices and get first-hand information about these valuable food adjuncts from the garblers—the staff of this Authority, who sort, sample, grade and lot the spices. It may be that our palates have lost the taste for subtly seasoned food, but as long ago as the twelfth century a Fraternity of Pepperers was formed in London. This was ultimately merged into the Grocers' Company, so I learnt from my visit to the Port of London. The camel which is the emblem of the Grocers' Company serves to remind us of the overland route by which in the past the spices were brought.

Pepper. Peppers are berries produced on pepper vines. They are hand-picked before they are quite ripe, and sun-dried, during which process they shrivel and darken, becoming almost black. In the production of white pepper the outer skin is removed by rubbing the berries before they are allowed to dry.

Cayenne Pepper is the ground pod and seed of a variety of capsicum, and, because of its "heat," sparing use only should be made of it.

Nutmeg and Mace. I wonder how many people realise the close association between nutmegs and mace, for mace is the outer shell of the nutmeg. It would also be interesting to know how many people use nutmeg for any other purpose than grating over the top of milk puddings. Those who limit its usefulness to this one purpose should try adding a little to stews, soups and gravies, but mace is probably even more useful in this connection, for it has a softer and more aromatic flavour than the nuts which it protects.

Cinnamon is native to Ceylon. The "sticks" or quills are made by rolling the inner bark of the plant, cutting it into lengths of 18 in. and drying it in the sun. They are then tied into circular bales and shipped to England and to other European ports. Cinnamon oil is distilled from the bark and leaves, and the "sticks" are ground finely to make powdered cinnamon. For the flavouring of milk puddings and hot and cold sweets, including stewed fruit, the cinnamon "sticks" are more convenient than the powder, because the flavour can be extracted without affecting the colour or transparency of the food.

Cloves are the dried flower-buds of an evergreen tree. Used whole or powdered, they give a peculiarly pleasant flavour to sweet and savoury dishes. It is a pity that they should be reserved almost entirely for apple-pie, pudding and bread sauce. Try adding one or two to a mutton stew along with ginger.

Allspice or Pimento. It is intentional that "allspice" is given first as the name of this particular spice, because it is better known by this homely title, which explains that it combines the flavour of several spices. Grown in Jamaica, it is sometimes referred to as Jamaica pepper.

Ginger. The white root ginger is largely used for the spicing of vinegars for pickles, or, when ground, for adding to spiced cakes, puddings and gingerbread. Here again British housewives might take a lesson from Chinese cooks, and use it occasionally for flavouring savoury dishes. We have tested many Chinese dishes at Good Housekeeping Institute, and found the ginger an improvement.

In conclusion, I should like to point out that one cannot hope to make preserved ginger from the dried root. Fresh young stems are needed, and consequently I never advise that this preserve should be attempted at home.

What *Makes* a Savoury?

A PEEP BEHIND THE SCENES

The backbone of good feeding is the savoury dishes of the meal.

I mean "savoury" because I cannot think of a better way of describing those main dishes—soup, fish, meat or fowl—which, leaving out the sweet, take us right up to the savoury itself.

A sweet, however much you love it, is but the tail-piece of the average meal. We get, or should get, our real nourishment and our real enjoyment out of the savoury dishes which preceded it.

If I had to instruct young housewives in cookery, I would teach them, in the first place, correct chef methods of producing really savoury fare: and I would stress, above all things, the very great importance of good seasoning.

Seasoning!—the essence of good cooking.

Seasoning!—precious spices from the Orient, herbs from lands far away, vegetables, exotic fruits.

It would be folly for me to suggest that you yourself should blend together these ingredients and make from them a flavouring-seasoning sauce which you could use so advantageously in all the savoury dishes you prepare.

To begin with, you couldn't assemble them. But even if you could—and even if you had the necessary knowledge and equipment and facilities for a long period of maturing—the cost would be prohibitive.

That's why I recommend, sincerely, Lea & Perrins Sauce.

For as little as sixpence, you can buy a bottle of the "essence of good cooking" made from spices, herbs, vegetables and fruits gathered from the finest sources of the world by experts whose job it is to select only the very best of the essential ingredients.

Obviously, when a product has held first position for 100 years, its makers kept it there by using nothing but the very best. None but the best methods, too.

The ingredients, once assembled, have to be matured in the purest vinegar and soy. The process employed by Lea & Perrins produces a strong and concentrated *true* essence extracted from the spices, herbs, etc., employed.

Perhaps you've used Lea & Perrins at your table but never in cooking? I now suggest that you get another bottle for kitchen use. It's a nuisance to be carrying the one bottle back and forth.

Lea & Perrins can make you a good cook—and "make you" as one!

Ask any chef what makes the difference between his simple but delicious Braised Beef and that of another, equally tender, perhaps, but "uninteresting," and he'll tell you it's because his dish is seasoned right. If he is as generous-minded as one of my chef friends, he'll tell you, "I use Lea & Perrins Sauce."

I've actually heard a chef admit, in front of a large class, to using it, for, as he said, "How can I possibly make an essence as good as Lea & Perrins is?"

He used it, on this occasion, in his Bœuf à la Mode. So do I.

Use Lea & Perrins to add zest to your gravies. Use it in all soups and stews and casseroles. Use it in such dishes as veal or beef olives. (In Mock Duck, it's indispensable to me.) And if you've never thought of it as a cooking part of liver and bacon, make up your mind to do so at once.

I know what will happen!

You'll find yourself so interested in Lea & Perrins that you'll invent your own ways of using it. That's what I've done—still do.

Your name will soon be made!

★　★　★　★　★　★　★　★　★

free COOKERY BOOK

To Lea & Perrins Ltd.
7, Midland Road
Worcester

Please send me your 70-page recipe book "Subtle Seasoning" which shows hundreds of different ways in which a dash can make a dish.

Name...

Address...

....

Let's be practical..

Practical is a good word to use in connection with cookery. McDougalls think a lot of that word and that is why their Self-Raising Flour has to pass very stringent *practical* tests before it is ever allowed to be sold to you. It isn't enough that McDougalls use only certain graded wheats, that the raising ingredients are mixed with scrupulous exactness. Every batch of McDougall's Self-Raising Flour is tested by actual cooking tests. These tests are your assurance of getting perfect results every time you use it.

RECIPE FOR CARD CAKES

FOUNDATION SPONGE

5 oz. McDougall's Self-Raising Flour
Pinch of salt   4 oz. margarine
4 oz. castor sugar   2 eggs
2 tablespoonfuls milk
A little vanilla essence

Line a shallow oblong tin measuring 9″ × 13″ with greaseproof paper, brush with melted lard.

Beat the butter until soft, add the sugar and beat again until the mixture resembles whipped cream. Add the eggs one at a time, together with a tablespoonful of the sieved flour and salt. Beat in each egg thoroughly. Stir in the remainder of the flour, the milk and vanilla essence. Spread the mixture evenly in the prepared tin and bake for 20 minutes in a fairly hot oven. Turn out and cool.

Regulo 6. Other cookers 400°F. Just above the middle of oven.

Trim the edges off the sponge, cut into four lengthways and widthways, making 16 cards.

Make a small quantity of almond paste by mixing 1 tablespoonful of ground almonds, 1 level tablespoonful each of castor and icing sugar and blending with a very little beaten egg. Divide into two, colour one portion a deep red with carmine, and mix sufficient cocoa into the other to make it a very dark brown. Roll each out thinly on sugared greaseproof paper and cut into suits with small aspic cutters.

To Finish the Cakes

GLACE ICING

10 oz. sieved icing sugar
2 teaspoonfuls lemon juice
2½ tablespoonfuls of warm water (approximately)

Put the icing sugar into a saucepan, add the lemon juice and warm water. Beat well and stir over gentle heat for one minute. The icing should be thick enough to coat the spoon.

Using a tablespoon coat the top of each cake, putting the hearts and diamonds, etc., in place as soon as this is done. Leave to set.

✳

RECIPE FOR BRIDGE CAKE

This is another idea for a Bridge Party cake. Playing cards decorate a larger oblong cake.

FOUNDATION

1 lb. McDougall's Self-Raising Flour
¼ teaspoonful of salt   12 oz. butter
14 oz. sugar   6 eggs
5 tablespoonfuls of milk
1 teaspoonful of vanilla essence

Make the cake following the directions for the Card Cakes and bake in a lined oblong tin measuring 12″ × 9″ × 3″ in a moderately hot oven for 1 hour.

Regulo 4. Other cookers 380°F. Middle of oven.

To Finish the Cake

Prepare the suits from almond paste as previously described.

Level the top of the cake and tie a double band of greaseproof paper around it close to the sides and one inch above them.

Prepare glace icing as before, using 14 oz. icing sugar, 2 tablespoonfuls of lemon juice and 4 tablespoonfuls of warm water. Pour over the surface of the cake and leave for several hours to set.

Prepare a tablespoonful of thick green glace icing and with a writing pipe divide the cake, into nine. Pipe around the edges of the cake finishing with spirals where the lines cross. Pipe a small dot of icing where the suits are to be placed and press lightly into position.

  making

Menu

by LEONORA MARY ERVINE

Simplicity, quality and balance—these are the keynotes of a well-planned meal

IT is surprising how few cooks can plan a meal. Few people, indeed, seem to know the simplest rules of drawing up a menu. All white, all brown, all stodgy meals are far too common. As a housewife, I am frequently in search of ideas for varying meals, but although I have a large selection of cookery books, some of which contain suggestions for menus, I seldom find them any help at all. Pork is sometimes recommended in months without an "r," and a recipe which included oysters was published in one of our most superior newspapers in June! I was once given suet pudding for dinner in an expensive seaside hotel in August! The simplest meal needs thought, if it is to be a success, and here are some of the factors to be taken into consideration:

(*a*) The average age of those who are to eat the meal.

(*b*) Are any of them on a diet? If so, can they be catered for so that the other diners are not penalised?

(*c*) Have any of them marked likes or dislikes?

(*d*) What is the temperature?

(*e*) What is in the larder or in the garden?

The good housewife has to ask herself such questions as these every morning, and has, in addition, to consider the capability of her cook and the capacity of her purse.

Below are examples of what I consider to be good menus for a household of six persons of moderate means, in each of the four seasons of the year.

They are menus for active people, and they satisfy most tastes.

For elderly people, lighter meals must be planned, as old people rarely eat meat more than once a day, and those who cling to the solid breakfast usually lunch lightly, while those who lunch lightly look for substantial dinners. Undoubtedly one really "filling" meal is all we need a day, but everyone cannot eat fruit in the early morning, and for those I recommend a good breakfast and a fruit or salad lunch. Fresh fruit juice is usually good for most people once a day. Freshly cooked vegetables or salad should appear most days. Remember that many people cannot eat twice-cooked meat. It is bad catering to need to recook any meat more than once a week, when curry, shepherd's pie or rissoles may be allowed.

"Good and simple" are the new rules for smart entertaining. The grander your guests, the more they will appreciate simple, *well-cooked* food. It is still the dreadful custom, in hotels catering for the well-to-do middle classes, to provide six and seven courses for dinner, often badly planned and badly cooked, which look far finer in print than they taste. In really good hotels people order *à la carte*, and rarely eat more than three courses. A typical autumn dinner would be:

Oysters
Roast Game   Salad
Ice Cream or Cheese Soufflé
or Fresh Fruit

WINTER	SPRING	SUMMER	AUTUMN
Breakfast			
Orange Juice or Stewed Apple	Grape Fruit	Fresh Fruit	Stewed Prunes or Plums
Porridge or Cereal	Cereal, Cream and Sugar	Cold Ham	Finnan Haddock
Bacon and Scrambled Egg or Sausage	Fried Whiting	Boiled Eggs	Toast, Jam, Marmalade
Toast, Jam, Marmalade	Toast, Jam, Marmalade	Toast, Jam, Marmalade	
Lunch			
Irish Stew or Stewed Steak	Cold Lamb and Salad	Fish or Egg Salad	Liver and Bacon
Boiled Apple Pudding	Fresh Fruit Tart or Stewed Fruit and Junket	Cheese and Biscuits	Spinach
Cheese		Fresh Fruit	Jam Roll
Dinner			
Vegetable Soup	Veal Cutlets	Roast Chicken	Roast Game and Salad *or*
Fried Cod Cutlets	Carrots and Spinach	Peas and Potatoes	Tournedos of Beef
Cheese Soufflé	Cold Lemon Soufflé	Fruit Salad and Cream	Cauliflower
			Blackberry or Apple Fool

. . . AND THIS IS LAURA'S RECIPE

FOR MORE DIGESTIBLE FRIED POTATOES

FRIED POTATOES. Peel the potatoes, cut into slices $\frac{1}{4}$ inch thick and then into finger-length strips. Soak in cold water for 1 hour, and dry well in a clean cloth. Put into a wire frying-basket and lower gently into hot Spry and fry until the potatoes are golden brown. Drain on crumpled paper. Sprinkle with salt, and serve very hot.

TO TEST HEAT OF SPRY. Drop in a small piece of bread. If it turns brown in 1 minute the SPRY is ready for frying potatoes.

For fuller details of digestible frying see the Spry Recipe Book.

FREE COOKERY BOOK—FREE ADVICE

Send for a free copy of the Spry Recipe Book. Send 3d in stamps to cover cost of postage and packing to—
THE SPRY COOKERY ADVISORY SERVICE,
Messrs. R. S. Hudson Limited (Dept. D.J.1), Bebington, Cheshire. (Your envelope must be sealed and bear 1½d stamp.)
Have you a cooking problem? Then write to the Spry Cookery Advisory Service explaining your trouble. This Service retains a staff of experts ready to give helpful advice on all cookery matters. It is entirely *free* of cost, and there is no obligation whatsoever.

The better your cooking is the easier it is to digest, and Spry makes *every* type of cooking better. Use it for pastry, cakes, puddings and frying; in each case you'll get the lightest, most delicious results. And because it is "ready-creamed" by a special process Spry is ever so much easier to use.

Spry

½-lb. size 5½d.   1-lb. size 10d.   3-lb. size 2/4.

. . THE "READY-CREAMED" ALL-PURPOSE COOKING FAT

SPR 77-5

Seasonable Salads

by OLIVE EDWARDS

☆

SALADS of fresh vegetables and fruits should be introduced liberally into the daily menu, for they are essential to good health. Although their nutritive value is low they contain relatively large amounts of mineral matters and vitamins A, B_2, C and D, without a liberal supply of which the health of the body and resistance to disease is considerably impaired.

Vitamin C is the anti-scorbutic vitamin; that is, it prevents and cures scurvy. Unlike the other three mentioned, it is unstable and is destroyed if it is exposed to high temperatures or becomes oxidised. Oranges, lemons, grapefruit, tomatoes, and all green salad foods contain an abundance of vitamin C and therefore must be taken liberally. Many other vegetables also contain this vitamin, but as for the most part they are cooked before being eaten their value from the aspect of the vitamin C content is lessened or lost.

Vegetables and fruit have another function besides acting as protective foods. They contain a large proportion of cellulose—a material which is not absorbed by the body but forms a bulky residue, which, as it passes through the intestinal tract, acts as stimulus to it.

These few facts indicate the importance of salads in the daily diet. They can be made into extremely palatable and attractive dishes so that even those who have no natural liking for them will be prompted to eat them.

Green Salad

Lettuce
Bunch of watercress
A few uncooked carrots

Wash the green salad vegetables carefully, using several waters if necessary, drain well and dry in a cloth, being very careful not to crush the leaves. Arrange in a bowl and grate a little raw carrot over the top. Serve with a French dressing.

Picnic Salad

1 cupful shredded cabbage
1 cupful sliced uncooked carrots
1 cupful chopped celery
2 cupfuls diced fresh tomato
½ cupful sliced sweet pickle

Mix the ingredients and moisten with French or cooked dressing. Serve on lettuce.

Sliced Tomato Salad

Tomatoes
Cooked French beans
Uncooked cauliflower
Celery
Diced beetroot
Lettuce
Watercress

Slice tomatoes and place on the lettuce in a circle. Cut the cauliflower and celery into small pieces and add to French beans, beetroot and watercress. Place the mixture in the centre of the circle of tomatoes. Serve with mayonnaise or spicy French dressing.

Ham Salad

Two hard-boiled eggs
1½ cupfuls diced cooked ham
1½ cupfuls diced celery
½ cupful whipped cream
½ cupful mayonnaise
2 tablespoonfuls of grated horseradish
Lettuce

Shell the eggs and cut into thin, even slices. Cut ham into small cubes, dice the celery and add to ham. Whip the cream and fold in the mayonnaise and horseradish. Season well and add the ham and celery. Serve the mixture piled on lettuce and garnish with the slices of hard-boiled egg. Add stuffed olives or sweet gherkins if liked.

Yorkshire Cream Salad

Cream cheese
Tomatoes
A few chopped chives
Crisp salad
French dressing

Season the cheese well, and add the chives. Cut a small piece off the top of each tomato and hollow out the centres. Fill with the cheese mixture and serve on a green salad. Diced celery and beetroot, grated carrot, cooked French beans or peas may be added. Serve with French dressing.

Celery and Tomato Salad

Celery
Tomatoes
Lettuce
Watercress

Wash the celery carefully, scraping off any brown and dirty pieces, and cut into strips about an inch long. Immerse the tomatoes in boiling water for about 1 minute, then skin and slice thinly. Arrange the celery and tomatoes in alternate layers on lettuce leaves. Garnish with watercress and serve with French dressing.

Bean and Beetroot Salad

½ lb. young French beans
1 Spanish onion
1 small beetroot

Boil the onion, and when cold cut into slices. Cook the beans carefully so that they remain whole. Slice the boiled beetroot. Arrange alternate layers of beans, beetroot and onion in a bowl and serve with French dressing.

New Potato Salad

Cold cooked peas
Cold cooked new potatoes
A little chopped parsley mixed with tarragon
1 hard-boiled egg

Slice the potatoes and mix with the peas and parsley, arrange in a bowl and garnish with slices of hard-boiled egg. Serve with mayonnaise dressing.

Mayonnaise of Cold Vegetables

Cooked potatoes
Cooked carrots
A little raw celery, onion and cauliflower
Cooked peas

Cut the celery and cauliflower into small pieces, and add to the diced potatoes, peas and carrots. Add a little very finely chopped onion and mix all ingredients together with 1 gill of mayonnaise sauce.

Fresh Fruit Salad

3 oranges
1 apple
3 oz. black grapes
2 bananas
1 lb. sugar
¼ grapefruit
Juice and rind of 2 lemons
3 oz. white grapes
2 pears
½ pint water

Boil together the sugar, water and a few pieces of thinly peeled lemon rind. Skim off any scum and add lemon juice. Allow to cool slightly and pour over the prepared fruit. Allow the salad to stand for a while before using.

Grapefruit and Apple Salad

4 oz. white grapes
2 grapefruit
1 lb. cooking apples

Core, peel and quarter the apples and cook them carefully, keeping the sections whole. Allow to cool. Prepare the grapefruit and cut into sections, removing all skin. Add to the apple. Wash and stone the grapes and add to the salad. If liked, a few glacé or tinned cherries may also be added.

Orange, Apple, Date and Nut Salad

Oranges
Dates
Apples
A few walnuts
½ lb. sugar
1 gill water

Make a syrup with the sugar and water and allow to cool. Core, peel and cut the apples into thin slices. Prepare the oranges, removing all skin, and cut into sections. Clean and stone the dates. Chop nuts. Mix all ingredients together and pour syrup over.

Pineapple and Raw Carrot

1 small tin of pineapple
Raw carrot
Watercress

Drain the pineapple and cut into small pieces. Arrange on lettuce. Grate raw carrot over top. Garnish with a few pieces of watercress. Serve with spicy French dressing.

Apple and Celery Salad

Apples
Celery
Lettuce leaves

Core, peel and cut the apples into small pieces. Chop the celery. Mix together with a little mayonnaise, pile on to lettuce leaves.

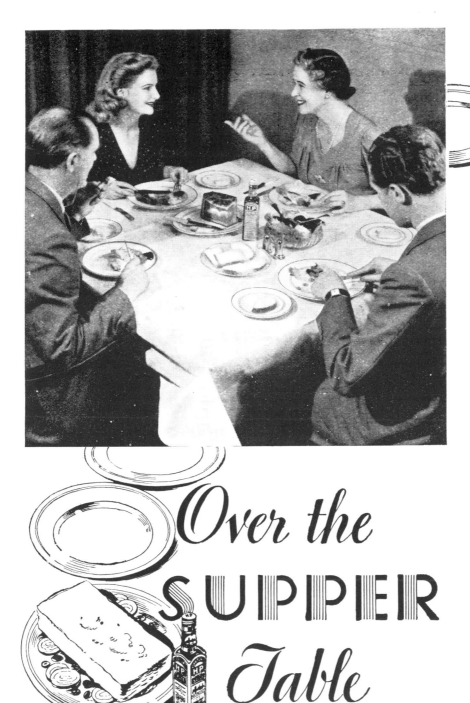

Over the SUPPER *Table*

Nancy. "I'm afraid it's a very frugal meal, aunt, but is seems unpatriotic to have anything else these days."

Aunt. "Of course, my dear. I understand. I've been cutting down myself. It's very kind of you to invite us in times like these. Catering isn't too easy even for an experienced housewife like me."

Nancy. "Well, in some ways it isn't so bad as I expected. I've the doctor's wife to thank for that."

Aunt. "Why, does she have legs of mutton to give away or something?"

Nancy. (*laughing*) "No, she has to put up with meat rationing like everybody else, but she manages to make her ration go much farther."

Aunt. "What, with a fairy wand?"

Nancy. "No, with a bottle of H.P. Sauce."

Aunt. "But, my dear, surely H.P. isn't a *secret* weapon. I thought everybody knew about H.P. by now."

Nancy. "Well, *I* didn't, though I must say I think it's a crime on Mother's part to have sent me out in the world not knowing what a blessing H.P. can be."

Uncle. "Now look here, you two, what about letting us get a word in."

Aunt. "Why of course, dear, what did you want to say?"

Uncle. "Well, I'm ready for a second helping of this excellent pie."

Philip. "And so am I if I'm not too greedy."

Nancy. "I'm glad you like it, because as a matter of fact it's only odds and ends of meat and vegetables well flavoured with H.P. Sauce."

Aunt. "Delicious, my dear. I could give you several good recipes with H.P. Sauce if you would care for them."

Nancy. "I'd love them."

Aunt. "I'll send them to you, then. In the meantime, here's one I know by heart—I use it so often. Have you got a piece of paper? Good. It's called English Hamburger. Take 1 lb. of corned or pressed beef. Break it into small pieces with a fork, mix the meat with 6 ozs. fine white bread crumbs, a beaten egg, a tablespoonful of H.P. Sauce and a little grated onion. Thoroughly grease a fireproof dish, or meat tin. (The former is better because it can be sent to the table.) Mould the mixture into an oblong about $\frac{1}{2}$ an inch thick. Cover with a well greased paper and bake until brown. Serve garnished with chopped gherkins and beetroot mixed and flavoured with a few drops of H.P. Sauce. Chip potatoes are excellent with it. The whole thing makes enough for six people."

Nancy. "It sounds lovely. I must make it tomorrow."

Aunt. "And don't forget H.P. —it makes all the difference."

What Shall We Have for Supper?

by N. H. Ramsay of the Institute Staff

Food Glorious Food

1940

To simplify the preparation and serving of supper or lunch in these busy days it is a good plan to provide one substantial course, and supplement it with foods needing no cooking, like salads, fresh fruit, and wholemeal bread.

For a nourishing and well-balanced meal the main dish should include protective foods such as oily fish, eggs, milk, cheese, and potatoes. Full use should also be made of home-grown vegetables, which can be combined with eggs or cheese to make a variety of attractive dishes. Here are suggestions for simple supper menus. The quantities given are for four people.

MENU 1. *Potato and Ham Casserole. Loganberries and Cream or Milk*

Potato and Ham Casserole :

2 lb. potatoes	2 oz. ham or bacon	Pepper and salt
2 onions	Chopped parsley	Milk
	Margarine	

Peel the potatoes and cut in thick slices. Peel the onions and cut in thin rings. Cut the ham in small pieces. Fill a casserole with alternate layers of potatoes, onion rings, ham, chopped parsley, and seasonings. Then three parts fill the dish with milk, and place some small pieces of margarine on top. Cover and cook over very gentle heat, until the vegetables are tender, or, alternatively, bake in a moderate oven, for about 1 hour. If the casserole is cooked in the oven, remove the lid half an hour before serving, to brown the potatoes on top.

MENU 2. *Risotto. Cheese. Green Salad. Fruit*

Risotto : 8 oz. rice   2 onions   4 tomatoes   3 oz. margarine   About 1¼ pts. stock   Pepper and salt   1 red pepper, if available
3 oz. grated cheese

Peel and chop the onions. Melt 2 ozs. margarine in a saucepan, and fry the onions lightly, then add the rice, and fry for several minutes. Add the stock, the tomatoes cut in slices, and the seasoning. Put on the lid, and cook very gently until the rice is tender, and the stock nearly absorbed. During the cooking stir once or twice, being careful not to break up the rice, and adding a little extra stock if necessary. Add the remaining margarine just before serving. Pile the risotto on a hot dish, and hand the grated cheese separately.

N.B.—Chopped mushrooms, a pinch of saffron, and pieces of chicken or rabbit may be cooked with the risotto, if available.

MENU 3. *Eggs with French Beans. Brown Rolls. Butter. Honey. Fruit*

Eggs with French Beans :

1 lb. French beans	2 eggs	Pepper and salt
2 oz. margarine	¼ pt. milk	4 diced cooked potatoes

Wash and string the beans, and cut in strips. Cook in boiling salted water until tender (about 15 minutes) and drain thoroughly. Melt 1 oz. margarine, add the beans and seasonings, heat through, dish up and keep hot. Beat the eggs with the milk, and add seasonings, the diced cooked potatoes, and a tablespoonful of grated cheese if liked. Melt the remaining margarine in the pan used for cooking beans, and cook the eggs over a gentle heat, stirring until the mixture thickens. Pour the scrambled eggs into the centre of the beans, and serve at once.

Tested by the Institute and approved by the Ministry of Food, these thrifty menus solve an ever-recurring problem

Holiday Catering, 1941

CHRISTMAS DAY
DINNER:
Celery or Artichoke Soup
Roast Chicken, Turkey
Goose, etc., or Boiled Fowl
Stuffing, Gravy
Bread Sauce or Apple Sauce
Potatoes, Brussels Sprouts
Christmas Pudding
with Sauce
Mince Pies
Coffee

We can't be lavish this Christmas, and we mustn't mind abandoning some of our traditional dishes, but we can make the most of what we have. Here we suggest a scheme to help you—especially those who have not had to undertake it before—to plan and carry out your Christmas catering with ease and success

THE DAYS BEFORE . . .

Remember that smooth running depends on careful planning, so decide on the menu and order the stores in good time. Plan and prepare the decorations, too, so that you are not rushed at the last moment.

The cake, pudding and mincemeat, being less rich than usual, should not be made more than one or two weeks in advance. Incidentally, if one variety of fruit is not available, substitute a rather larger proportion of one of the others, if you have sufficient. Here are the recipes we suggest:

Wartime Christmas Cake

½ lb. flour	½ lb. currants
¼ teaspoonful salt	¼ lb. sultanas
4 oz. fat	¼ lb. raisins (if available)
4 oz. sugar	
½ teaspoonful mixed spice	1 oz. mixed peel (if available)
¼ teaspoonful bicarbonate of soda	1 or 2 eggs
	Milk to mix

Stone and chop the raisins; wash, dry and pick the currants and sultanas; chop the peel. Cream the fat and sugar together very thoroughly, until light and creamy in texture. Add the beaten egg by degrees, mixing very well, and adding a little of the flour if the mixture appears to curdle. Add the prepared fruits, and lastly the flour, salt, spice and bicarbonate of soda, adding enough milk to make the mixture of a dropping consistency. Put into a greased, lined cake tin about 6 to 7 in. in diameter, and bake in a slow oven at a temperature of about 325° F. for from 3 to 4 hours.

Wartime Christmas Pudding

½ lb. flour and breadcrumbs mixed	¼ lb. sultanas
¼ lb. suet	¼ lb. home-dried plums or apple rings
¼ teaspoonful salt	
½ teaspoonful mixed spice	1 oz. mixed peel (if available)
Little grated nutmeg	1 egg
A pinch of ground ginger	Approximately ¼ pint milk
2 oz. sugar	A little caramel to colour
¼ lb. currants	

Wash, dry and pick the currants and sultanas. Chop the peel and the dried plums or apple rings. Mix together the flour and breadcrumbs, suet, salt, sugar and spices. Add the prepared fruit, and mix with the beaten egg and milk to make of a soft dropping consistency, colouring with a little caramel. Put into a greased basin, cover with greased paper and a cloth, and steam or boil for about 6 to 7 hours. Cover with a clean cloth, and store in a cool, dry place until required.

Wartime Mincemeat

¼ lb. currants	¼ lb. carrot
¼ lb sultanas	¼ lb. apple (weighed after peeling)
¼ lb. raisins (if available)	3 oz. suet
2 oz. mixed peel (if available)	½ teaspoonful mixed spice
3 oz. sugar	

Prepare the fruits in the following way: wash, dry and pick the currants and sultanas, and stone the raisins, if used. Peel and core the apples, and scrape the carrot. Put all these, together with the peel and suet, through the mincer, and mix well together. Add the sugar and spice, and stir for a few moments. Cover, and keep in a cool, dry place, stirring every day for about a week. Put into clean, dry jam-jars, cover as for jam, and use as required.

This mincemeat should be used within 2 or 3 weeks, as it is likely to ferment if kept for longer.

ON CHRISTMAS EVE . . . .

To avoid a last-minute rush, much of the cooking can be prepared on Christmas Eve. Make the stuffing, stuff and truss the bird, and leave ready for roasting. Prepare crumbs, etc., for bread sauce. Stew giblets for gravy. The stuffing can be made with sausage meat or chestnuts, or may be a bread-crumb forcemeat flavoured with herbs.

Make and bake the mince pies, and while the oven is still warm cook the biscuits. Here is a good recipe:

Chocolate Short Biscuits

3½ oz. wheatmeal flour	2 oz. margarine
	2 oz. sugar
½ oz. cocoa or chocolate powder	A very little cold water
¼ teaspoonful baking powder	A few drops vanilla essence
A pinch of salt	

Mix together the flour, cocoa, salt and baking powder, and rub in the fat very thoroughly until it completely disappears. Then add the sugar and a teaspoonful or so of cold water, with a few drops vanilla essence, and knead to a firm dough. Turn on to a floured board, roll ¼ in. thick, and stamp into rounds or fancy shapes. Bake in a slow oven (350° F.) until firm and somewhat browned (about 20 minutes). Cool thoroughly before putting in a tin.

The picture on page 31 shows how you can decorate the Christmas cake, using only 4 oz. granulated sugar, a few silver balls and about 2 yards of Cellophane ribbon. To make the icing,

Put it in the bank, it'll help to buy a tank.

by E. J. M. CRESWELL
of the Institute Staff

TEA :
Anchovy Toast or
Savoury Sandwiches
Biscuits
Christmas Cake
Tea (China or Indian)

issolve the sugar in ½ gill water and ring to the boil. While it is boiling emove any scum that rises, and keep he sides of the pan free of crystals, sing a brush dipped in cold water. When the temperature of 229° F. is eached, pour the syrup into a clean asin and beat until it thickens and ecomes opaque, then pour on to the ake and place any decorations in osition. Do not ice the cake more han one day in advance, or the icing ill become discoloured.

Prepare the custard for the trifle or ruit fool, and make the mock cream o serve with it.

Mock Whipped Cream

pint milk	1½ oz. unsalted mar-
teaspoonfuls corn-	garine
flour	3 teaspoonfuls sugar
A few drops vanilla essence	

Mix the cornflour to a paste with little of the milk, heat the rest of the milk and when boiling pour on to the lended cornflour, stirring well. Return to the saucepan, bring to the boil, and cook for 2 or 3 minutes, stirring continuously, then allow to get quite cold (it should set like a blancmange). Meanwhile cream the margarine and sugar together until *very* light and creamy. Whisk in the blancmange mixture, a little at a time, beating with a wire whisk. Lastly add vanilla.

Prepare the Christmas Platter dish as far as possible. This is made with the following collection of cooked garden vegetables, cold meats, and fish, set out on a large dish like a giant hors d'œuvre :

Christmas Platter

1 small cauliflower	A variety of cooked
1 small white-heart	sausages and
cabbage	smoked and pickled
A heart of celery	fish
A little grated onion	Watercress
Salt and pepper	A few cooked carrots
Mock mayonnaise sauce	

Cook the cauliflower (and carrot, if necessary) and allow to cool. Shred the crisp raw cabbage and celery very finely, mix them together with a little finely grated onion, and bind with mock mayonnaise sauce, adding salt and pepper to taste.

To dish, place the cauliflower in the centre of a large platter and coat it with the mock mayonnaise sauce. Arrange the slices of cooked sausage or canned meat down one side of the dish, and filleted tunny fish,

smoked herring or other piquant fish on the opposite side. Pile the cabbage and celery mixture in heaps at each end of the dish, with strips of carrot and sprigs of watercress in between.

ON CHRISTMAS DAY . . . .

The Bird. Allow a young chicken about 1 hour to roast, a duck about 1¼ hours, and a goose about 1½ hours. Turkeys up to 14 lb. (weight after dressing) require 15 minutes per lb. and 15 minutes extra; allow rather less if larger. Steam a boiling fowl 2½ to 3 hours, then roast for ½ hour.

The Gravy. Use the giblet stock for this, and make plenty, as it comes in useful when cooking up the remains of the meat.

The Potatoes. Roast these with the bird, allowing them 1 hour.

The Sprouts. Cook in a little boiling salted water for about 20 minutes. Take care not to overcook them.

The Pudding. Steam or boil 3 to 4 hours, and serve with good white sauce made with ¾ oz. each of margarine and flour and ½ pint milk, flavoured with vanilla or almond essence, and sweetened to taste.

THE DAYS AFTER . . . .

You will want to make the remains of your bird go as far as possible. One way is to use a little of the meat in **stuffed pancakes.** Mince the meat, and any left-over vegetables, season well, and bind with gravy or a sauce. Fry some small, thin pancakes (a prepared batter mixture is suitable for these) and fill with the hot meat mixture. Serve with a green vegetable and the rest of the gravy.

A **plate pie** is another good dish with cooked meat. Make the mixture as above, adding a little grated onion, if possible, and bind with gravy or sauce. Line a tin plate with shortcrust pastry, fill with the mixture, and cover with a pastry lid. Bake in a hot oven (450° F.) till the pastry is well browned. Serve hot or cold.

Keep some of the neater pieces of cold bird for a nourishing **salad** with all manner of winter vegetables. Cut the pieces of meat into neat strips and marinade them in a mixture of two parts salad oil to one part vinegar, with salt, pepper, mustard and chopped herbs. Mix together some diced cooked root vegetables (carrot, turnip, beetroot) and place in a salad bowl. Arrange a ring of cooked sliced

potato round the edge of the bowl, place the meat and marinade in the centre, and garnish with bunches of watercress or winter endive.

Collect all the bones, of course, and the carcase of the bird, and add them, together with a bouquet garni, a bay leaf and a few bacon rinds, to the remainder of the giblet stock and boil gently for several hours. This gives an excellent stock, which makes many delicious soups.

Gravy Soup. Thicken the stock and season well, adding a few drops of vinegar or piquant sauce. Colour a good rich brown with gravy browning, and serve with croûtons of bread, fried or toasted.

Broth. Add diced or shredded vegetables to the stock and a little barley, season well, and simmer till tender. Add fresh chopped parsley before serving.

Christmas Hotch Potch. Cut up a few carrots, a small turnip, a small swede, an onion or leek, and a few sticks of celery, and sauté them in a little dripping or bacon fat. Add half a cabbage, shredded finely, and enough of the stock just to cover. Lastly, add seasonings and a bouquet garni, and simmer until all is tender. Add more stock, if necessary, but the soup should be thick with the vegetables. Before serving remove (*Continued on page* 82)

SUPPER :

Christmas Platter

Wheatmeal Bread
and Butter (or Margarine)

Fruit Trifle
or Fruit Fool

Mock Whipped Cream

Coffee

A sailor's blood is on your head if you waste a scrap of bread.

How do you Cook Fresh-salted COD?

THE fresh-salted cod which comes from Iceland is a welcome addition to our food supplies at a time when fresh fish is scarce. Priced at a modest 9d. a pound, it is very good value, as there is practically no waste with it. It is obtainable ready for use from the fishmonger, who washes the salt out of it. Cook on the day it is bought.

Here are some ways of using it, including two quickly made savouries:

Creamed Cod with Tomatoes

1 lb. fresh-salted cod
½ pint milk and water
A bunch of sweet herbs
A sprig of parsley   2 peppercorns
1 bay leaf   1 cupful bottled tomatoes
1 oz. flour   ½ oz. margarine
Sauté potatoes to garnish

Put the cod in a saucepan with the liquid, the herbs and peppercorns tied in muslin, the sprig of parsley and the bay leaf. Cover, and cook very gently until the fish is tender—about 15 minutes. Remove the fish and divide into large flakes. Strain the liquid, and use a little of it to blend the flour for thickening, then put the remaining liquid back in the saucepan with the margarine, and when boiling, stir in the blended flour. Stir and boil for 2 or 3 minutes. Add the flaked fish and the tomatoes (cut in pieces, if necessary) and season to taste. Re-heat, and turn into a hot dish. Garnish with a border of sauté potatoes.

Curried Cod Hot-pot

½ lb. cooked fresh-salted cod
½ lb. cooked carrots
½ pint curry sauce
1 lb. cooked potatoes
A nut of dripping   Brown crumbs

Make a good curry sauce, using some of the fish boilings. Flake the fish, dice the carrots and add both to the sauce, then turn the mixture into a fireproof dish. Cover with a thick layer of sliced cooked potatoes, then sprinkle on a spoonful of browned crumbs and cover with fine shavings of dripping. Put in a hot oven for about 20 minutes, until the potatoes are lightly browned on the top.

Baked Cod au Gratin

1 lb. fresh-salted cod
Little milk and water
¼ pint white sauce
2 or 3 oz. grated cheese
1 teaspoonful made mustard   Pepper
1 or 2 teaspoonfuls vinegar
Browned breadcrumbs
A little grated onion, if available

Lay the cod in a greased fireproof dish. Pour round it a little milk and water, cover with margarine paper, and bake in a moderate oven for about 20 minutes, until tender.
Make a white sauce, adding the liquid from the baked fish. Stir in half the grated cheese, the seasonings, the vinegar and the flaked fish. Fill greased scallop shells with the mixture, or place it in a shallow fireproof dish. Sprinkle with the remaining cheese, a few browned crumbs and the grated onion. Bake in a hot oven for about 15 minutes, until golden brown.

Boiled Cod Provençale

1 lb. fresh-salted cod
1 teaspoonful vinegar
A little minced onion, if available
1 oz. margarine
1 or 2 teaspoonfuls salad oil
4 peppercorns (crushed)   Grated nutmeg
1 teaspoonful vinegar or lemon-juice substitute

Put the cod in a saucepan, with cold water to cover and a teaspoonful of vinegar. Bring slowly to boiling-point, and simmer until tender—about 10 minutes. Drain the fish, divide into large flakes and keep hot.
Fry the onion lightly in the margarine, then stir in the salad oil, peppercorns and nutmeg, and mix well. Add the fish, and shake over the heat until thoroughly mixed, without breaking up the flakes. Sprinkle in the parsley, then dish the cod on a bed of nicely mashed potatoes. Serve very hot, sprinkled with vinegar or lemon-juice substitute.

Piquant Fish Toasts

6 rounds of toasted or fried bread
3 oz. cooked fresh-salted cod
1 tablespoonful white sauce
1 tablespoonful tomato sauce or purée
Seasoning
Pickled walnuts, olives, capers or any other pickled vegetable available

Mash the fish, mix with the thick white sauce and the tomato sauce, and season rather highly. Pile the mixture on rounds of toasted or fried bread, and garnish each round with half a pickled walnut or a piece of olive, or decorate with chopped mixed pickles. Place the rounds on a baking tin, cover with margarine paper, heat in a hot oven.

Anchovy Fingers

Scraps of shortcrust pastry
2 oz. of cooked fresh-salted cod
2 tablespoonfuls white sauce flavoured with anchovy essence
A pinch of curry powder
2 salted anchovies or anchovy paste
Chopped parsley

Roll out the pastry ¼ in. thick, cut in fingers and bake in a hot oven. Mash the fish and mix with the anchovy sauce. Add curry powder to taste. Wash and pound the salted anchovies, and mix into the sauce. (If anchovy paste is used, spread this on the pastry fingers.) Pile the fish mixture neatly on the pastry. Reheat in a hot oven, garnish with parsley.

Paper is a munition of war—never waste a scrap.

*Illustration by
L. G. Illingworth*

THE greatest dietetic revolution of the War in our village has undoubtedly been the change-over to the national wheat-meal loaf. Before its enforcement, Tom Stoner, our local baker, seemed to send round specimens more as a polite gesture to Lord Woolton than as part of the regular and serious purposes of his trade. And indeed, the customers at the end of the round, who were left with the choice of that or nothing, had sharp comments to offer which were soothed only by the vanman's off-the-record sympathy with them.

"I can't abide the stuff myself," he would confide. "But I s'pose they Government folks mus' ha' something to show fer all the talk they gets up to. I could understan' it if anythin' were bein' wasted. But it ain't. It goes into the pig meal and the poultry food, and wheer's that comin' from if they wants us to stick it in the bread?"

Those who subscribe to *The Times* may remember the arguments waged in its columns for many weeks between eminent medical authorities, who saw bread as the instrument by which the obstinate general public could be forced to take their vitamins whether they would or no, and highly varying bodies concerned either for their personal predilections or for live-stock rations. Not all the curt reminders about the shocked surprise of the black-bread-eating Russians that in the third year of the war we should still be arguing so fine a point won over the dissident individualists, who might or might not have suggested that the substitution of such trash as pure white bread in Russia would provoke an equal tendency towards

rebellion there. Only Lord Woolton saved the discussion from becoming perpetual and our disgrace international by making his wheatmeal loaf compulsory and universal.

At that juncture Colbourne, of necessity, fell into line with strangely little articulate objection. It is not, perhaps, unamusing that our evacuees were at least one of the causes of this lack of enthusiastic revolt. Always more finicky and unyielding in their tastes than our huskier country children, always ready to yelp at the first presentation, their plainly avowed objections to the innovation killed every foster-mother's own hankerings for the mixture as before, and stiffened her resolution to make the best of the new with-

* Paper is a vital war material—save every scrap.

COTTAGE Loaf

Marjorie Hessell Tiltman and her delightful Sussex village folk once again!

tuals. For the most part, the less material seed seems to remain dormant. Occasionally, when circumstances make it politic, it sprouts forth with surprising vigour. "Please, M's Til'man, may we come and pick some rabbit food? . . . Please, M's Til'man, may we take out Jenny? . . . Please, M's Til'man, may we play in the field? . . .''

For these two, Mum washes and cooks and works and sews and generally labours, dratting as she does so the *prolapsus uterus* which interferes with the freer exercise of her muscular activities. Expostulated with, she offers the perennial promise that she "be a-goin' to see 'bout passin' of 'em on soon.'' Old Dad proffers a more convincing reply as he reminds us of the occasion on which "th' ole gal was spoken to by the Queen'' and congratulated for her public spirit in starting a new family at the age of sixty-five. "No,'' repeats Dad, biting on his pipe a trifle vindictively, "mark my words! we be landed wi' they varmints now fer good; th' ole gal'll never git rid on 'em while the Queen wants 'er to keep 'em.''

The last collection from the post office, viz. 4.15 p.m., coincides nicely with the hour at which Mum wipes down the nasturtium-pattern American cloth on the kitchen table and "lays up'' for tea—bread, margarine, shrimp paste, plum jam, and lettuce or mustard and cress. The National Loaf is still apt to bob into the conversation. What, I asked, did they think of it now?

Dad pushed his plate a little farther away from him, the better to lean forward across the table towards me.

"Well,'' he said slowly, peering down at the hunk beside him, "I don't reckon it's too bad, if it don't get no worse. But theer!'' he added, catching up a trifle with his notoriously pessimistic outlook, "I spec's it'll be as bad this turn afore they've done wid it.''

"What about you, Mum? Everyone says it's more sustaining. Don't you agree?''

Mrs. Jackson paused in her slicings.

"Seems to stay in their stummicks longer,'' she allowed. "But mind youse, they ain't properly got goin' yet; *(Continued)*

out more ado. And although it is true that a large proportion of visiting children have returned to their town homes and parents, enough still remain to make a noticeable bulge in our stationary population of four hundred.

Of these, old Mum Jackson still harbours a couple—strapping, rosy-cheeked boys into whom she labours to inculcate old-fashioned courtesy as she has known it, along with good honest vic-

* Travel as little as possible, and then outside rush hours.

Cottage Loaf
(Continued)

Stoner's man tells me they had a purty good store o' white flour as they ain't worked through yet."

"I tells you what, marm," interposed Dad, "s'long as it's only corn as goes in, I don't mind, but Lor' lumme!" he whistled, turning to Mum, "do you remembers what stuff they dosed us with last war? Pretty nigh killed me, it did, I tells yer straight, marm. You'd tak' a bite for breakfast an' be doubled up for a coupla hours. Then, as soon as yer got over that an' had to tak' a bite o' dinner, it'd start all over agin. Yer inside were allus pinched, same as yer were takin' salts. An' it's not to be wonnered at, neether, fer any ole muck were good enough to shove in—black beans, taties, maize an' all."

"But it's changed now, ain't it?" Mum appealed to me. "All inspectors and such-like. You can't do nothing without they passes it. An' 'sides, if it come to that, why the bakers allus did use taties for bread in the country in the old days. We were as careful as could be to c'lect every small 'un in the field and save 'em in a sack till they'd call fer 'em an' fetch 'em."

"But didn't you bake your own bread, Mum?"

"Well, my mother did, but I on'y used to knock up a bit when us got short'. Not much time wi' eight little 'uns on me hands. Sunday mornin' were bakin' day. Oh, I minds it well enough. Gettin' the wood fire lit in the brick oven, keepin' it goin' wi' oak an' elm till the bricks was white-hot, then sweepin' out the ashes wi' a rake made o' that green broom you has in yore garden, all but a ridge by the door to keep the heat in."

Dad blew an extra whiff from his pipe to the memory of those days.

"Ay, an' that *was* bread, too. None o' yore puff-an'-powder stuff, dry in a few hours, like 'tis in these days."

"I suppose it was all stone-milled flour," I suggested. "That makes a great difference."

"Oh, Lor', yes, an' ground from our own corn, too. When the farmer'd cleared the field, he'd let us go leasin'—or gleanin', as you might call it," reminisced Mum. "Off us'd go, to march up an' down the 'lands,' the whole fambly, wi' lap bags tied round us fer the short ears, leavin' our hands and arms free to 'bunch up the long 'uns.'"

"O' course, you couldn't do that now," broke in Dad. "The machinery takes it off too clean. But in them days it was all scythed by hand."

"An' then," went on Mum, "when the farmer'd had his own corn ground, we'd take ours, an' the miller'd do it fer kindness like. As much as a sack or a sack an' a half, an' we'd lug it home an' stand it on two old chairs in the kitchen, nice an' handy. It'd pretty well last us then till next harvest, if we took care."

"There was pretty nigh a mill to each village then," put in Dad. "I know to fourteen or fifteen o' them not eight mile from here—an' mos' o' them still grindin' in the last war."

"Yes, that's right," nodded Mum.

"Ay, an' they ground corn as it should be ground," continued Dad, warming up. "These yere steel rollers takes all the swell out o' the stuff. You takes bran. They serves you up wi' nothin' but sawdust if you gits it now, but in the ole days, it'd come in great flakes. If I wanted a poultice fer one o' my hosses or cows, I'd put a han'ful in a bucket, and it'd mos' burst the top off of it, wi' a drop o' boilin' water. But now—now . . . I don't know what they can do now; fer sure I don't," he muttered.

I looked into the scullery as I heard footsteps coming up the path.

The footsteps sounded on the step and a head peered round the back door.

"Same as usual, Mrs. Jackson?"

"If you please, Ted," Mrs. Jackson called, and six full-size loaves were deposited on the side-table.

"They know you, Mum!"

"Well, they ought to," said Mrs. Jackson. "They bin' servin' me ever since I war a gal o' twenty an' jus' married. An' that's—how many?—forty-seven year ago. It were ole Sam Stoner then, Tom's father, o' course, and neither on us were ones fer changin'. But Lor', bless you, it were fourteen loaves three times a week in them days, at tuppence a time."

And she breathed a sigh, to think that such cheapness and spaciousness were things of the past, though she smiled again at the realisation that the friendliness still remained.

Fruitful results from vegetables

Eating fruit is a pleasure we don't often get nowadays, and there's no denying we miss it. But, from the point of view of *health*, we can more than make up for the lack of fruit by eating extra vegetables.

The main health value of fruit is in its Vitamin C. Vitamin C clears the skin, prevents fatigue, and helps you to resist infection. And it's by no means confined to oranges, as people are apt to imagine. Some vegetables, indeed, actually contain *more* of this health-giver than oranges do.

To get your requirement of Vitamin C you should eat daily a salad which includes a good portion of at least one of the following :

Watercress (all the year round)
Raw shredded sprouts (December to February)
Raw shredded cabbage (May to August, October to March)
Raw shredded spinach (all the year round)
Shredded swede or turnip (September to March)
The Vitamin C value will be increased if you use parsley or mustard and cress as a garnish.

Increased servings of
Cooked green vegetables
Cooked swedes and turnips
Cooked potatoes
will also help to maintain the Vitamin C value of the diet at a high level.

Vegetables are most "fruitful" of Vitamin C when you serve them raw !

And, by the way, the dark outer leaves of vegetables are richer in vitamins and minerals than the paler insides. So when they're too tough to eat raw, or to cook in the ordinary way, be sure to put them into soups or stews.

Our old friend the carrot, although not so rich in C, is important for its anti-infective Vitamin A.

Have YOU tried DRIED EGGS yet ?

Dried Egg from America is now in the shops—soon there'll be enough for one 1/9d. tin on every ration book. They are *extra* to your regular egg ration. Each tin contains one dozen fine fresh eggs, dried, and in powder form. Nothing is taken away but the shells and water. All the rich goodness and fine flavour of fresh egg remain.

You get your Dried Eggs from where you are registered for shell eggs. Mix with water as directed on the tin and use just as you would use freshly beaten egg.

ISSUED BY THE MINISTRY OF FOOD

* Keep on saving Paper zealously—it is needed more urgently than ever.

MAGPIES AREN'T POPULAR

MARJORY doesn't realise it, of course, but she's a magpie. And a magpie—in these days—is a most unpatriotic bird!

It isn't that she steals things, nor even hoards food to such an extent that the Ministry of Food could prosecute her. But she KEEPS things, and keeps them long after she needs them.

Altogether Marjory was brought up as a model housewife, and she doesn't see that a world-shattering war should move her one inch from the nice little rules her mother made.

Now and then she hears on the radio an appeal for waste paper. But, she says solemnly, she buys only one newspaper a day and *that* can't help the war much. Her books? Dear me, she can't be expected to part with them; most of them were 7s. 6d. editions, and she does feel sentimental about the old school prizes. Magazines? Oh, she *always* keeps them. It's lovely to look back through the old numbers at the recipes and the advertisements. Some day her grandchildren are going to get such a thrill out of them!

It doesn't seem to dawn on Marjory that this nice, sentimental thought may be her contribution to *no* grandchildren, or at least no land fit for them to live in.

Since clothes rationing came in, Marjory has been congratulating herself that she has always kept her old clothes. She has chests and cupboards full of them, and many of them will certainly never be worn again by anybody. In a chest of drawers she has bundles of cuttings and patchings for garments that vanished years ago. "But these aren't *rags*!" she said indignantly when somebody mentioned the Government appeal for rags of all kinds. "They are perfectly new, and I might want a piece of odd material. . . ."

She *might* want. The country DOES want now. A pad for an aircraft in 1942 is really much more important to Marjory than a patchwork cushion in 1952.

In Marjory's attic, in the cupboard under the stairs, and out in the garage, there is quite a nice little collection of stuff that might be useful some day. Old kitchen tools and pots and pans, Grandma's brass fire-irons, the bronze horses that sat beside Grandpa's presentation clock, old rubber Wellingtons (oh dear, perhaps they *have* a hole in them), tyres from the 1930 car and the 1935 one as well, and a garden hose that perished years ago. Some day, of course, she is going to clear them all out, but what with her canteen work and housekeeping without a maid, and John away, she's never got round to it.

Marjory is a good and thrifty housekeeper. She buys three-pennyworth of bones from the butcher every week and makes soup. But when she has drained off the last stock, she tosses the small bones to the dog to play with and buries the big ones in the garden refuse heap. Bones, that are so vitally needed for fertiliser and glue!

Marjory, chiefly because she is such a good housewife, has a little spare time. Not much—just about a couple of hours on an occasional afternoon. "But, of course, you can't do any useful war work in that time."

You *can*. Marjory could quite easily, if she would just cast her 1902-vintage magpie feathers. She could begin in her own home, gathering up all the little but vital pieces of material she was saving for a "rainy day." That day is NOW, and it is raining hard on all the world. She could collect salvage in neat piles, newspapers in separate bundles from magazines and mixed waste paper; rubber, rags and scrap metal tied in groups; and the bones (as clean as she can get them) in a tin.

Then, when her own house was in order, she could volunteer to spend an hour a week sorting salvage at the local depot. She might learn then how terribly, tragically important salvage is. A strange job for a life-long magpie. But it can be done!

Illustration by Emett

ANNE BLYTHE MUNRO.

Food for the picking

Blackberrying is a traditional custom that most of us have enjoyed at one time or another. There are other Hedgerow Harvests too, that provide good things for the larder. So why not take the children and go a-harvesting ? Be sure, however, that in their excitement they do not damage bushes or hedges, or walk through growing crops, or gather mushrooms, for instance, in fields without getting the farmer's permission.

Elderberries are delicious stewed with half-and-half apple; or made into jam with an equal quantity of blackberries. Wash and strip them from the stems before using.

Sloes look like tiny damsons. They are too sour to use as stewed fruit, but make a delightful preserve with marrow.

Crab Apples. For a drink or flavouring, Crab Apple juice is a good substitute for lemon juice. Put the apples to sweat, choose only the sound ones, take off stalks, beat the fruit to a mash and press the juice through a thick cloth. Leave for a day or two until bubbles appear. Put into clean dry bottles and cork well, securing the cork with wire. Store in a cool place. The juice will be ready in about a month's time.

Rowan-berries (Mountain Ash) make a preserve with a pleasant tang, admirable to serve with cold meats. You can make the preserve of the berries alone, or with a couple of apples to each pound of berries.

Hips and Haws should not be picked until perfectly ripe. Hips — the berries of the wild rose, make a vitamin-rich jam. Haws — the berries of the may-tree, make a brown jelly that is very like guava jelly.

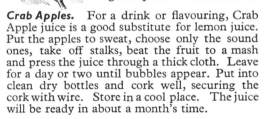

Nuts. Cobnuts, walnuts, chestnuts and filberts, are good keepers. Choose very sound, well-coloured nuts. Remove them from their husks, spread them out and leave to dry overnight. Pack cobnuts and filberts tightly into jars or crocks and cover with an inch layer of crushed block salt. Pack walnuts and chestnuts in a similar manner but cover with an inch layer of sand instead of salt. If the containers have lids, put them on top as an extra precaution against shrivelling. Packed in this way, your nuts should keep till Christmas. Beechnuts make good eating, too. Store them as you would cob-nuts. Use as almonds.

Mushrooms are very easy to dry and make an excellent flavouring for Winter soups and dishes. Small button mushrooms are best for drying. Gather them in the early morning; before the mushroom fly has had time to attack them. Simply spread them out to dry in the air.

Blackberry and Apple jam. Here is a favourite recipe :—*4 lbs. firm blackberries, 1½ lbs. sour apples, 4½ lbs. sugar, 1 breakfastcupful water.* Core and slice the apples. Put in the preserving pan with the water and cook till quite soft. Add the blackberries and bring to the simmer. Simmer for 5 minutes, then add the sugar (warmed) and boil rapidly until setting point is reached. (Make first test after 10 minutes.) Put into hot jars and seal.

Hedgerow and Harvest Leaflet containing many useful recipes for using wild produce will be sent to all who ask. Please send postcards only, addressed to The Ministry of Food, Room 627E, London, W.1.

(S.46)

ISSUED BY THE MINISTRY OF FOOD

* There is still too much waste in Britain—don't be a guilty party.

By Christine Palmer

AND AGAIN— POTATOES

Don't forget—every time you use potatoes in place of bread you're helping to save British lives. "Potato Variety" —fourteen stimulating suggestions for varying the menu—send 1d. stamp to Good Housekeeping Institute, 28–30 Grosvenor Gardens, London, S.W.1.

Potato Cake with Onions

1½ lb. potatoes	1 oz. dripping
2 large onions or leeks	1 oz. grated cheese
Seasoning	

Cut the onions into thin slices and cook them slightly in the dripping until they are a golden-brown. Bake the potatoes in their jackets, then remove their skins and beat them up well with a fork. Mix the onions with the mashed potatoes; season well and put into a greased, flat earthenware dish. Sprinkle with the grated cheese and brown in a hot oven.

Scotch Potato Scones

2 lb. potatoes	½ oz. margarine
2 oz. flour	Salt

Choose large potatoes of the mealy variety. Cook and mash them thoroughly, add the margarine and salt and sprinkle in a little flour, the remainder being used for flouring the board and rolling pin. Roll the potatoes out to about ⅛ in. thickness, cut into circles the size of a dinner plate and cook on a girdle or very thick iron frying-pan until lightly brown. Cut into four and serve hot, buttered and rolled like a pancake.

Hampton Pie

½ lb. cooked sausages	1 dessertspoonful chopped
½ gill stock	parsley
1 tablespoonful made mustard	2 tablespoonfuls tomato ketchup
1 onion, chopped and fried	Mashed potatoes to cover

Slice the cooked sausages and mix with the parsley, ketchup, mustard and stock. Arrange the sausage mixture and fried onion rings in layers in a pie-dish. Cover with mashed potatoes and bake in a hot oven.

Potato and Leek Hot-pot

12 leeks	1½ lb. potatoes
1 oz. margarine	Pepper and salt
Little mace	Water

Well wash the leeks, cut off the stalks and remove the outer skins. Melt the margarine, without allowing it to get very hot, and steam the leeks in it, using a very slow heat: after 5 to 10 minutes add the sliced potatoes and continue to cook for another 5 minutes. Add sufficient water to half cover the vegetables, add pepper, salt and a very little mace, and let it simmer until the vegetables are tender—40–50 minutes. You must cook this over a very slow heat, or the mixture boils dry. When the vegetables are tender, remove the leeks, keep them in a casserole, and mash the potatoes. If there is too much moisture in the pan after removing the leeks, take the lid off the pan and boil until it is reduced. Add to the leeks and serve in a casserole. (6–8 portions.)

Potato and Cheese Galantine

6 medium-boiled potatoes	2 tablespoonfuls white sauce
½ teaspoonful made mustard	1 tablespoonful tomato sauce
3 oz. grated cheese	
Pepper and salt	

Boil the potatoes, mash while still hot, and add the rest of the ingredients. Turn on to a floured board and shape into a roll. Bake slowly, covered with greased paper, for about 30 to 40 minutes. Serve on a hot dish and pour tomato sauce around it.

Winter Salad

1 lb. cooked potatoes	1 tablespoonful shredded raw beetroot
1 teaspoonful chopped parsley	1 tablespoonful shredded carrots
1 tablespoonful chopped onion or leek	2 eating apples
1 tablespoonful chopped celery	2 tablespoonfuls salad dressing
2 tablespoonfuls shredded raw cabbage	1 tablespoonful grated cheese
Pepper and salt	

While the potatoes are still warm add the parsley and onion, then the rest of the vegetables and the apples, and finally mix with the salad dressing. Sprinkle with cheese, pepper and salt.

With the Compliments of the Season

*O*ur compliments and thanks to you all. For it is thanks very largely to you for so loyally and so helpfully working with us that at this, the fourth Christmas at war, the nation's health is on a sound footing. But though "good living" must now be taken in the sense of healthy living, instead of luxury living, and we all must go carefully with fuel, we can still make Christmas fare hearty, appetising and tempting to look at. 'Here, with our very best wishes, are some ideas which may help you:

❋ Christmas Day Pudding

Rub 3 oz. cooking fat into 3 tablespoonfuls self-raising flour until like fine crumbs. Mix in 1½ breakfastcupfuls stale breadcrumbs, ¼ lb. prunes (soaked 24 hours, stoned, chopped) or any other dried fruit such as sultanas, 3 oz. sugar, 1 teaspoonful mixed spice, ½ teaspoonful grated nutmeg. Then chop 1 large apple finely, grate 1 large raw carrot and 1 large raw potato; add to dry ingredients. Stir in a tablespoonful lemon substitute. Mix 1 teaspoonful bicarbonate of soda in 3 tablespoonfuls warm milk and stir thoroughly into pudding mixture. Put into one large or two small well-greased basins, cover with margarine papers and steam for 2½ hours. This can be prepared overnight and cooked on Christmas Day.

❋ Emergency Cream

Bring ½ pint water to blood heat, melt 1 tablespoonful unsalted margarine in it. Sprinkle 3 heaped tablespoonfuls household milk powder into this, beat well, then whisk thoroughly.

Add 1 teaspoonful sugar and ¼ teaspoonful vanilla. Leave to get very cold.

❋ Christmas Fruit Pies

This mixture is a good alternative to mincemeat.

Warm 1 tablespoonful marmalade (or jam, but this is not so spicy) in small saucepan over tiny heat. Add ¼ lb. prunes (soaked 24 hours, stoned, chopped) or other dried fruit, 1 tablespoonful sugar, 1 teacupful stale cake crumbs, or half cake, half breadcrumbs, ½ teaspoonful mixed spice. Stir together until crumbs are quite moist. Remove from heat, add 1 large chopped apple; also some chopped nuts if you have any. Make up into small pies, or large open flans. The mixture keeps several days in a cool place.

❋ Stuffed Mutton *With apple or bread sauce, this is as delicious as any turkey!*

1 leg of mutton, or loin of mutton (half a leg does, but is more difficult to stuff). Bone with a sharp carving knife and small kitchen knife, or get your butcher to do it. Spread the meat flat, stuff one end with your favourite savoury stuffing, one end with sausage meat, the two meeting in the centre. Fold meat over, re-forming into shape, sew with sacking-needle and stout thread, place sewn side down in baking dish, spread liberally with dripping. Put halved potatoes, peeled or in jackets, in the baking dish. Allow about 40-50 minutes before joint is done.

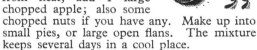

ISSUED BY THE MINISTRY OF FOOD (S50)

Don't waste elsewhere the fuel you save at home.

Patriots must know . . . .

War — world war — has imperiously reminded us that all food comes from the soil and the sea — and that the labour of harvesting is man's primal task.

To Government and Governed alike has come the realisation of the vital importance of the canning industries in overleaping the seasons, and bringing food at its sun-ripe maturity to the humblest kitchen table on any day of the year.

The 57 Varieties have long inspired liking and trust throughout the community — therefore they were sorely missed when the grocers' shelves gave evidence of temporarily diminished supplies.

But patriots must know that all the time Heinz have been doing a big job of National feeding (supplying the Services, the national food reserves, etc). More — they must realise that Heinz have steadfastly refused to lower that standard of quality which gave the 57 its great good name.

It may be difficult to secure them, because the demand is large and retail output restricted, but Heinz 57 Varieties remain unchanged in purity, flavour and excellence.

57

H. J. HEINZ CO. LTD.

LONDON FACTORY

* Make your Salvage pile really worth while — to-day and every day.